An Extraterrestrial Conspiracy

A Case Study

An Extraterrestrial Conspiracy

A Case Study

By Marian Greenberg

Introduced By Christopher S. Hyatt, Ph.D.
With An Epilogue By Neil Freer

1988
FALCON PRESS
LOS ANGELES & PHOENIX

ISBN: 0-941404-74-9
LCCN: 86-80657

First Edition 1986
(The DownSide Of Up)
Second Revised Edition 1988

Falcon Press, 3660 N. 3rd. St
Phoenix, Arizona 85012 USA

Manufactured in the United States of America

ACKNOWLEDGMENTS

Kahil Gibran, from *The Prophet*, Published by Alfred Knopf, 201 East 50th St. New York, NY 10022

Carolus Magus, from *The Magian Gospel of Brother Yeshua*, and Charles C. Wise, Jr., from *Pictures Windows on the Christ*, Published by the Magian Press, PO Box 117, Penn Laird, VA 22846

Swami Jyotir Maya Nanda, "Past, Present and Future," from *Yoga Mystic Stories and Parables*, Published by Swami Lalitanada, 6111 Southwest 74th Ave., Miami, FL 33143

James J. Hurtak, from *Keys of Enoch*, Published by The Academy for Future Science, PO Box FE, Los Gatos, CA 95030

A *Course in Miracles* Published by The Foundation for Inner Peace.

Neil Freer, from *Breaking the GodSpell: Genetic Enlightenment*, Published by Falcon Press, 3660 N. 3rd. St. Phoenix, AZ.

In addition the author would like to thank Mark Mawrence, Christopher S. Hyatt, and the seminal ideas of Zecharia Sitchin, Claude Vorilhon "Rael" and Bud Hopkins.

Efforts have been made to gain permission for all reference material. If a source has not been acknowledged formally, notify the publisher for such acknowledgment in subsequent printings.

INTRODUCTION
By
Christopher S. Hyatt, Ph.D.

MODEL MUDDLES

Don Juan tells Carlos that we all live in a "bubble of perception". We know our world through inference and the one we *choose* to see is selected from an infinite warehouse of possibilities. The language used to describe the "bubble" we live in, is created by our models of interpretation and the tools we have available to understand and measure our universe.

The purpose of models provides a filter to the infinite, for it appears that when the *'lens of perception'* is clear we are frequently overwhelmed and terrified by the wealth of information available. Sometimes we even experience 'neurotic or psychotic symptoms' when information overload forces us to shift our perspective. The frequently violent clash between world views can be seen everyday in the diversity of cultural models used to interpret and explain life.

During the Dark Ages, the Church did an outstanding job of closing the doors of perception, limiting not only information, but expression of new conclusions. By use of selective perception their world view was established and fiercely defended. If new data did not fit the prevailing paradigm, they simply forced it into existing models or excluded it entirely. Those who refused were simply sacrificed as heretics.

MUDDLED MODELS

Before inventions to detect and understand the structure of the atom, we had no real knowledge of its nature. However, the idea of the atom or primal material had a place in primitive cosmological theory, myth, religion and philosphy from the beginning of time.

Aldous Huxley makes a similar point in his discussion of the constellation Orion. With the naked eye, we see a "small faint smudge" and there is no doubt that we can construct from this a grandiose cosmological philosophy. However brilliant or complex this theory might be, it can never provide the depth and wealth of information gained through direct observation by a powerful "telescope, camera, and spectro-scope."

Our brains sensory/motor system is tuned to a very narrow band. Surrounding us are all types of phenomenon to which we remain completely unaware. Numerous devices have been developed to detect this *something* which our senses and reason deny. As with the narrow detection of our senses, our rational mind functions as a screening device, categorizing experience into concepts, world views and models that are familiar. Yet, data is being processed peripherally all the time of which we are not cognizant. If information can escape the inhibitory processes of the senses, rationality and ego, what emerges is a hunch, an intuition, an unexpected something which leads to discovering a world which far outstretches our normal understanding.

T.S. Eliot once said that, "humankind cannot bear very much reality". In this sense our models are tranquilizers, teddy bears and security blankets. Man takes the complicated and strange, and often reduces it to the 'banal and ordinary'.

An alternative to this obsessive reductionism is to search for that which is not apparent to our normal senses and reason. This will allow our hunches the opportunity to develop into new inventions, technologies and theories. Perhaps myths are as Whitehead noted, but "belief in a science yet unborn"; they are the hunches not yet fulfilled as workable models as man continues his search into his own origins

CREATION MYTHS
THE CONSPIRACY OF WHOS WHO

The origins of man appears to be a complete unknown, though numerous speculations exist, each a function of culture and mythology. There are myths portraying single creators as well as multiple ones. We have Maori cosmology, with its notion of a swelling embryo, or the Gnostic myth of Ennoia where the creator first conceives of a thought within himself. Creation by thought also exists in certain North American Indian myths and in some Eastern Indian myths. In comparison, one Chinese myth views creation as murder, for in their system you can not create without destroying.

Science has tried to identify steps leading toward the origin of life through chemical reactions and physical processes. The problem for science is to answer the baffling question of how complex bacteria could originate from non-living material.

Scientist, Robert Shapiro theorizes that the early biosphere exerted a heavy influence on the emergence of life, as chemical complexity evolved through a process of primeval cycles.

So, within the possibilities of our origin, stems these two primary competing systems, each containing numerous theories.

The first system is magical-religious and the second is scientific. Occasionally, we have mixed systems which attempt to use science to explain the observable events of creation through theories constructed from research and reason, which only fall again into a mystico-religious conclusion.

An attempt at unification between Judeo-Christian myth and Darwin's theory of evolution, two apparently contradictory models has been made, hypothesizing that God created the evolutionary process, or that God added something at some point of the evolutionary process to create man.

ANCESTORS IN THE SKY

The creationists conception of the bible is the exact word of God. Some hard-core scientists have dismissed it simply as poetry while Jung and others view the bible as an expression of the religious spirit in man.

Recently a new possibility has emerged in a book written by Zecharia Sitchin, *The 12th Planet* (Avon, 1978, now in its ninth printing). He speculates that ancient legends, myths and biblical tales are indeed true, reflecting a primitive attempt to express the events of the time. His ideas are not incompatible with evolution theory or modern science.

Civilized man, according to our present historic models appeared about 7000 years ago in the Middle East, when an advanced race emerged seemingly overnight from roots to primitive to have spawned it. Sitchin, refusing to accept this historical premise used his scientific intuition to pursue thirty years of arduous research.

Sitchin's brilliant and life-changing work is based on hundreds of thousands of unearthed archeological findings in the Mid-East, supporting his thesis that the biblical God (or Gods) is not an infinite being, but rather an advanced race of humanoids from another planet.

These extraterrestrials or Nefilim, mentioned in Genesis, created what we know as the human race by the direct result of genetic engineering. Thousands of years of folklore and myth have muddled this knowledge of our birthright into models which now retain only traces of truth.

In essence, Sitchin's scholarly creation thesis reads like modern science fiction becoming fact. The overwhelming evidence demonstrates that these extraterrestrials, through artificial insemination, fertilized the ovum of a paleolithic woman with the sperm of their own 'God-beings', and implanted it into a 'Birth Goddess', thus creating the first homosapien, 'Adam' of the earth. So it appears, **the human race was begun as a genetic hybrid!**

The notion of an engineered human race has had its play from our very beginnings. The mating of God(s) and animals is an ancient myth finding expression in many cultures. Unlike common historical interpretations of events which appears as biased ego-centric clap-trap, technology provides us with empirical evidence of how we are extending our nervous system and new models are being used to explain the universe and our place in it.

Sitchin's work begins to take on the reality of the believable when we begin to understand our own technological breakthroughs in the areas of genetic engineering, space exploration, and artificial insemination.

I do not believe it wild speculation to imagine future earthlings discovering new life forms in outer space and then applying genetic manipulation for their own purposes perpetuating our own beginnings.

According to Neil Freer, *Breaking the GodSpell -- Genetic Enlightenment* (Falcon Press, 1987), "The ramifications of such knowledge produces an immediate illumination of both the present and the future. Our institutions, social forms, political modes, customs, traditions, philosophy, religion, are all, when re-examined, shown to be influenced profoundly by our concept of ourselves as a result of that redefinition. The essence of the synthesis put forth is that, almost without notice, the last piece of the puzzle of the human condition has fallen into place and the revelation is the impetus for the unfolding of the next stage of the maturation of the race. And what exciting magnificent potential we have for that transition. . .The game has changed. The truth is beyond our expectations. The ramifications are inescapable. . ." *What an extraordinary freedom! What will it take to use it?*

When we lose are old ideas of the Monotheistic God(s), and replace it with our own god-sense, created by technology, there is a fear (technophobia) that our self-worth will be lost. However, this does not have to happen, if humans begin to trust, think and value themselves.

SEX
Genetic Propriety Rights -- Or Who Owns The Genes?

Throughout history, sex and religion have often been associated in literature and myth, one being reduced or amplified into the other. For example, Freud believed that 'religious experience' could be reduced to sexual drive. Reich attempted to unify the 'religious experience' with the notion of orgastic potency versus erective potency. He even began tying these notions, albeit in strange fashion, to a malevolent flying saucer conspiracy.

Tantra yoga has also attempted to combine such notions into a religious sexuality (Western interpretation). The essence behind tantra and orgastic potency, is that this 'mystical' experience frees the human from bondage and master. Total sexual-religious orgasm, is one of the mysteries, that has been held secret by religions-governments. *Genetic Propriety Rights -- Or Who Owns The Genes?*

A new idea has recently emerged from the devious mind of Dr. Hyatt. He speculates that from the power of organically liberated sexuality, a person can simultaneously make contact with his/her own genetic ancestry and uniqueness. In otherwords, *depth sex can release archetypal memories of our historical roots.* In this sense sex, genetics, and religion are tied in the collective unconscious. Could it be that Dr. Reich was on the right track, except he did not have the advantage of Dr. Sitchin's research findings. *Can we speculate that the profound*

sexual experience links us to our memories of extraterrestrial origins?
Genetic Propriety Rights -- Or Who Owns The Genes?

OUTER SPACE AND THE ILLUMINATI

I recall a number of years ago seeing a book illustration entitled *A Spiritual Pilgrim Discovering Another World*, which according to Jung represents a Rosicrucian illumination. The pilgrim beholds another world, with symbols representing the wheels of Ezekiel, disks and spheres. Remembering that I saw this picture in Jung's, *Flying Saucers: A Modern Myth Of Things In The Sky*, I immediately noticed Plate VIII, titled *The Quickening of the Child in the Womb*, which depicts the animation of the infant in the mothers womb from a source in a higher world. It appears as if something is entering the fetus.

Jung uses these and other pictures, as well as dreams, and novels to demonstrate the unconscious attempting to express itself through UFO symbols.

Some may interpret this as a simple wish to be saved from the problems of earth by technically superior, wise and benevolent beings, thus dismissing the entire experience as nothing but a need of the psyche. While Jung postulates a similar reason, he rejects the notion of "nothing but" and forces his reader to contemplate the idea that there is evidence for the possible existence of UFO'S and extra-terrestrials. To paraphrase him, he felt that there are very good reasons why UFOS cannot be easily dismissed by the process of psychologizing. Jung believed that science has not explained away the UFO, nor does psychology, but implies an alternative explanation, where psyche and reality may be working symbiotically.

Leaving these older pictures behind, John Wyndham presents an interesting story in his Sci-Fi book, *The Midwich Cuckoos* (1957). He weaves a tale about an extraterrestrial force which hypnotizes or sedates humans. Weeks later it is discovered that all the females are pregnant. In due time, the children are born with golden eyes, possessed by higher

intelligence as well as other unusual qualities. In other
words, an advanced species arrives on earth to perform
genetic experiments using a form of artifical insemination.
Could such an imaginative story symbolize a 'hunch' expressed
before a scientific model evolved?

More recently the titillation of science fiction has been
replaced with *bizarre reality*. Bud Hopkins in *The Intruders*
(Random House, 1987), reports a compilation of case studies
concerning UFO abduction experiences. Using hypnotic
regression he probes deeply into hidden memories of the
abductees.

After collating his information, the hypothesis projected is
astonishing. Extraterrestrials are indeed abducting individuals,
collecting sperm and ovum samples. It appears their purpose
is to create a *genetic hybrid!* This is not much of a quantum leap
from Sitchin's artificial insemination by the 'Gods'? Perhaps
some sort of genetic manipulation *is* going on by the Nefilim
or other groups on the Adam seeking to understand or
monitor where we are on the evolutionary cycle?

IMMACULATE MIS—CONCEPTIONS?

If we regard all of this as wild speculation bordering on the
insane, then we must also ask ourselves why a significant
portion of the human race believe in the idea of immaculate
conception?

Does civilization simply rely on paradigms created from a
faulty historic belief system? Could it be that the words
'immaculate conception' are merely a phrase expressing a
similar idea to artificial insemination?

Scientific advances are opening up new perspectives for
everyone willing to pay attention. They provide alternative
world views which include, immortality, genetic engineering,
and space travel. Compare this to our image of the cave man
sitting in terror of dinosaurs. What was his world view? If we
can imagine this juxtaposition for a moment, we may begin to
envision possibilities that the models of the last two thousand

years will meet the same fate. The difficulty for many of us however, is that we are too close to the old patterns. Regardless, if we can not completely accept the emerging new world -- its ideas at least stimulate us to begin to think about change. We may have to go without miracles, but this new world view allows us to entertain the miraculous.

A CASE STUDY

The sensual and compelling true story that follows is a personal montage of patterns repeated over and over, from relationship to relationship, life after life. Patterns that mirror many of the challenges facing all of us, as we wrestle with change.

This story is not a science fiction thriller, nor a chilling mystery of invading aliens. It is rather an exploration of innerspace that can lead to a deeper knowing of the universe and our place in it.

The essence of Ms. Greenberg's experience may be perceived in a number of ways:

First, we may accept it as mystical or as miracle.

Second, it can be seen psychologically, either as pathology, or as the search for wholeness.

Or, it can be understood as an extraterrestrial conspiracy to bring wisdom and understanding to this planet. In otherwords, are the Gods adding to their handiwork? Perhaps!

Regardless, I feel the deeply human story that follows will muddle many models as it unfolds the miraculous. I request simply that the reader allow him/her self to be open and join me in a fascinating tale which just might be the beginning of a new page of history in the search for truth, meaning and the revaluation of our religious models.

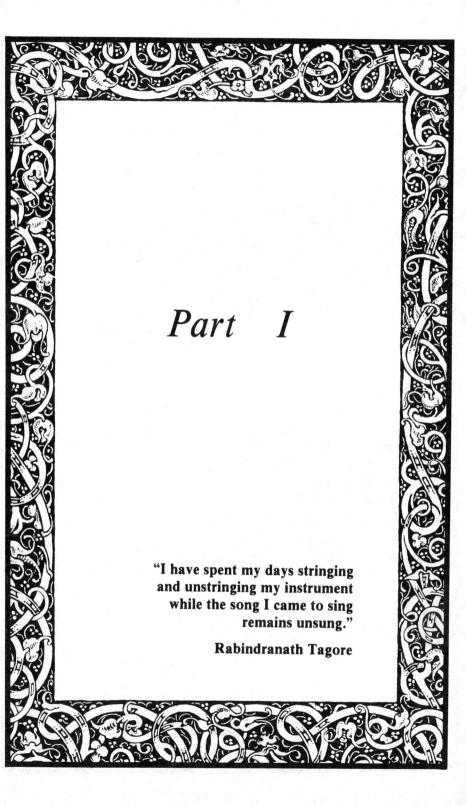

Part   I

"I have spent my days stringing
and unstringing my instrument
while the song I came to sing
remains unsung."

Rabindranath Tagore

Chapter I

Endless drive. Night lights and neon. Crystal avoided asking questions or making small talk. I couldn't handle any more variables entering in. My decision had been made, and the time was now.

The clinic was staffed with young doctors who moonlighted by keeping unorthodox hours. Husbands and wives crowded the waiting room in anticipation of birth. Their exuberance contrasted with my resigned despair, the light and dark of it. I wondered what they would think if they only knew my story or if my life would ever be normal again. How could that be when normal is not knowing? There was no unlearning what I now knew. Oh dear God, what am I doing? Is it all simply mortal fuss?

I'm missing the gold ring! There's no Sam or Sydney waiting, only a picture of Raphael's *Madonna and Child* hanging over the tray of instruments. The table so cold as my feet slip into stirrups. Quieting a scream, traveling inward on my pain. All these births and deaths.

Is destiny something out there separate from now, always in anticipation of? Or was destiny living , unfolding even back then, without the players knowing? So many veils to stagger through.

Oh yes, Gibran, perhaps life is not in the youth of spring but in the soil of winter . . . preparing.

Could all this decision and choice be a great cosmic joke? We believe we're given free will and in fact we are, but the irony is, it doesn't matter. Free choice only computes in the same earthbound horizontal plane of reality as material form, ego and results. No matter if I choose Sam, Sydney or Peter, I still have to learn what I came to learn in an endless array of stage sets, players and scripts--ancient, modern, science-fiction. Because the *master computer* in the sky doesn't compute form, it only is programmed in essence, connection and process. So the cosmic joke is there's really no choice, for the plan is already perfect.

Was the plan perfect back then, too?

Remembering another cold hard surface lying in the back of a station wagon. Another endless drive, night lights and neon. . . another hospital.

Oh God, how can ten years seem so many eternities ago . . . .

.   .   .   .   .

"Do you take birth control pills?" This was the first medical probe. Quickly my thoughts computed the consequences of Dr. Bradford's warning months ago. Oh God, am I to be cursed for the one thing I had refused to eliminate from my past bad habits -- the pill? Was Nothing sacred? Was I to have no entertainment in bed for my two months' confinement? Damn, it must have been the sixteen-day fast that increased the harmful side effects of the pill. My heartbeat quickened as I realized what I had done. Staring, disbelieving, I looked down at my leg now distorted, turning blue with swelling, veins pulsating beneath thin stretched skin.

His ski sweater stuck out from his white surgical gown. He was obviously the high priest of the hospital. "It's thrombophlebitis a blood clot in the leg. There'll be hourly injections directly into the stomach to thin the blood, and this tube", gingerly held between two fingers, "is for intravenous feeding. I'm afraid it's necessary since you can't lift your head to eat. Of course, your legs will be in traction to help the circulation."

I shook my head half from shock and to make sure I wasn't dreaming. This couldn't really be happening, not now. Not after all I've been through. He'll never believe this. I guess they seem competent enough for a little mountain hospital. An involuntary release of tears cascaded down my cheeks. The doctor bent over to dry my face. Taking my hand in his strong one, he went on in a compassionate tone, "We're attempting to dissolve the clot, but if it should dislodge before that time, it could return to the bloodstream in seconds with one of two destinations. The first possibility is the heart," his eyes shifted to a downward gaze, "and death would be instantaneous, or it could bypass the heart and take a route to the brain . . ." His words marched on, but I shut off . . . to the brain, creating the living dead! Was I to die now? But I'm so young, only 29! Is it possible the life I've lived is all there is? What did it all mean? Did I miss the boat? If I could do it differently, would I? To simply die would eliminate the need for questioning, for wondering, of painful confrontations. Slipping into a soft blackness, an enveloping comforting void, I sit on the edge of knowing death. Facing the ultimate enemy so intimately, my confrontation somehow carried with it a sense of relief. Certainly it would make life easier, this death. Maybe when you take fear to its extreme and live there, the energy dissipates. It becomes a known. Is fear then simply the unknown? I see you fear, I know you now.

The discomfort of my body demanded attention. If the clot does dislodge, oh please God, make it go to my heart. Eve, I must call Eve and make her promise to pull the plug if it should go to my brain. I'll tell her she can have all my clothes. My Porsche won't move her, she still can't drive.

Strange, my heart hurts. I wonder, is it the physical organ

itself, the heart house, where feelings and emotions live, or are they separate and simply a creation of the mind? And where's the mind located anyway?

He'll finish skiing soon and come looking for me. I'd rather the clot had already put my heart to rest than have him see me like this, looking at my legs straight up in the air suspended by pulleys, tubes and machines everywhere. Tasting the blood on my tongue, I released my lip. Voices . . . his voice; he's in the corridor talking to the doctor. Framed by the doorway, he just stares at me, disbelief and anger contorting his handsome face.

"How could you do this? You must really hate me!" His venom deliberately shot at me. Those were the only words that passed between us that night. Sinking back once more into blankness, I preferred the comforting inner darkness to his black anger.

Morning brought the daylight, but the nightmare continued. The doctor announced officially, "The news is, my dear, you need two more weeks without any movement before you can manage the nine hour car trip back to the city."

Then he burst into my room, "Look, I'm not listening to the diagnosis of some hick doctor. I've rented a station wagon, and hooked up a traction device for your legs. We'll get a more cosmopolitan opinion in the city. It's probably all psychosomatic, anyway, induced by desire to finalize our relationship!"

Amazing how someone else's reality can be so infectious. I began to wonder, is the mind capable of creating disease in order to manipulate itself. Would I be sick to punish him? To punish myself? Truly I love him and want things to work out, but is it possible that destiny has something else planned and my unconscious is making sure its scenario carried out? What of free will? It's probably a cosmic joke . . . .

In a few hours, we'll be on the road--destination: another hospital, *if* I make it. Does it even matter anymore? What an ending! The beginning seems so long ago . . . .

.   .   .   .   .

Nineteen-forty-five was a traumatic and terrifying time to be a child. The world was at war and there was no escaping fear in the air -- a time of black and white, lights streaking in night skies. Everything seemed larger; a sense of urgency in all things, but even air-raid blackouts in Los Angeles didn't stop my family from the monthly 'cousins club' dinner.

Uncle Irving reluctantly uniformed in army khaki was home on leave. Aunt Shirley's pompadour stayed up with the help of a rat. I'm not sure what help she was getting under her tight red sweater, but it was obvious from his frequent fondling, that Uncle Irving would soon find out. Tempting smells made my mouth water as Daddy's favorite potato pancakes were being deep fried in the kitchen. A trill on the piano -- the highlight of the evening was about to begin, a family talent show. My older sister Eve showed her paintings of Bambi and other Disney fantasia, followed by cousin Lorna singing "Because, you came to me . . .," and I waited to dance. My name is Mary.

This particular evening was the tenth wedding anniversary celebration of my parents, Jake and Lenore Rosenbloom. Jake was a man of passion. A sensuous, dimpled smile set off his Damon Runyon image. He looked especially handsome tonight in a bright Hawaiian shirt with palm trees and naked women. Jake loved people, and people loved Jake. Our house was a club, a gathering place for the boys amply supplied with Jack Daniels and a deck of cards. Living hard in work and play was the simple philosophy Jake understood.

Zady, his dad, left Russia to avoid the draft just before the revolution. By the time he made it halfway across the country, he had bought a horse and wagon and began to sell junk and settle down. And so, his son inherited the family business and graphic title, "Jake the Junk Dealer", offending my aesthetic sense. Once filling out a school form, after father's occupation, I wrote "deals in rare metals". This romanticizing left me with pangs of guilt, but more, longing for my father to be something he wasn't. How I wanted him to be perfect. Incredible, such a simple childhood response set up a pattern affecting my relationships with men for years to come. The model was beyond any movie hero -- someone I knew, evasive but familiar, divine yet human -- a subtle, etheric model. Lurking inside, lost in the cobwebs of my soul, was the memory of a Christ-like perfection in men.

For an anniversary present, Jake gave Lenore ten professional driving lessons, though she quickly decided the danger of maneuvering in big city traffic was not worth the independence. She feared the fast lane and anyway Jake drove.

Mother came from a family of twelve. Her father, whom I never knew, came from White Russia to mid-America and also bought a wagon. But instead of peddling junk, he spread the word of God through tales of Jewish folklore as a country Rabbi, an easier profession to romanticize about. Lenore would proudly tell us how simple life was when she had only one white cotton dress. No decision to make about what to wear, she would just wash and iron it at night and slip it on in the morning. And being white, it didn't fade. Now Jake, who did all the shopping, would lavish her with five new dresses at once, adding confusion to Mommy's life. My memory always dresses her as she was that summer night -- a sapphire blue matte jersey dress clinging to her long legs and those full pale blue sleeves with a wonderful slit from the shoulder to the tight wrist, subtly revealing her arm as she moved, sweetly vulnerably, someone you wanted to take care of, easy to love. She felt like a swan.

"We purchased her from a tribe of Blackfoot Indians" was the joke about my sister Eve, because of her dark olive complexion. Taking this very seriously, such jokes confused my own sense of who I was and from where. Crying, I'd ask, "How much did I cost?" Would then I know my worth? Strong memories of other places often made surroundings feel foreign and other worldly as though I'd been dropped off at the wrong house into a grosser vibration with smells of stale cigars and beer and frayed towels hanging in the bathroom. I felt offended. Where were the jasmine scented oils, the fine white linens? Where was the complaint department? Who could get it straight? Maybe I was really a queen and all this, a mere dream?

Still waiting to dance, the fear of performance created a deep pit gnawing inside my stomach. The fruit began to slip from the turbanded headdress. The costume was a Carmen Miranda imitation for a *Chiquita Banana* number. Dancing gave me a place to retreat, a deep silent space to float into daydream, choreographing great dance sequences on the stage of my mind. The memory of dance was so familiar, even then, but I never questioned the unknown source of my talent. Perhaps, the innocent can still remember a life before this until they learn not to listen. Could life be just a set-up, a continuing non-ending mystery school?

A constant childhood companion in sleep was a reoccurring dream.

This window into the night always brought the same handsome white horse proudly prancing on a carousel to the sound of carnival music. Urgently, I ran to mount him. Each time I reached out for the gold ring, the momentum and thrust of the merry-go-round would swing me forward on endless cycles as though some stronger force had taken over. Turning and turning, my frustration and fear deepened. I desperately searched my mind for the answer,"What will it take to get off?"

Somehow the moment was out of time -- ancient, ritualistic, eternal. The sound of applause for Lorna's rendition of *Because* brought me back. I found myself looking at my three-tiered skirt instead of an expected temple robe, staring into the maroon and yellow floral pattern of deco drapery instead of a columned sanctuary, and observing the performers instead of priestesses and initiates. "Here, be here" my soul cried. And once again, I experienced the rush, the conflict before the resolve.

"Princess," called Jake, "you're on."

Chapter II

There was no stopping him. He stood pushing his authority as he fondled his new growth of beard. "I'll sign whatever papers you need, taking full responsibility in case the journey proves too much for your patient. Is that sufficient Doctor!" He lit a cigarette inhaling deeply as though another brand and signed the release.

Carefully, I was stretchered into the back of the large rented station wagon; the innards had been gutted. They pulled my legs in the air by the ingenious traction device he had rigged, probably taking him all night to perfect.

"Take this, you'll need it for this nine hour endurance test." Tactfully, the gentle giant of a doctor slipped a bedpan by my side. "I'm afraid results of the suppository to relieve your other condition won't wait for the trip's end." I could overhear the doctor telling him as we drove off, "And remember, drive carefully. You're doing this against my advice. One bump could be fatal!" The sound of second gear faded out his final warning.

We've only been on the road for ten minutes, why is he pulling over? Meticulous sounds. I don't have to see. Preciously taking out his leather pouch of pre-sifted quality Tijuana Gold; then evenly pouring it across cupped paper. Now the

11

smooth one-handed roll, sealed with a lick. The match strikes, then the inhale, long enough to touch the base of his spine. The ritual complete. Oh, if only he made love to me with such intention. I can't believe he's attempting this gamble with my life, stoned! Biting my lip to keep silent, I'm certainly not in a position to rile him by criticism. My back feeling cold indentations of metal coming through the makeshift mattress, I adjust my position in an attempt at relief. *The Princess and the Pea*, Lenore's favorite bedtime story. Was I the Princess or the Pea? Now that he's handled his pain, he's driving like a madman, trying to race time, or erase time or recall a time . . . .

Along with the realities of growing up was another world inside me, simultaneously living, distancing all others, feeling separate. From where did this history come that gave me a mysterious sense of continuity? Life was a movie and I was the star but also the audience.

All that summer carried fantasies of the impending first day of high school. Closing my eyes, I tried to capture an image of the boy I would soon meet, for I was ready to make a fist and pull his stardust down if I had to. The alarm rang.

The day had arrived.

Eve spewing toothpaste all over the mirror, shouted from the bathroom, accusation already in her voice. "What are you wearing?"

"Oh, I'm not sure." Not then a lie for I hadn't yet taken the green angora sweater from her drawer. Dressing, the reflection in the mirror was unappreciated, as I ran my fingers through long dark hair, only vaguely aware of my growing beauty. Could I change myself as easily as I created Jake, the dealer in rare metals? The sound of the horn jolted me into the reality of this day. The green Studebaker belonged to Harry Bloomfield. My best friend Tess had met him over the summer. Tess lived down the street, but it seemed like another world, a normal home, something I privately longed for; where the smell of chocolate chip cookies made milk tolerable and cloth napkins made dinner so special. Dinner was late afternoon. Her father would twist his waxed moustache before picking up a fork, the mother giving an adoring smile while awaiting his approval of the meal. He died early, but she continued to set the table. How often habit takes over when the life has gone out of it.

I tiptoed into my parents' bedroom. It smelled of cigars and sex. There was a large economy size jar of petroleum jelly on the night stand. Jake must have gotten home early. They were in love. Discreetly, I took lunch money from the jar of coins on the dresser. Lenore was still asleep.

Inhaling a deep breath, I ran out the front door. "Are you ready?" Tess asked as she signaled me to sit in the back, squeezing herself against the dashboard as she pulled the seat forward. I climbed over long legs covered in pants obviously from last year for they were far too short, leaving six inches of pink iridescent sock showing. The legs were attached to a lanky body outgrowing itself and the most poetic face I'd ever seen. Instant recognition touched that responsive memory bank where a wealth of past history was stored. How far back it went seemed unclear, but the feeling definitely went beyond chemistry. Fears of the first day of school were silenced by sounds of my heart. Surely, everyone in the car could hear it. Who was he? No matter, he didn't say a word all the way to school making him far more interesting. My imagination could supply the details. Right then I created him. Strong yet sensitive, different from the rest, sent here for a special mission -- he would change things ... I could help him! Each morning for two weeks, the color of iridescent socks would change. All else remained the same -- silent. The stillness was finally broken when Sam Golden asked me, Mary Rosenbloom, to a dance.

Sam had spent a year of high school in a kibbutz in Israel. The Holy Land was right for him. So, although he was a year ahead, we began high school the same day. At sixteen and 6' 2" he was already above all the others. Sandy hair obeyed the wildroot command in a proud wave that occasionally would fall over his soft green eyes. What was so attractive about him was not just good looks or a wealthy family, but his deep sensitive nature so unlike any other. I wanted to handle him gently.

The dance blending that wonderful mixture of pain and ecstasy finally came. I was determined only to go as far as a kiss.

"Mary, I've had a wonderful night." I stood on my toes to meet his gratitude as the sky opened and stardust fell around us. His full sensual lips soft warm on mine were so very familiar. But this was enough for one night. I turned to go as he lowered his mouth once more to mine, his long surgeon-like fingers slipping behind my bra. My resoluteness to stop at a kiss was overruled.

Oh God, I see now how the pattern started even back then. Determined to get him to stop, with kindness I asked, "Can you pull over? I've got to use the bedpan."

"We're behind schedule, so do the best you can. You never minded roughing it!" His sarcasm, as usual, was controlling.

Nothing in my experience before this time could have prepared me for meeting Sam's mother, Esther Golden. Stately, prematurely gray, with soft braids neatly packed on the nape of her neck, no makeup was needed to adorn her chiseled face. Her clothing suggested expense but not extravagance, pearls not diamonds, ethnic shawls not furs. She was a matriarch of the first order. Although Abe Golden, a soft kind man had built a great fortune and was highly regarded in the business community, Esther was the dominant force in the domestic arena.

This particular evening, Esther had arranged a family outing, the opening of the ballet at Shrine Auditorium.

Sam walked in first. "Welcome, I call it home."

I tried to act unintimidated. Surely, I've lived in palaces in one life or another. I felt naturally noble. Two shining black grand pianos sat back to back taking up only a corner of the huge high-ceilinged living room. Tokens of travel everywhere displayed definite leaning to the Middle East. Several cozy seating areas invited relaxing in front of the fire but somehow didn't ease my presence. I wanted the flames to melt me away. Instead, my density seemed to expand.

Esther and her daughter Rachel were performing a Bach duet as we walked in. Esther graciously met us halfway across the room. I was thankful for it shortened my trip. Rachel felt continuing the fugue a priority. Sam's sister was the eldest of three. More than peculiar, she verged, even at seventeen, on being slightly crazy. Perhaps if she had had more style, she might have been considered simply eccentric. Her body sprouted up so quickly it appeared stretched out, forgetting to stop and form the basic female necessities. Adolesence had left its mark on her skin. She seemed to flaunt the scars provoking guilt feelings about the smoothness of my own. Brother Michael was a dark suave, version of Rachel. *Shortcut Mike*, named for his mastery of avoidance was the youngest.

Running late, getting dinner on was rushed. The table was masterfully set with elegantly cut glassware in deep burgundy, gold rimmed heirloom china from Austria, monogrammed silver and starched linen napkins. No cigars or football talk. No after dinner t.v., dessert and beer chaser. At fifteen the outer packaging certainly took first position and this was a blue ribbon family.

"Dear. . .," I jolted as Esther approached. "Would you mind putting milk on the table? Caroline's frazzled in the kitchen. The oven broke."

Her familiarity felt reassuring. I took a large half gallon of milk from the refrigerator and placed it on the table. This time, the voice was bittersweet, "Oh no, Mary, one does not put a milk carton directly on the table." She hastily removed it, almost expecting this error in etiquette, and poured the milk into a silver pitcher. I had quickly gone from "Dear" to "Mary" to "one" with my first mistake. Flushing red, I felt set up and retreated to Sam.

"Why didn't we ask the nurse at the hospital to pack a picnic. I'm starving!" No response from the front seat. The wheels pounded methodically on the pavement luring me back to that other time . . . .

"Let's have a picnic in the mountains. We'll show the road who's boss." Sam was anxious to try his new scarlet Triumph on the highway. The romantic in me dressed for the occasion, a soft summer dress, floppy hat and ballerina slippers. Ayn Rand must have created her *Fountainhead* heroine for me and Sam was an inspired Howard Roark.

"Your mom sure is a good cook, Sam offered. I smiled. Brisket was the main stay of Lenore's culinary repertoire Everything looked perfect. I had borrowed the wicker basket and red checkered tablecloth from Tess.

"O.K., are you ready for a hike?"

"Sure, I can't wait!" Oh God, please make it more of a walk than a hike, inwardly acknowledging my love/fear relationship with nature. Soon, we had left the trail behind for more adventurous terrain, my heart beating faster when our journey through the trees led to a deep ravine. Over the edge of the cliff we peered down into its bottom, a trickle of water running between jagged rocks and dead trees. The span from one cliff to the other side was about forty feet with a giant log lying conveniently across the gorge. Balancing with his arms, Sam gracefully ran across the log, leaving his heroine on the other side. For a moment mesmerized by the *cross* his body formed, I felt dazed.

"Come on, it's fun. You're not afraid, are you?" He shouted what seemed like a judgement.

Infiltrated by fear, I was sentenced to a plank over a deep abyss. Damn, it was no fun being tested out in nature it would have been far easier to dance *Giselle* for the Bolshoi. "I'm coming." Jewish and young, and oh-so anxious to please, even to my own demise, I tentatively began the journey across the log.

Halfway across, a voice coming from a man on the hill, bolted through me like lightning. "You dumb kids! Get off that log! Someone was killed falling off it last week!"

Sam looked scared. I froze. "Damn you! Damn you; get me off of here!" Blaming Sam helped a little, but it didn't change my situation. Mixed with his fear of my unillustrious end was a tinge of indulgence in his masculine superiority. So there I was--my upright position, mimicking a tightrope walker reduced to an unglamorous squat. Soaked with sweat, my hands slipped over the bark. Just as damaged were the pink ballerina slippers stained and wet.

Sam's next tactic was to use authority. "Come on, he's just trying to scare us; if you don't come, I'm leaving!" Now tears made the crossing even more difficult. The floppy hat went with the wind; I didn't dare move my hand off the log to retrieve it. So inch by inch, I crawled across the abyss separating us.

Down into the gorge I had gazed -- so afraid. Now staring up at the roof of a rented car -- so afraid. At this moment, it seems more than thirteen years ago -- probably because I'm feeling so old. God, life is long.

How humbling, a twenty-nine year old woman, lying in the back of a station wagon with my legs hanging in the air, unable to move, to communicate, being taken to a hospital, driven by an angry, stoned man with the backseat company of a bedpan! We must be going way over the speed limit, the snow is moving by so quickly. Strange, being at this pivotal point between life and death, memories become so vivid.

Oh, if I could be anywhere but here. When you look back, time takes on enormous speed; it's only the moment that seems to stand still and tomorrow so slow in coming . . . .

My higher education remained local. Sam was off to a private Eastern college to study design; he took Howard Roark very seriously. My fantasy of him became larger than life. Funny, imagining Sam always took him back to that log, crossing the abyss with arms outstretched, his body forming a *cross*.

Buses and more buses left me with no choice. I needed a part-time job. A car would change my life. One of Jake's cigar-smoking friends, Issy, owned the Beverly Health Club for Men. So, for three nights a week, I sat behind the reception desk of this posh club, smiling at celebrity clientele.

"Wow, it's a sizzler and I need a Coke." The bookkeeper came out of her cubbyhole office stretching. As we talked, a tall, tanned young man walked up to the reception desk and signed the register. The bookeeper, reading backwards his signature, asked, "Are you *the* Lance Reventlow?"

His face became stern and answer indifferent. "I don't know what you mean, Madame!"

She continued, unruffled by his aloofness. "Well, you know, is your mother, Barbara Hutton?"

In a low condescending voice, he indulged her. "Yes, she's my mother."

My naivete prevailed, "Who's Barbara Hutton?" The effect on Lance was positive; He was instantly enamored. The bookkeeper later filled me in. Barbara Hutton was one of the wealthiest women in the world, "The Million Dollar Baby in the Five and Ten Cent Store." Indulging my curiosity, I pulled his card; the statistics read: Age: twenty-one; Hobby: sports car racing; Occupation: retired. Jake's fast lane looked like slow motion compared to this jet stream.

Each Wednesday night thereafter, Lance would keep me company as I smiled at passing clientele. "Let's leave here. Go to my house. My houseboy will prepare a Philippino feast." I coyly rejected the idea. After the fourth week, Lance firmly demanded, "Why?" unaccustomed to being refused.

The truth was simple, "I'm not allowed to go out with anyone who's not Jewish." Saying the words aloud brought the humor in focus and we both had a good laugh. After all, in addition to being handsome and stimulating, he was also the richest young man in the world. Even Jake finally agreed an exception should be made. But when the night arrived Jake acted out second thoughts.

"Daddy, get up off the couch. Lance is coming any minute. Can't you put a shirt on!" He finally succumbed, crushing his empty beer can with his left hand, muttering something about Gentiles.

Something inside me, even then, knew he was a deviation from my destiny. I had the same kind of feeling about dance -- unnecessary to pursue, somehow already complete in another time and place. This time, I knew fate had something different waiting for me.

Summer finally arrived after a difficult first year in college. The extra money from working meant mobility and an apartment of my own. A small room with a hot plate was home in a converted old stately house in the Hollywood Hills on Queens Road. My sense of drama forced immediate acceptance for Sam lived on Kings Road. A giant oak stood outside my door; its shadows darkening my room but its beauty worth the hidden sunshine. Colors splashed -- in pink and black pillows and lush green plants in brown woven baskets. With a little time and much imagination, my one room took on a magic of its own.

Sam was coming home! I tried to sort out what that meant to me. How strange we humans are in going directly to the mind for a reading on our heart. What would it be like to simply follow feelings? But how can you trust feeling not to change? Can you pin it down and make it constant, or give it room to expand and contract. If only Mutual of Omaha insured a fickle heart.

Sam now filled his tall handsome body with a new command, kind of a time-to-take-charge attitude. I wondered if this new confidence touched the soles of his feet grounding him in reality or if this were merely a preppy affectation? Looking into those green sensitive eyes, always asking not to be hurt, I knew for me, he was in charge.

With our first kiss slipping into feeling, I was quickly brought back to mind as Sam laid out an ultimatum, "I'd never marry anyone without first testing our sexual compatibility. Really Mary, what if it didn't work?" His words spinned me off into daydream, the momentum picked up by the merry-go-ground, carrying me on endless cycles. Was I to miss the gold ring? I remembered Lenore's ultimatum to Jake -- he had to stop boxing professionally or she wouldn't marry him. Her last bit of control went with his acceptance. Must relationships always be so manipulative? Choices. Was the basis for decision always no choice? The absurdity of an academic argument that it was time for sex replaced romance and spontaneity with achievement and performance. There had to be something else. But what?

That night we initiated my new apartment and terminated my virginity. The real idiocy was that I gave my consent to his ultimatum. The controllers and the controlled -- both simply afraid to lose. Sam was staying with Harry, who was studying to be an actor and in preparation for possible seduction, Sam had taken a condom from his roomate's bedside drawer.

Hard sex was not nearly as much fun as foreplay, penetration was awkward and painful. I felt violated. So *this* is what he demanded before he married me? I think we were both short-changed. There was a wetness inside from all the friction; the condom had broken.

The next six weeks moved in slow motion; the thought of pregnancy hung heavily over our relationship. When nausea began accompanying breakfast, I went to a doctor. I expected an unwanted result. Loneliness filled me -- separateness from everyone, including Sam. This certainly didn't satisfy my need to have everything look right.

How fickle form is! Making Sam marry me wouldn't work, just like making me have sex didn't work. Choice, what choice? There was no choice. Caught in the form of it, plans were made for an abortion.

To avoid the dark guilt that rode in on every wave of nausea, I kept occupied. It was Bubby's birthday, my old Jewish grandmother; Zady my grandfather, was dead. She was one of the last of her kind, orthodox verging on occult. On the Sabbath, she sat, a shawl draped over her head moving in rhythm to prayers, as she hovered over the candles. Infused by the cadence of it all, I found myself rocking back and forth with prayers of my own. A familiar ancient rhythm echoed of synagogues and sanhedrin.

Her skin was radiant and her eyes knew an inner secret; but her connection to God was blanketed in superstition and tradition -- surely God didn't mean it to be that way. Her greeting was always in the form of question, laden in a thick Russian Jewish accent, "Ven vill you come to see me again?" She continued, whining, with heavy hand gestures ushering me in, "And I hear you h've your own apartment; a nice Jewish girl doesn't live alone." My mind silently added, "Nor get pregnant." Her prayers over, she folded the shawl neatly and placed it in a cedar chest as smells of mothballs escaped. This time she put an apron over her head and turned to making bread. Shaking her finger as she kneaded the dough, the flour dust left a trail in the air. This whole scene, the smells, textures, even the preaching, made me feel secure and forget for a while.

"You're twenty years old. Like your name, you're a Rose-in-bloom, soon you'll vilt. Who'll vant you then, a spoiled flower? You must get married and have a baby." Leaving, I wondered whether compassion or support were something only given when accompanied by a certain belief system. If one goes against the rules, love becomes arbitrary. Can compassion be controlling too?

A passing ambulance speeding someone else off to a hospital interrupted the stillness of my thoughts. But within our confined space remained silence . . . .

Endless drive. Sam didn't speak all the way downtown. The same intellect that decided premarital sex was imperative, now concluded abortion the logical answer. The tears we both held back created a density of their own. That might have been the beginning of a lifelong protection of the poet inside him, a cornerstone being laid for the building of a solid brick wall.

Finding someone to perform an abortion in those days was no easy task; for Sam and Harry the investigation announced their virility. For me, my reputation became cloaked in promiscuity. No name was etched on the glass door of Suite 204. Feeling uneasy, we walked in and sat down. As if greeting our common enemy, Sam held my hand tightly. A tall bony woman came in and coldly addressed him.

"Did you bring the five hundred dollars?"

"Yes." Sam answered curtly.

Came the order, "Put it on the table and leave. You can come back in two hours."

Sharing a frightened look, Sam tried to take command.

"No, I want to stay."

She accentuated her refusal by pointing to the door. Sam's smile attempted encouragement as he shyly kissed my cheek. "Don't worry, Mary. It'll all work out."

At that moment, I wanted Sam to take me away, to mount the white horse on my carrousel and give me the gold ring, but the glass door closed behind him. Following the authoritative nurse like a lamb innocently being led to slaughter, I was taken into an adjoining room where my eye immediately spied the cold, blunt instruments on the table. I could feel them pierce my heart as the nurse placed a blindfold across my eyes. My last glimpse caught a painting on the wall of Raphael's *Madonna and Child.*

"The law doesn't look kindly on this, and the doctor can't take any chances." All my other senses heightened as my eyes were covered." I could feel a large man enter the room for he gave the impression of taking up alot of space; his voice impersonal as he lay me down on hard plastic and placed my feet in icy metal stirrups. He disguised any empathy that might hinder his work.

"This will feel cold," he said as he used an instrument to widen his view. My teeth and fists clenched. If Jake knew, he'd kill me.

Pleading, "When will I get a shot?"

The nurse endorsing her own lack of compassion emphasized, "An anesthetic would be far too dangerous; after all, we don't want a corpse on our hands!"

"Oh God, please help!"

"He didn't get you into this, a man did. Call on him!"

My thoughts had, but he refused to mount the white horse. The next hour was a nightmare.

On the ride home, the tears had gone. And left was the stark reality of now -- vivid greyness, blacks and whites. "It's so hard for me to tell you this Mary, but I've decided it's best if we stop seeing each other. There's a part of me that wants to hold and take care of you, but I've had a long talk with my dad . . ."

"Well, the conversation apparently injected you with courage to be detached." I felt betrayed and the hurt deepened. How simple life was when sexual gratification came from climbing the maypole at school, or security was dear Jake joking about his three girls, "Buy me, give me, take me."

After that day, a love-hate feeling was seeded inside me toward Sam. We had been through something together that created a strong bond; ironically, it also tore us farther apart. I wasn't sure if the breach could ever be healed.

Peculiar creatures that we are, the first thing you do when you dissolve one relationship is immediately desire to seek refuge in another, making sure someone out there thinks you're all right. I dialed the number for Lance Reventlow. The Philippino houseboy announced that he was on a honeymoon with his bride, Jill St. John, the actress. The irony was hilarious, for while I was going out with Lance, Harry had introduced his acting school pal, Jill to Sam. But after changing partners, Jill ended up with a husband, and I with memories. Maybe our world is smaller than we imagine and the players have many roles.

"Can you turn up the heat? It's freezing back here!" Louder, "It's freezing back here." I could hear my voice in attempt at graciousness. Sarcasm, along with smoke from another joint came wafting to the back of the station wagon where I lay.

"It's nice and warm up here!"

Damn you, you controlling bastard. My hand firmly pressed my mouth closed as not to let the words escape. Calm down. We must be halfway to Los Angeles by now. Only a few more hours. The snows turned to rain. My bones feel brittle. My view about mid-window offers freeway signs and telephone poles. All those words traveling over hundreds of miles of wires unheard except in two little receivers . . . like memories over the years. Who really cares? Sam had left . . . .

Europe seemed the perfect salve for wounds of the heart. I sold my mobility and was ready to go with Jacqueline Jacobs, a young artist I had met through Sam. Jacqueline was on the hefy side, but her face offered potential though she sabotaged her resources by insisting on tying waist-length hair back in a pony tail. I have to laugh when I think of gorging on pasta trying to put myself on a more even scale with her -- the pleaser in me surfacing again, like a rubber ball held under water.

We rented a Citroen 2CV, a French version of a tin-can on wheels. London, Paris, Geneva, Rome . . . .

In Rome, the quaint pension across from the Fontana de Trevi was home for one month. Each day, we succumbed to the coin-throwing ritual asking the Bernini created Gods to grant our wish . . . mine always the same, for *perfect love*. At the end of the first week, we naively watched as the fountain was drained for cleaning. The Gods stood nude in the sunlight as half the city youth filled their pockets with loot from romantic wishes of the tourists of Rome.

Of course, there were a few short-lived romances, although I was now sexually over-protective and any exploration by these foreigners was limited to the top half of my body. In Rome, we met Pietro and Fabrizo, quite a pair. As fate would have it, I later found out that Fabrizo's first love was not me, but Pietro.

At the same time during the five months of the trip, visits to American Express for mail were never a disappointment, for a letter from Sam was always waiting. My independent stand had provoked his passion. Sprawled across the bed reading his letters, I felt a twinge of jealousy from Jacqueline; she always had a weakness of heart for Sam. I wonder now if it were my own projection or truly what she had been

feeling. When you really love someone wouldn't you think that everyone felt the same attraction? Was this the basis of much unfounded jealousy? The last important news item from Sam was that he had decided to finish college in Los Angeles and had already moved back. Could I ever trust him again to be all that I wanted, or could I trust him again to do exactly what he had done before?

We chose a quiet mid-week day to visit St. Peter's Cathedral. The sun was bright in the piazza -- all the tourists adjusting their cameras. The grandeur demanded reverence as you walked through the doors and entered this awesome space of cloistered spirit. And then, as if all the splendor of architecture were simply to house what came next, there just to the right, lit by candles and the brightness of white marble was Michaelangelo's statue of the *Pieta*. The mother held her son's broken body in her arms. Time stood still. Conscious thought knew not why, but somewhere in the archives of eternity was written my understanding of the pain of it. Overwhelmed with emotion, I surprised myself falling to my knees and weeping in compassion for mothers and sons.

Finally, after visiting half the churches and museums in Europe, I knew I wanted to live there amongst the paintings. I'd return to school! Art history would be a perfect major and with three hundred dollars miserly saved from my travel money, I would pay tuition. Now, with my own plan, I was anxious to get home; school would fortify me against falling into merely a support system for Sam.

Rigged, steel, support system -- my life at the mercy of a contraption -- looking up at my legs. Thank you powers that be, he's finally turned on the radio. "He's got a ticket to ride . . . . He's got a ticket to ri-i-de." It must be a red light. Funny, the driver in the next car is moving his mouth in rhythm to our music, singing away, "He's got a ticket to ride. . ." Everyone with a ticket and a different destination. What an incredible connecting and healing force music is, yet each sings the same song separately. . . .

Only the second voyage of the *Leonardo da Vinci,* but since it was departing from Napoli, hundreds of Italian immigrants boarded, bound for America. Docking in New York brought out all my red, white, and blue emotions. Chaos was the scene at the dock. January snow covered the ground all around the outdoor tent facility making it look like an open air market. Hundreds of Italian immigrants searching for their American family and exploding with emotion when they were found. Salami and garlic smells wafted through chilled air. Screams of panic softened by sounds of laughter, harmonicas and guitars. All senses were awakened by the vitality of the city. There was no mistake, we had landed in New York. Scanning over this remarkable scene, my breath stopped short. There in the midst of it all, was Sam standing tall as if he could control confusion. Harry was next to him. I guess everyone needs a little support. Sam had journeyed cross country to deliver another ultimatum -- this time, marriage.

Chapter III

"Oh Sam, Sam, the controlling man . . ." my silent song sung to the rhythm of passing telephone poles. With a deep breath, I allowed the exhale to carry me back into memory . . . .

All my emotions churning inside confused my priorities. Always so concerned with what things looked like -- function following form. Now I was changing, beginning a new decade and a passion to explore inner workings of the mind. The convoluted brain, I wanted to delve into its creases, gaining secret insights.

The *The Foxes of Harrow* and *Wuthering Heights* had once satiated the girlish romantic surge in me and travels opened me up to writings of Anais Nin and Herman Hesse; somehow, I aligned myself with the intricate workings of these brilliant minds, their words like twisted road maps into the bowels of personal thought -- a depth for which I longed to know more. Was it to be found by way of the kitchen?

Still I was trying to understand Sam's needs, his change of heart, for somehow, getting married right now felt contrived . . . he wrote his script, acted it out, and marriage was the next scene. Maybe guilt lingered from the abortion or perhaps, he wanted sex on a regular basis.

"Hey, don't you think I understand your need to learn.

Our life together won't stop your going back to school."

"But you still have two more years of school. Who's going to foot the bill for this educational extravaganza?" My question was as sincere as his answer.

"It'll give my father endless joy. His life's devoted to making money for this end -- educated children. What else are rich Jewish parents for?"

"O.K. here's the plan," Sam excitedly shared his orchestration of the event. "The wedding's going to be at Harry's uncle's apartment overlooking Central Park -- very posh. The rabbi is a re-constructionist, part of a new group considered avant garde by orthodox standards. They're more into cultural heritage. He said their founder, Mordecai Kaplan, was a great leader. The rabbi even has a brother in California who's doing research on a new drug called LSD. Both obvious disappointments to their nice Jewish mother who no doubt thought she was educating a simple rabbi and Beverly Hills doctor."

"Somehow, I don't feel like a white bride. What about a green A-line dress with matching pillbox hat?"

Jacqueline was non-committal about the dress but insisted on buying me a luxurious nightgown, strangely inappropriate, for I was convinced by then she would prefer sleeping with Sam herself.

The morning of the wedding I woke crying; "It's Jake's birthday."

"Baby don't cry, we can't chance a call home . . . I know I'm right. Somehow, someone would put a damper on the way we're handling things."

My crying continued all day as I prepared myself. Where was all this deep sadness coming from and why? Was I too just acting out my own script and this proper time to insert marriage into the scenario, so caught up in the world of form? Would Sam be all that my soul longed for in a man? My motives and desires turned over in my mind -- was this truly part of my destiny? Was I weaving the future in enchantment with the right threads? Never mind! From then on, I would know who I was, Mrs. Samuel Golden . . . It was late. We rushed out the door, forgetting my bridal bouquet. . .purple orchids.

Harry's aunt was the nervous, impeccable housekeeper type. The plastic slipcovers were just removed, their impressions still visible in the sofa's velvet cushions. In greeting she nodded, left me standing in the doorway and pulled Sam aside, "Dear boy, I'm using my best crystal wine goblet for the rites, so just before you crush it with your foot, substitute this water glass. Don't forget now, it'll be on the floor in a napkin. Then we'll shout 'Mazeltov'. O.K., come in, take off your coat."

Degas dancers caught in pirouette assembled on the coffee table. A Louis XVI desk whispered its heritage of time . . . Harry's uncle had spent a lifetime collecting works of art. All the walls were lined from Rembrandt to Gauguin, stopping only for the window and a nature scene overlooking Central Park covered in snow.

A flashbulb went off. Excitement was high. Photographing the wedding, Jacqueline's big project, captured the precious moment in black and white. Harry in his Oscar Levant fashion, succumbed to tradition and played the *Wedding March*. Gathered in front of the Central Park scene, the ceremony was about to begin. Wishing I had my purple orchids or Jake or Lenore, I watched the skaters dancing on ice.

The Rabbi read from Kahlil Gibran:*

**"Give your hearts but not into each other's keeping,
For only the hand of life can contain your hearts.
And stand together yet not too near together,
For the pillars of the temple stand apart.
And the oak tree and the cypress grow not in each
other's shadow."**

"The purity of the Hebrew language is like kissing the bride on the mouth rather than through many veils. May this bride be blessed by the lifting of the layers."

We each sipped from the crystal wine goblet. The substitution was made, crystal turned to glass. Sam raised his foot and forcefully crushed it. Harpsichord music of Vivaldi's *Spring* resounded among shouts of 'Mazeltov.' We kissed long and hard, when Jacqueline screamed, "Oh God, I forgot to take the lens cap off!" And there were no black and white memories.

During the celebration dinner at the Plaza, Sam ordered caviar to chocolate souffle for everyone, already preparing for his role as 'Big Daddy.' As he picked up the tab, his free hand lodged between my legs under the table.

"Do you have any cash?"

The three hundred dollars for tuition, so miserly salvaged from my travels was packed neatly in the bottom of my purse. "Well darling, I've been saving this particular three hundred . . ."

Sam snatched it up. "You don't have to worry about money now!"

God how I loved him, but unfortunately, that love was inhibited in our sex life; even on our wedding night the lingering thought of our first time and its results were always with me. Penetration/Abortion. Dropped in the midst of kissing, fondling and sips of champagne were intermittent warnings of our future. "You know Esther wants a perfect daughter and she'll mold you like putty into her image."

"That doesn't sound like such a terrible fate. After all, I've found the perfect man, why not mother?" Yet unaware of the conflict that Sam already lived in, trying to please a woman whose disdain for making money set up a father whose life was devoted to earning it. I wonder if he chose a creative career to bridge the gap.

Now his voice a tone more serious, "As for me, please

don't put me on a pedestal . . . I'm bound to fall off!" He recognized something in me I couldn't yet see. He warned, "Listen Baby, when you encourage my potential, I feel pressured. Like I have to perform. The abyss between your reality and my actuality is an easy pit to fall into. I'm afraid disillusionment will trail not far behind." A setup Sam was very uncomfortable with and I refused to see. Would I become like his Mother? Did I expect him to build cities, not houses, as Jake dealt in rare metals not junk? Is he, are we, caught in the marriage trap -- a pre-conditioned, pre-determined, pre-life setup? . . . Turning over I climbed on his back and wrapped my legs around him. It'll all work out for Mr. and Mrs. Golden.

Our return home was triumphant; Jake was thrilled his daughter now true royalty, at least in the Jewish scheme of things and even if it did mean giving up my virginity. Esther's mother expressed the only noticeable disapproval. Austrian Jews tend to have an Aryan superiority over their Russian counterparts. Still, Esther Golden saw great potential in me -- perhaps someday I would fall into her abyss. She immediately began plans for a gala wedding reception in the Golden's garden with large ice sculptured swans swimming in the pool along with hundreds of water lilies. The day arrived, a chamber music ensemble strolled through the umbrellaed tables while enough smoked salmon, caviar and champagne were served to put an enormous dent in Jake's bank account although in the end Abe refused to let him pay. The February temperature reached ninety-five degrees that day . . . the ice swans melted.

Sometimes some handsome student or exciting professor made me wonder why I had tied myself down in marriage, but after dinner my fantasies were diluted in dish water. I loved Sam.

Still questions, hovering and omnipresent, haunted me like what connects all things to each other? Is there one

all-encompassing law that rules? Are things all relative until
they reach an absolute? Is that God? What is the beginning
and is there an end? And most importantly, what is the
purpose of life? What's it all for? My soul demanded a
search. The lure of the intellect still left a major void in the
puzzle; sometimes I felt figuring it all out was simply mental
masturbation. There must be layers and layers of knowing
before leaving the confining circle of the merry-go-round.
Motivating this quest for a universal plan was my own deep,
personal fear of the greatest unknown, death, for the
thought of a final letting go terrified me.

What a wonderful sense of security wrapped up in the warm
blanket of past answers or even seduced by the veil of future
questions, but somehow in the present you feel like you're left
holding a philosophic bag of garbage . . . or a full bedpan.
Damn, I wish, I wish -- Oh hell, I don't know what I wish. It
could have been so unblemished . . .

A weather-perfect Sunday, not meant for indoors. Combining our creative abilities, we played a game to come up with
the 'perfect Sunday.' Sam's response was so quick, I thought
he manipulated the whole sequence. "Of course, sailing --
let's buy a sailboat!" I wondered wherein did perfection lie,
the act of buying or sailing? Confronting my fear of death by
riding its number one phantom, the ocean, when I couldn't
even swim was not my idea of an ideal Sunday selection.
Sam's masculine image of himself satisfied as captain of
his own ship, his excitement peaked as he rushed through
his Spanish omelet. I could tell this was serious when he
started mixing his eggs and potatoes. He looked across the
table at me, "And you're the perfect first mate."
Was I never going to be captain? My own romantic
self-image was offended. We walked through the marina
looking for boats for sale. "Oh, Sam look at this one. You

can see yourself in the wood. It looks like a Victorian drawing room."

"Yes, and are you willing to become a fulltime varnisher?" As he pushed his poet down deeper inside, my poet was forced along for the ride.

We settled on a more practical 32 foot fiber glass sloop with bright blue sails and multicolored spinnaker. Sailing soon became a way of life, that wonderful sound of silence -- only wind against the sails. Watching Sam behind the tiller, he wore his role well. God, he was so handsome -- his hair turned the color of the sun, his skin a golden tan. He made me feel safe. I learned to love the sea, as long as I was on top of it. After all, it was under the surface that was wet, dark, deep and unknown.

The snow turned rain drummed hard on the roof of the station wagon. I feel underwater, caught in that dark, deep unknown -- a victim of my own pattern, anchored firmly in marriage. Looking up I see the steel support system making sure blood doesn't forget its journey back to the heart. Refuge in the past . . . let's see, where was I in my saga with Sam?

He finally graduated. And along with the graduates, all the wives were rewarded with an honorary degree. We were growing up and along the way, our roles becoming well defined. Once you lay your major course in life, everyday navigation becomes directed toward that end. Our ground-work subtly but firmly planted my role as first mate, and I felt a growing victimized reality as I became more and more caught up in the play.

Each Sunday, a new entrepreneur attitude budded in both Sam and me making real estate on the sand more enticing than a sail on the sea. A new marina was just completed and rumor had a freeway connecting it to town . . chance for a new Sunday game!

My moon in Capricorn helped creative juices flow in the direction of business. All this ocean front property with scattered beach shacks, oil wells and wild daisy fields, was just waiting to be discovered! If Sam could design, package and build apartment houses, I could certainly lease and manage them. Our excitement was infectious and a limited partnership was set up with Sam, General Partner and me, his assignee, a kind of legal appendage -- a position with no control.

Now we had to find investors. Zak Black, in school everyone called him zexy Zak, was the first boy I ever fell in love with. Crazy, all those telephone calls just to hear his voice then my ten year old courage quickly faded and I'd hang up. But one day that pattern abruptly ended when I overheard Zak, in the lobby of Temple on the Jewish High Holidays, telling friends how some inconsiderate jerk kept calling and hanging up, disturbing his father who was recuperating from a heart attack. I was mortified! Right then, on holy ground, I swore to give up telephone intrigue forever. Even so, my infatuation with Zak's sensual and powerful nature was to sustain itself well into my adult life. Sam and Zak were close friends, and now that Zak was a major personal manager in the entertainment business, he had many famous clients, all in hot pursuit of a tax shelter. What a deal! Zak would harness all green energy. Sam would design and build a beachfront fortress, demonstrating that his business prowess was a patriarchal, genetic triumph. Having Zak on our team was exciting male energy. His certainly wasn't a handsome face; my daydream appraisal was more on the lines of ethnic and sexy. Ah well, I wondered if anyone would ever think of me as sexy again, placing my hand on an ever growing stomach.

Climbing into a pink chiffon maternity dress was no easy task, for the past two months, I had lost sight of my feet. The celebration -- another wedding -- my sister Eve was finally

getting married. As I applied extra makeup to compensate
for my bulbous condition, memories of Eve filtered through
my mind. Always a strange one, emotional and amazingly
fragile, she felt like a fawn, dutifully attached to family and
tradition. Eve painted her world with rosy colors, but
behind the Disney watercolor wash, were dark clouds and a
frightened Bambi. As a child, more than I, she had been
exposed to Jake's other women. Eve had dealt with them as
make-believe, suppressing her feelings. The cake had fallen
but the icing would cover it all up. How different we were. In
contrast, I would lie awake at night listening to my mother
crying because Jake hadn't come home. My heart would
break for her and smoldering would turn into rage against
him. Fury would prod me out of bed, I'd pack his clothes,
and throw the suitcase out the front door. The next day's
scenario was always the same, forgiving wife would force
her headstrong daughter to unpack her misunderstood
father's belongings.

A smile came across my now overly madeup face as I
remembered finding out about Louise from a nurse in the
hospital where Lenore was having a hysterectomy. Jake's
girlfriend, Louise, was also in the hospital with some
gynecological problem, sharing doctors, nurses and husband
with Lenore down the hall. Mother's tests had come back
positive for syphillis, and Jake was on the spot! My reaction
was predictable; I stormed into the hospital room of his
mistress, where Jake was visiting at the time, and bluntly
demanded a divorce.

"What are you laughing at?" Sam called out from the
bedroom.

"Just some funny memories." I answered then cursing the
mascara misplaced in my eye.

I sat between Sam and Zak at dinner. Part of Sam's adult
role was heavy drinking and Zak kept encouraging one
more as he toasted the bride and groom. "See that blond

over there?" Sam perked up at Zak's question. "She likes you, Sam. I've been watching her watch you. Why don't you ask her to dance?" Sam snapped at the bait.

"Sam!" My outrage surfaced.

"Why are you so upset? I'm me just being me." He was off to meet the challenge.

"You're still the most beautiful girl in the room." Zak whispered in my ear longing for an attentive word. His subtle advances playful at first, were now contrived. Why not? Sam deserves it.

"Ow!"

"What's wrong Mary?" Zak protectively put an arm around me.

"The baby kicked!" This time Sam controlled the situation more than he knew. Midnight past, Sam barely managed to maneuver around the dance floor with some Beverly Hills Barbie, when my indignance peaked.

"Mary let me take you home and put you to bed."

Picking up my lumbering body from the chair, I refused Zak's invitation; then deferring goodbyes, wedged myself behind the wheel of my classic Mercedes 300 and headed home. The car's aesthetic lines usually pacified its Sherman tank performance, but not tonight, and all that extra mascara was finding its way down a tear-stained face when a jolting noise and swerve announced the rear tire was flat. There wasn't any humor left, even for such an absurd predicament as a seven month pregnant woman, looking like a pink Easter egg, hitchhiking down Sunset Boulevard in the middle of the night. Home never looked so good, nor felt so lonely. As the key turned in the latch, rage welled up inside, along with determination to punish Sam. Deliberately, I placed the chain across the door. I lay waiting in bed. Where could he be so late? He's trying to punish me. He won't come home at all. My anger was given extra time to fester. First came a knock, then a bell.

"Mary." Softly, no response altered the next "Mary" into a shout.

"Mary, I'm going to kick the goddam door in!" Then a loud crash.

A large imprint of a foot in the door forever served as a reminder of that drunken evening. Odd how sex is always better after conflict -- somehow mixed with fear of losing and reward of winning.

Expecting a baby meant a grander house was needed. Now I would know who I was not only by my man, but through a child and a home in all its architectural splendor of glass and steel set dramatically facing the sea. The recession had put a halt to building, times were hard and lack of work was depressing Sam. But Abe came through with a loan which he referred to as an advance on Sam's inheritance. Now with money and time, Sam not only designed his dream house, but actually put hammer to nail and built it. So each day as our child grew inside me, Sam externalized the womb to house our family. I planted a tiny coral tree in the garden.

The huge boughs grew to cast a dark shadow over the house seemingly indifferent to the people problems within. Still not all trips to the hospital are bad . . .

The waiting room was filled with Goldens, Rosenblooms and an assortment of friends. For seventeen hours, labor persisted. Those mysterious excruciating pains that begin in the spine and slowly sneak around the side exploding front on, got closer and closer together until my body seemed encircled in torment — not so very different from the pain of abortion. Could it be the same soul I once refused? Oh yes God, please give me another chance. Finally, the doctor called Sam in. "Well, the head is hung up on the mother's pelvic bone; if we wait any longer, the baby will be born dead. It's up to you if we should do a Caesarian section."

The imbecilic question confirmed for Sam the state of the art in the medical profession. It was all he could do not to attack. Instead, with face turned red, teeth clenched and a strained voice, "Yes, I think that's a prudent choice. Do it now!"

A Golden boy heir, all eight and a half pounds, bald head and blue eyes. The birth battle waged marked only the beginning for the raising of a son. My feelings were all mixed up in memory. Was that child to have been a son too? Oh God, please let him be the same soul I once denied.

Nursing him at my breast, I wiped my tears from his face as the wonder of this miracle of birth overcame me. I held him closely wanting to protect him from all harm. Veils of past cloaked in mist. Images of a white marbled mother and son, and the pain of it all. A peculiar but familiar fear swept over me at the thought of ever losing my son, while a new kind of love stored and just waiting to be released empowered me. Still, the profundity of birthing, I wasn't quite prepared for. What an enormous blessing, this motherhood! How could I ever have made the choice to give it up?

Sam called Harry in New York to announce the birth of his godson. The two decided on an appropriate name, Alexander, since at the time Harry was playing Alexander the Great on stage, and we could placate my family as well, for my great grandfather's name had been Alex. Anyway, 'Alexander' was always a favorite of mine. Feeling radiant, I tied a baby blue ribbon around my hair and wearing a matching gown and bed jacket, readied myself to receive guests.

Jake had a joke he couldn't wait to tell me.

"How do you know that Jesus Christ was Jewish?"

I shrugged.

"Number one, because he was thirty and still lived at home. Number two, he was still a bachelor. And number three, his mother thought he was God!" The joy of laughter was instantly replaced by the pain in my stitches and an inordinate amount of gas in urgent need of release. Zak walked in just as the gas was on its way out.

Sitting in the sand, we watched the waves coming ashore. "Someday, you'll discover things yet unknown, uncovering the cloak of life's mysteries." I looked down at Alexander's tiny face smiling at the soothing sounds of my voice. "Whatever makes you happy, my darling -- building pillars and temples -- conquering worlds . . . " I listened to my strange words as they seemed to resonate in the sea.

I think I must have held Alexander in my arms for the first four months, taking him to museums, listening to classical music and even lectures when school began. Managing the new house, family and life as a student required study at four in the morning. And then there were Sundays; why do Sundays feel so lonely, anxious to fill the space, like an empty dance card. They began with phonecalls requesting a beach weather report; friends would arrive for morning volleyball or a late afternoon sail. Wanting everything to give the appearance of perfection, especially after our house was published in *Architectural Digest*, I would clean, cook, take time to look good, and assume the role of hostess. While our external world was acknowledged in print and my efforts willingly enslaved to form, internally, my emotions became more confused and hidden.

One thing I couldn't act out was prowess at the net. Volleyball was not my sport and I was always the last choice as a partner. Sam was always the first. So the pattern emerged. He would be victorious and I would see to everyone's needs and wait for the games to be over. Was life just a game I was waiting to be over? How was I to die to it all?

I had learned well as a child to wait. Even then, each Sunday morning the phone would wake me. Eve could sleep through anything. Most often it was one of Jake's cronies setting up their weekly card game. For the entire day, I would keep a vigil and wait. Every hour or so I'd tug at his sleeve, "Daddy, when can we go?"

"Soon Princess. I've got to catch up so I can afford to take my girls out."

If he won, the reward was dinner and a movie. The chance then seemed worth the wait but now the payoff was serving lunch -- unaware of how deeply I remained an emotional prisoner of my past. How far back I knew not.

Zak came through with investors for the beach apartments and building began as well as the need to entertain a different social set. Going to a concert in a chauffeur-driven limousine simply meant the back seat was occupied with dope-smoking impresarios trying a new high in the form of an expensive habit. Feeling foolish always refusing, I would reluctantly join in as the cigarette was passed, setting everyone's behavior back ten or twenty years.

I remember one evening, Sam came home from work early to change. "I'm going to a preview tonight; sorry, Darling, Zak says it's only for the boys."

Unhappy that being female excluded me from the fun, I went to bed early. Sam came in late, making the seven A.M. alarm seem earlier and louder than usual.

At nine the phone rang; it was Zak, well aware that Sam left the house by eight. "Sorry you couldn't make it last night Mary. It turned into a great party."

The hurt of deception gripped my heart. "But Sam told me it was only for the boys!"

Pausing, as though he was covering up for Sam, "Oh yes, of course, it was an all male party!" I hung up, not sure whether I was being manipulated by Zak or lied to by Sam.

Already late for my morning class, I kissed Alexander, by this time in the midst of the terrible twos, and gave the day's instructions in my kitchen spanish to Marta. The phone rang again. It was Esther planning another evening at the Music Center for us, having already bought the tickets, set up the dinner reservations at Chasen's and invited the other guests. She merely wanted to show off the perfect young couple. Oh, the deception of perfection. If the outer form could only tell the tale and stop my insides from caving in from lack of light. Control of my own life seemed further and further away.

Chapter   IV

Permeated with the weight of silence, the car seemed to be driving itself. We must have been traveling for hours, there's a sign for Los Angeles; oh, I missed it. He's pulling off the road; it's a restaurant. Thank goodness, I'm starving, freezing and in desperate need of the bedpan, and oh God, what I'd give for a stretch.

"Why don't you get something to go and we can have a picnic back here?" My charm strained.

He's stretching by the side of the car to be sure I can see. "I'm going inside for a good hot meal."

How can anyone be so cruel? Consciously controlling my emotions as not to reveal it in my request. "Get me something vegetarian!" Oh, the window's closed. I hope he heard me. Now comes the trick to use this portable toilet lying down without the help of gravity . . . that's one less physical problem. From now on I'll have deep appreciation for a simple flush. With that out of the way, there's just cold, discomfort and hunger. Oh God, is it necessary to go through this complete lack of control in such degradation? Ah, but the years I've spent in perfecting the role — I remember well . . .

In those middle years, Sam was not only head of our little family, but assumed more and more duties for Abe who was

showing signs of being twenty years Esther's senior. Each
little family problem sought refuge with Sam. Not to
mention clients; everytime it rained, I'd take the phone off
the hook and let them deal with leaks on their own. The
burden began to take its toll physically on him, rounding
and stooping his shoulders and more reliance on anything
that would ease the load. The joints lay in precision all
pre-rolled and available next to the bed for a midnight hit or
morning toke. Two martinis downed before he could talk
about his day. The mysterious vagueness of pain seems to
anesthetize all reason. That wonderfully sensitive face
began to fold in on itself -- gray began to replace the gold in
his hair. He was just twenty-seven. As usual the gap between
reality and desire created conflict for him.

Sam's sister Rachel was one of the worst offenders of his
peace. Her self-imposed alienation dramatically acted itself
out. In obvious protest to her Zionist parents, she left a
promising career as a concert pianist to run off with a
penniless Arab radical whose anger often manifested
physically against his Jewish wife.

"What an amazing setup! A woman dislikes herself
enough to seek out punishment so blatantly." The thought
angered Sam as he threw some essentials into a suitcase.
Rachel had made one of her many distress calls and Sam
was off to the rescue.

"Let me go with you darling."

"No, I don't want her dumping on you because of her
possessiveness of me. Rachel needs her little brother to save
her again. It was a game we always played as kids, only
Rachel doesn't know we grew up!"

This time, it was an island off the coast of Corsica, to a
village of ex-patriots and rejects. Rachel's husband had
barricaded the house with her two children inside, securing
it with a shotgun. The locals, having for hundreds of years
given the husband the privilege to work out his domestic

problems, were not sympathetic to Rachel's plight.

After a grueling journey Sam arrived to find himself at the wrong end of a rifle barrel with a mad Arab at the controls. Somehow after convincing the local police to help, they managed to disarm his brother-in-law and put him behind bars long enough to regroup. This meant Sam and Rachel had to literally kidnap her children out of the country without their father's permission. In the end all of the wisdom and caring Sam gave his sister was in vain for she insisted on yet another round and reconciliation. Her need for abuse was not yet complete. Returning home tired, beaten and out of control, he seemed to have lost another inch in stature, attained a few more creases in his face and a lot more dope. How well I could relate to Sam's defeat -- trying to make marital decisions for someone else was a familiar memory to me. So hard to accept was the method for dealing with his pain: each night after dinner, he'd light up a joint, retire to the sofa and rely on earphones to let music isolate him even more from any connection with his feelings or me.

"Darling" louder, "Darling . . . Sam! Can we go to a movie?" I shouted to compete with the music in his head. "I've had it. Just because you can't be everything to everyone, you think you've failed! Sam talk to me! Hey Baby, no one could live up to the role model you've created for yourself!" Oh God, which one of us created that role for him? "Sam, are you listening to me! God damn it . . . talk to me!"

He just lay there giving preference to the Rolling Stones.

Our bedroom was a dramatic loft over the high-ceilinged living room -- both facing out to sea -- the waves endlessly crashing. Every sharp angle of glass meeting steel seemed to coldly pierce me as I lie in the vast open space -- he on the sofa below, me waiting in bed above taking it all very personally . . . all so separate.

·   ·   ·   ·   ·

Lying here staring at passing cars everyone listening to their own music. No, I never knew the meaning of separateness till now. Oh dear God, how can we end it? I'll lick your wounds if you'll lick mine. Let me just escape into the past. For who knows what future loneliness awaits me . . .

Exam time and I needed to focus, which meant hours spent in the art library. Interesting how my deep questioning was silenced by the need to score high grades. I was finally learning that in college one didn't go romantically off in search of philosophical explanations to life; instead, you regurgitated information some frustrated academic expounded and expected to find reference to in a blue book. How indulgent, everyone demanding his own reality be supported! So many different realities, can we ever rediscover the source of a truth?

I forced my thoughts back to the book in front of me, the erotic sculpture of an ancient Indian Temple at Khajuraho. A magnifying glass helped as not to miss any detail. The subject matter made it even more difficult to concentrate. How free in body and spirit these little stone creatures were in a religious display of sexual intimacy. Contorted yet spiritual sex?

I read on . . . "Seated in the base of the spine lies the power of the kundalini waiting to be exploded in orgasm reaching up to God." What an intriguing and wonderful culture. Sex dedicated to the glory of God! Squirming a bit on the hard library chair, I felt a strong energy focus on me. Shifting my gaze above the rim of reading glasses, I met Jeremy. His were those kind of penetrating black eyes that don't just look at you, but into you, touching deep, personal and highly vulnerable places.

"Excuse me for staring. Your face, it's calling me to photograph it; please, the photography studio is just upstairs. I promise not to take more than a few minutes of your time." My blush was for more than compliments; it was evident he was looking beyond my face. I know he saw my wedding ring. Could he also see crashing waves and earphones? Were my wounds in search of a healer? Why not help a young photography major and besides, a break would be welcomed.

A week passed before Jeremy called. A rendezvous was set at his apartment to share the artistic results of our meeting. His photographs captured that very place in me he had made contact with in our first glance. They were very moving. My smile giving approval, I looked up at him. His hand touched me slowly turning my mouth to meet his. The contact was hot and wet. His shadow fell over me and all the agonies of guilt I felt in anticipation were quieted by the moment's excitement. I had never been with another man. The possibilities had been explored in conversation with Sam, he expressing no desire to go elsewhere, but giving me consent if I should need. His response was more like condoning a research project rather than a clandestine affair. Funny, if he had been jealous, I would have felt more loved. Jeremy gazed at my nude body with the appreciative eyes of an artist. Surely, he must be examining the stretch marks and scars left by motherhood. I looked down at his buried face, long dark hair falling on my body. Who was this stranger? What am I doing here? Could Sam have known how I would feel? Is that why he gave his approval? After only two afternoon meetings, I realized Sam's academic attitude was true for me as well, this was just a research project. Was I investigating that side of myself that was Jake . . . or something far beyond? For being intimate with a stranger touched some deep dark memory of a more illicit past. Brothels of pleasure and pain, money and magic . . . Unfortunately, the result was to last for many years, for in this brief interlude, I contracted herpes. Incredible, the first man I have sex with, I get pregnant; the second man, I get herpes!

Dissatisfaction often leads to a search, from the down side to up and both Sam and I had unconsciously begun. In the early Hollywood days of marriage a close relationship began with our neighbor, Sally. All the usual commonalities that bring two people together take a back seat to geographic convenience and a morning cup of coffee across the hall. But Sally would have made an impact on anyone's life. At thirty-five, her years brought the body of a full blown woman still able to cover the pages of Playboy and a face that left a map of where she'd been which only added to her sensual, radiant beauty. After a morning shower, a toss of the head would arrange her streaked blond hair for the day. Arrogance with ease, a kind of loose confidence and she wore it well. As a young bride married to an actor who overdosed, she now brought up their son alone, waitressing and sleeping around to pay the bills. There was something to admire in all this -- maybe getting paid for sex takes some of the pain out of relationship? Money and magic. I never judged her for it, I understood. Having a child kept her from going too far astray and finding us gave her a sense of family. So the move to the beach was quickly copied by our adopted family. As a free spirit, Sally readily explored any new idea that came along. When she heard of Dr. Kaplan's research at the university on a new hallucinogenic drug, actually paying people to get high legally, Sally enrolled. Life for her was a trip and she wasn't going to miss any free ride.

After her fifth exposure to LSD, she felt the need to expound upon its miraculous virtues. "Mary, you can visit places and dimensions that man has hardly even dreamed of. And this Dr. Kaplan really knows his stuff!"

"Oh my God, that's the brother of the Rabbi who married us, Dr. Kaplan!" Putting my hand over my open mouth, in response to the coincidence and wondering what reaction his Jewish mother might have to his research. All the wondrous tales of this newly discovered drug, LSD, were revealed through Sally's excitement.

"Come on, Mary. Take it. You'll tap into a place that has all the answers. Don't be afraid. I'll be with you. I'm an expert!"

The first thought that crossed my mind if I were to take the drug, was being very vulnerable and alone with Sally. She was all the things I wasn't, which made her even more seductive to me -- in the cold, Sally would fling open her arms embracing it as I used mine for warmth. Even though I sometimes felt intimidated, somewhere down inside me lived an attraction to all the openness and availability she wore so blatantly, almost mockingly. Would she try to seduce me, or did I hope she would? The key turned in the latch, Alexander cried out, "Daddy," and my fantasy sharply came to an end.

Describing Sally's experience with LSD to Sam, I realized my decision to take it had already been made. Now, I was looking for approval.

"I don't know, Mary, maybe if you take it first?"

"Oh Sam, Sam, you gentle-man. O.K., you're on. I'll try it."

So began my scientific research project -- reading the *Tibetan Book of the Dead*, Leary's and Alpert's writings on the newly found drug, this mysterious lysergic acid. Putting down the book, I turned off the light and climbed on Sam's back.

"Did you know that *secret teachings* in all religions talk about a greater consciousness, something beyond the limits of this life? Haven't you ever felt you were acting out a continuation of some ancient play? Could this drug pull back the veils of time and expose that unknown?"

"Well, you'll find out tomorrow! Now go to sleep."

A kind of fearful excitement ran through me.

Funny, I never asked what would happen if I suddenly knew the secrets of the universe -- how it would change my life from that moment on. I wasn't prepared for what came next. I remember well that clear Saturday morning at the beach, a perfect external setting . . .

Sally staged the scene; the capsule was ready, fruit and vegetables were prepared, laid out aesthetically on the coffee table and the proper music selected. She chose the Beatles, but I requested Vivaldi. "I'm afraid. I feel like an astronaut!" These were my last words as I swallowed the capsule with a chaser of water, hoping at the last moment it would flush through before dissolving.

Lying on the sofa, Sally tied a mask around my eyes. An involuntary flinch went through me in memory of another blindfold. I felt like I was again going to abort -- this time perhaps myself. She explained. "Covering your eyes makes it easier to look inside."

"But what if I don't like what's in there?"

"Just relax and go within."

Softly, *Winter* of the *Four Seasons* began.

My research carried expectation of the journey ending in the white light -- that promise made me determined to have the experience. It came upon me suddenly, confines of a dark tunnel encasing me. The destination was clearly marked by a light at the end. Diffused at first, but as I came closer, the white brightness magnetized my soul, the ultimate seduction. Finally, I was in it, not separate from it, caught in Eternity. Not an intellectual presence, but an experience so of the moment, it eliminated the gap between thought and action. I became the white light, made of that substance -- weightless, void of any emotion other than ecstasy, no distinction could be made between it and me. Separation ended. How to bring this to relationship wasn't a thought at the time. There's no room for question when in the midst of the answer.

Past and future were lost in the now. "Oh God, our understanding of time is so manmade!" Suddenly, from the right hand corner screen of my mind began to weave the web of a spider; working quickly until the entire frame was filled with this black menace. The pendulum had swung -- into darkness. A loud scream broke the silence and I realized the sound was mine.

Sally's calm hand comforted my trembling as her voice soothed my fear. "You're meeting life and death. You must choose to be alive, not just among the living dead." The words acted as a triggering device, jolting me back into the experience. Physical pain . . . deep excruciating abdominal thrusts . . . it was labor!

"Oh my God! I'm giving birth . . . to myself!" I cried . . . and cried.

The concept of time was irrelevant, yet hours passed. I finally sat up, took off the blindfold, and slowly looked around the room as if for the first time. Like a doll factory after dark, I watched all things come to life. The density objects are imprisoned in fell away as unnecessary supports and they were allowed to breathe and move. My understanding stretched as the rhythm and vibration of life were revealed before my eyes like a dance. The cosmic egg had broken. Looking down at my arm, I could see its internal workings, as though possessing x-ray vision and becoming mesmerized by the flow of my own blood. My mind accelerated. Thoughts began to flow as I tapped into the river of life. "Nothing I see has any meaning and everything I see has only the meaning I give it. Oh God, I even understand Einstein's theories, the nature of the universe -- quick, get a tape recorder before I forget!" I pleaded to my guide.

"You're all right, let it just pass through. You don't have

to hold on to it. Remember, you're already a part of it."
Sally was wise.

"It's so delicious!" I feel like a starving cat lapping up
bowls of caviar!" I sat holding my head in my hands, the
tears streaming down white cheeks. My words began with
reverence, then doubt crept in. "Oh God, it's so beautiful in
here. I feel part of something awesome and inspired, but
there's a deep pit inside of me that's empty. It feels lonely
and separate . . . the demons live here." I looked up and
began overindulging in food set out before me in a futile
attempt to fill the void, a black hole that took lifetimes in the
making. A man-made pit -- a hiding place for all he doesn't
want to see. Equipped with a bandaid, I futilely tackled the
giant wound.

As the Saturday afternoon sun dissolved into the sea, the
key that unlocked the cosmic door slowly closed. But my
real journey had only just begun! The glimpse into another
dimension left me in awe while new questions welled up
inside. Were the answers to be found inside that little
capsule or did the drug simply unlock a reservoir somewhere
deep inside, storing all the secrets of the universe -- an
ancient log written in the soul of everyman? If so, did the
soul enter life with this memory and then learn to forget?
And most important, how could I make contact again
without the drug?

Sam's experience the following day had as profound an
effect on him, although the results of his inner journey
mapped out a different direction. The question of tapping
into that consciousness without drugs was not an issue for
him, as in time he became more and more dependent upon
them. Layers gradually built a fortress around him, protecting
what he had found, creating his private refuge. On the other
hand, my search to become the butterfly once again began a
long process of shedding the cocoon. Strange, how our sex

life improved as outward communication deteriorated --
subtle sexual manipulation in attempt to hold on to one
another. Meanwhile, school no longer held fascination for
me, making it clear, answers were not held in the intellect.

Each day, anxiety built inside as I settled into *darkness*.
The pendulum had swung and all my clarity dissolved into
muddy water. I felt myself drowning in it, submerged in a
deep swamp of depression, the demons demanding to be
exorcised.

The Cabala warns that if the vessel isn't ready for the light, it
short-circuits. God, the struggle is so intense. Does it ever end?
Is a neurotic someone whose life doesn't mesh with the truth
the soul has buried? Looking up at my legs, I have to laugh. All
my life, I've had to work against the gravity of Jewish thighs.
What a vessel! My skin feels raw, layers of self peeling away --
how many left before exposure . . .?

Dr. Theodore Weldman was by consensus of monied
opinion, a psychoanalytic wonderboy. After the initial
interview, Dr. Weldman revealed to me that I could surely
be relieved of all neurotic symptoms through medication.
His diagnosis was a chemical imbalance in my body. Maybe
the LSD did foul up my chemistry.

So began my prescription-sanctioned drug experience.
Anxiety was easily treated with Valium, for fatigue three
grains of Thyroid, accompanied by one Dexamyl spansule
to put a zip in these sluggish glands. To keep depression
from the door, Tofranil was prescribed. He even anticipated
something for ensuing constipation. This apothecary became
my life support system.

Entering the private side door entrance to his posh
Beverly Hills office, no secretary to allow for any indiscretion,
there would be the high priest sitting behind his desk. The
ritual of opening his ten o'clock mail demanded his
complete attention, then casually, he leaned back in his

chair, squinted his eyes, admired his manicure and proceeded to take my blood pressure, first lying, then standing. The difficulty was in getting anything to register! My blood seemed to be standing still, waiting for direction. A new prescription was ordered -- Ritalin -- to stimulate the flow.

This mass medication being dumped into my pregnant body -- God, when I think of it now, I cringe. At delivery, the fifty-three pounds gained with Alexander were now held in check by the Dexamyl.

"A perfect baby girl!" I had to hear the words and count fingers and toes before totally succumbing to induced slumber. It was truly a miracle that Tara (meaning 'star' in some Indian dialect) hadn't been affected by her mother's medication. But, even such a beautiful helpless creature as Tara could not draw me out of the depth of depression I had slipped into. If only I knew what caused these precarious demons to shift from light to dark, titilating and teasing the lock to drop from my vaulted soul. The secret of changing emotions -- maybe it's all programmed in the DNA. Closing the drapes on my favorite Indian summer weather I refused to leave the refuge of bed. I threw Dr. Spock across the room -- what the hell did he know about being a mother? And picked up a book Sally had brought me, *The Magian Gospel of Brother Yeshua**. This story was about the personal life of Jesus (Yeshua was his Hebrew name), and what it was like for this man who knew of his divine mission yet was caught in a human body with desires and needs. As I read, I felt drawn into the drama beyond the mere fascination of a voyeur, an almost *deja vu*. Consumed, I fled the pages unable to stop. Here was a love affair beyond all love affairs, the greatest love story yet untold. Reading it threw me into an eternal sadness released through endless tears. Could it be true? Why not? *The Lord of Forgiveness* and *ultimate sinner*, Jesus and Mary Magdalene were in love? What divine *perfection*! To sing the song of the soul makes mockery of form. Could brothels become "Houses of Many Mansions" if divine love brought the forgiveness to change the stones? Holding the book in my arms, I fell asleep -- its memory lingering in my dreams. I preferred being there in that other time.

Lying in bed, I spent hours staring at the Roualt lithograph entitled *Guerre,* a wedding gift from Harry. The upper half shows Christ depicted with full halo in all his glory, but below the image of Christ is distorted and pathetic. Was the 'war' an internal one between the higher and the lower selves, the God-man? Could Jesus the man ever have lived in doubt of who he was?

A private nurse took charge of holding things together at home. Lenore hired Sally to tend her daughter's needs which only added to the frustration of my own inability to cope. It weighed heavily on me. The only joy that touched me in those dark days was being alone nursing my baby, and Alexander relieving his sister's distress by gently patting her on the back. I called her Star. Looking down at her smooth white skin with a dab of subtle pink blush. Those black expectant eyes looked up at me.

"What language do you speak, my Star? How can I let you tell me what you know?" Her eyes had compassion for my naivete. I wondered did she still have the memory of time beyond this life, and how soon would she learn to forget? The children truly entered my heart, but even that love couldn't quiet my demons.

The merry-go-round wasn't the only recurring dream of youth; a frightened child still lived in me expressing herself in the night. A dark dream came.

Bombs going off lighting up the night, fighting and killing. Filled with terror, I seek a safe place. I go to the closet open it, and on the floor a trap

door leads into a tunnel. Dark and nightmarish I tumble down the passageway falling, falling straight into the bowels of the earth. At the bottom is an army tank; I run to it. Climbing down inside its protected space, stopping breath to listen, pulling the cover closed -- I am finally safe.

But where would I find safety in life? Up tunnels of light. Down tunnels of darkness . . . Somehow, waking to Sam's subliminal snore didn't give me this deep sense of security.

The six week Caesarian recovery time had come, and Jake planned a day at the races for his daughter's coming out. All his best intentions were for naught for I could see the plan only as a manipulative, controlling device. Even the destination satisfied Daddy's need, not mine -- no one even asked. Jake waited in the living room, throwing his grandson in the air, then turning his attention to Tara, stroked her hair. Alexander maneuvered his way behind the T.V., sending the Flintstones crashing to the floor, his expression of jealousy straightforward. The noise jolted my fragile nervous system, and pressed some self-destruct button the demons were in possession of. Staring into the bathroom mirror at the well-dressed image, I suddenly turned on the shower, let out a violent scream, and stood under my self-made storm. This certainly put a damper on a day at the races. Sam, loving me as he did, understood my plea and his need to take action. I couldn't even appreciate the tenderness of a man in love.

"You're going to see a doctor, not the head variety but a real medical man -- and right now!" He quickly called for an emergency appointment. As we walked to the car the sun was unusually bright for eyes that had not seen daylight for weeks. Sam kept one hand holding my arm, preventing my jumping from the moving car.

"Stop, stop the car. I'm going to throw up!" At first, he thought it was a ploy to get away, but he saw my color turn gray and quickly pulled over. He put one hand on my forehead for support and the other around me in compassion. My body ejected all the medication I had force fed it, as I hung my head out the car window.

"Are you taking any medication now?" Sam could feel my body become rigid with the doctor's question. He held my hand tighter. I feared betraying Dr. Weldman.

"Dexamil, Tofranil, Ritalin . . . . " Sam began to list all the medication.

Shocked, I accused him. "How do you know that?! Did you go through my things?"

Tactfully, the doctor intruded, "He must care a great deal about you. My first medical order is to stop this pharmaceutical deluge."

I numbed at the thought of my support system being cut off. Within days, withdrawal set in. Getting up to go to the bathroom, my knees would buckle under. I could actually feel the chemistry in my body being altered. But, after two weeks, a fog lifted and light shone in. It was a miracle! I prayed the demons had been exorcised and not just a lid put on.

Growing a beard was Sam's way of distancing himself from me. He was well aware of my dislike of facial hair, so there was a slight edge of punishment thrown in. Now that I was getting better, he was getting angrier. He took it all very personally. Communication stopped altogether and going to a marriage counselor worsened the situation.

The therapist sat behind the desk professionally protected, thoughtfully cleaning his glasses about as concerned as watching a soap opera. Sam and I directed all our conversation toward him avoiding first person contact.

"I think she did it all to see how much I could take!"

"You must understand Doctor, Sam carries the world on his back. He stands behind me like a benefactor when I'm down. Ah, but the minute I show signs of strength, the subtle punishment is administered. Like the abortion -- remember!"

Sam condescendingly replied, "I see the pattern revealing itself. There are the controllers and the controlled!"

Strange, when you allow connection to lapse and merely act out a relationship, then come in telling tales in the presence of a third party, the effect can be devastating, destructive and permanent.

A timely but shocking bit of news put an abrupt end to my confidence in any professional guidance. Dr. Theodore Weldman, the wonderboy of the Beverly Hills 'couch set' shot and killed his wife and then turned the gun on himself, appropriately through the head. My high priest had only been a confused warrior. Doesn't anyone know how to get through life alive?

The pain and loneliness of living together yet so apart led to a brief separation, but the solution only deepened the symptoms. Settling on more neutral ground in an attempt to anesthetize our feelings, Sam moved back in. The facade of marriage remained intact, while the innards continued to decay.

Chapter V

The reality of the cold station wagon brought me back. All this remembering -- how precious even sad recollections become at the possibility of no more memories. When it comes right down to it, what are the most important things in life? Health, relationship, money and career -- the order changes according to which is in most jeopardy at the moment. But the children, they're outside that fuss. I can't bear to think of them burdened by the pain of my death. Who would raise them?

Thank God, here he comes. I'm starving. Opening the driver's door he slides into the seat without even turning his head around, casually throwing a dry piece of ham between two slices of white bread over his shoulder and into my lap as if I were an unwanted pet.

"That's all they had -- these are meat and potato people. This here's margarine country."

The bastard! I restrain myself from throwing the results of my bedpan in his face. That last sign said a hundred and eighty miles to Los Angeles. About three more hours. My bones ache. When you're flat on your back you can only see the *down side of up*. O.K, let the past take me out of here . . . Let me think, of course, my life was just about to take a real turn. I love remembering how we met . . . .

$$\cdot \quad \cdot \quad \cdot \quad \cdot \quad \cdot$$

Although breakfast was over and Sam had already left for the office, it seemed too early in the morning for visitors. From the upstairs bathroom window, I could view the front door and investigate arriving guests. The bell was persistent. It was Marta's day off. Opening the louvres, I saw Sam's brother, Michael, lighting up a new Marlboro with the old one he was about to put out in my potted geraniums. With him was someone I had never seen, but from that moment on, would never forget. For a moment, I thought Michael (who Sam referred to as a 'Star Fucker') had brought Mick Jagger over to wow Alexander, a three year old Rolling Stones fan. But, as he turned into the ocean wind, it swept back his long unkempt hair, revealing a face that brought all the romance of the Renaissance to memory. Of course, it's from DaVinci's paintings -- that etheric face used over and over again -- in the *Madonna of the Rock's, St. Sebastian*, and St. Anne. Whether man or woman, here was that androgenous Christ-like look I fell in love with in the pages of art books. The face had found its perfect body and now was being delivered to my doorstop.

Why couldn't they have waited another hour, letting my favorite grey-and-red chenille robe, a thrift shop gem, dry my damp body. "The back door is open. Come in, I'll just be a minute." I called down directing them towards the back through an open louvre. "Well my handsome stranger gets to see how I look in the morning right off, no surprises!" I muttered to myself coming down the stairs. The purity of that just-washed look was in obvious contrast to the passion that immediately passed between us.

"Mary, this is my friend and new business partner, Jess Weber." Michael introduced him. Extending a hand, I feared my feelings revealed by the electricity generated in our touch.

"I love morning faces!" He smiled. It felt like a dual compliment, that I was the most beautiful woman in the

world, and an invitation to bed. Jess's charm was not the
manufactured variety; it simply exuded from the very core
of his being. He was a sensual Pan, a poet in the raw!

"Would you like coffee?"

"Yes please, with all the accoutrements."

There's something so intimate about sharing morning
coffee, loosening conversation. Wanting to know everything
about him, I questioned, "It's hard to detect under all that
charm, but you seem troubled Jess." My immediate caring
allowed entry into his personal thoughts, voluntary, at the
level of conversation and involuntary, impinging on the
psychic. We shared a knowing deep look. I knew he wanted
to tell me.

"Oh, there's a girl. I slept with her. Now, there's a
paternity suit. We go to trial tomorrow!"

Michael intruded; we both had forgotten he was there.
"Hey, we better split . . . things to do . . . people to see . . .
places to go . . . .

Jess added, "Before we meet again!"

Jess became a regular visitor winning all the Golden
hearts. A camera always hung around his neck ready to
make the most of a moment . . . music from the mundane.
Another 'Sand Sunday', Jess had an audience of all the kids
on the beach as he demonstrated the art of building sand
castles. He had lost the paternity suit, but never spoke of it
again. That same day, Sam wasn't himself. He had awakened
with an ironic and embarrassing affliction -- his testicles
were outrageously swollen. Maybe his masculinity was in
outrage. Lying in the hot sun, although comforting, didn't
reduce the localized pain and probably added to his rising
fever.

"Damn it, the throbbing is getting worse!"

"Better have Dick look at it." I urged. Signalling to stop
the volleyball game, I whispered Sam's plight to our
physician neighbor.

"Does this have to be so public?"

"Come on Sam it's easier out here." A makeshift tent acted as an examination room and attracted more attention than a Sunday supplement on sex.

"You're going to the hospital boy, right now."

Jess was there on the spot. "I'll take him; he can lie down in my van." The blood left Sam's face . . . he couldn't control it.

Whatever induced this strange affliction, the cure kept Sam bedridden for weeks. Typically, Jess walked in just before dinner time -- wearing a safari jacket, pockets stuffed with little presents for the kids, his hair in perpetual motion. First, he'd run upstairs and throw the latest copy of *Architectural Digest* over to Sam lying in bed. "You've got to keep up to date on your competition!" Then he'd whistle a tune, taking two stairs at a time down to the kitchen, where I was setting the table. He'd slip up behind me and put a copy of some sleazy sex magazine on top of a plate, with a knife and fork crossed over the cover. Life was his art piece, running from bizarre to childlike but always making me laugh. There was something in the way his mouth slanted in a smile that spoke seduction -- and it was me that was being seduced. Three way Scrabble was the outward game being played as we sprawled on the bed after dinner, but a more emotional contest was brewing underneath and the rules had not yet been defined.

No doubt we all really cared for each other, although I wasn't sure how Sam saw Jess fit into the scheme of things but he encouraged him to take me out with the crowd and relieve my Florence Nightengale monotony. Leading a separate life while in the same house for Sam meant being isolated, detached and private. I knew his pain for I shared it. Jess was there for me. I wanted him -- how could Sam not know that?

The guilt about my fantasies prompted prayers that my

powerful thoughts of desire for Jess didn't create the situation. Could thoughts manifest events? What irony if, in fact, simply by thinking something, it becomes reality. That would certainly say a great deal for purity of thought!

Sam's illness had speeded up the deterioration of our relationship. The Fourth of July -- an appropriate day for independence and the end of a decade which marked Sam's move out. As he packed his bags, flashes of Jake filtered through the shadows falling on our bed. This can't be happening. "Please Sam don't go!"

"I've said it all here. You can sit with it after I've gone." He placed a letter on my pillow and left.

That night, I stared for hours at fireworks on the beach falling over the water and quickly fizzling out. Over and over I read Sam's words:

Friday night
My Dearest Mary:

As I sit here in the attempt to gather my wits sufficiently to write this note to you, I am perfectly amazed with my love for you. There have certainly been times during the past seven years that we've lived together that I've not liked you, disliked you even, yet loved you, perhaps even more during periods of strife. There has never, my Darling, been the slightest fraction of a second, that I did not feel so. And you ask, why? As you have asked it so many times in the past. I can remember in the early years of our marriage your asking that question, and my own reply; some silly sentimental answer which you wouldn't believe, because I guess I really didn't know the answer then, yet tried to verbalize it in order to be kind. Yet how clear the answer seems now. I imagine that I stumbled upon it during those periods of strife when the house was under construction. If we had had an argument, I felt myself utterly unable to work. I thought to myself that this was probably due to the fact that work was

so closely tied up with providing a home for you. Yet
working on other projects proved equally impossible. In
short, I found myself incapable of functioning in my normal
manner without the peace that only the harmony of our life
together could give me. There was a time in my life when I
thought of my work as a very noble gesture in itself, yet as
such, I see now that this kind of behavior was no less a
product of gross self gratification than what other people
derive from common vices. I don't mean to say that I no
longer enjoy my work, for on a higher level I gain more
enjoyment from it than the old me was ever able to perceive.
Yet I see my work not as an end in itself but as a link in the
chain of life's process. Not my life, but our life. In short, all
that is petty and self indulgent in my character is a function
of our common destiny. You have, my darling, given me a
reason to exist above the superficial level of awareness that
is my brother's lot and would be mine without your love.

And what have I given you, my Love? A car, a home, a
servant, a thousand material objects which seems so important
for the moment, but which show their true value all too
quickly as bursting bubbles of disillusionment. You know
that the only lasting values are those of the spiritual world,
yet try as I might I cannot make you see the way. I imagine
your intellect is too demanding to give way to such simple
truth, yet all you have to do is open your eyes and see now;
listen and hear now; let the blood course thru your veins and
feel now. Not good or bad, hot or cold, beautiful or ugly,
yesterday or tomorrow, just now and whatever it is you
want it to be. Just life my Darling; everything, in you now.
As you have given meaning to my life, let me show you the
way to peace.

Yet I am a man, my Darling, and as the poem goes -- when
you prick me I bleed, when you strike me I feel pain. Yet I
have pride too (some little bit left) and so I will dress and

leave here and drive somewhere and have a drink and be miserable. My pride and I, sick with love for you.

Sam

If only I could have heard him then. If only he could have heard himself -- years for both of us to catch up to the meaning. I watched the telephone poles passing by, all that silent communication. God, if I could go back to that moment
. . . .

Part of me was dying -- put to rest before my time. It can't be over between Sam and me, I still love him too much. God, I never realized how much he loves me. Why didn't he show it more, kiss me instead of lighting up a joint, at least take out those damned earplugs. Maybe after just a short affair with Jess, there'll be time to heal the wounds with Sam. Quickly, I tried to erase that thought from my mind. Weeks passed. Alone, I faced this death devastated. What it was like for Sam -- I didn't want to think about that.

And so there was Jess. The magnetic pull existing in the air between us compelled a physical coming together -- a surrender to an energy that seemed predetermined. Like a runner's high, a chemical must be released in the body when you fall in love. Could this chemical be stored in the DNA, programmed many lives ago? Maybe you could have a bad relationship surgically removed.

Falling in love with his friend's wife was a complex position, for Jess had great admiration for his predecessor. He could more easily accept the children almost as a penance for the one he legally denied. Strange, he's so perfect with the children, what a tragedy rejecting his own. Who am I to judge? I made that blindfolded decision once myself . . . .

There were fringe benefits of the pseudo-family connection to Golden wealth and prestige, including my brother-in-law, Michael, whom Jess loved. Strange, how this love relationship between men can be physically acted out with a female contingent of the family. It's interesting to ponder on incestual aspects of our group's interaction. No doubt, we all have things to work out together in this thing called life -- left over from another time and space. All programmed in the DNA or written in the stars.

Jess began spending so much time with the children, they considered him their friend, not mine. Curious, how his guilt about Sam made him appear to be such a good guy, as he overindulged the children. Making up a bed on the sofa and setting the clock for five in the morning, became the nightly routine.

"This is insurance that daylight will find a house guest sleeping in the living room, rather than a lover in bed with mom."

"Jess, I'm afraid. What would happen if the children wake up in the night and discover our secret?"

"They'll think what you think and not what you act. If guilt's in the air, for sure their little sensitive psyches will pick it up, but if joy and love are undercover, excuse the pun, my dear, that will be their experience."

Jess was wise, but there it is again -- the idea that thought creates experience. Will my own fear send my children running up the night's stairs? Now all I need do is learn the formula for controlling the mind. Sometimes, I feel so victimized by my own emotional behavior, bypassing the mind, and having a life of its own.

Am I really in love with Jess or my own fantasy of who he is? Will he fall into the black hole I create for my loves? Where did I get the idea that a man has to be perfect? The answer still hidden behind many veils.

Sam was back after months in Europe, his trip highlighted by the Cannes Music Festival. This will be a fine test of control, I thought, dressing the children for the first outing alone with their daddy. Being three years old and two days before Halloween, Alexander insisted on previewing his costume. He was precious. Sam was to arrive at ten o'clock and my anxiety about getting Jess out before that deadline added to the confusion. A honk instead of a knock at the door, pierced me, for it indicated the situation was not as compatible as I hoped. Rudolph the Red-Nosed Reindeer ran out the door and Marta carried Tara close behind.

"Daddy, Daddy . . ."

"Oh my sweethearts, how I've missed you."

From behind drapes I watched their touching and tearful reunion. As they pulled away, Sam looked back at the house and I uncontrollably wept never having experienced such loneliness . . . isolated in the midst of it.

Oh my babies, how are you doing now? They must be frightened not knowing what's happened to me. I bet the dialogue was priceless as Sam explained it -- something condescending but subtle like only the weak get weaker and the sick get sicker. Thinking about it now only makes me helplessly furious . . . .

"Venturing Out,"the film documentary company Jess and Michael began, seemed mostly an excuse for the avant garde artistic community to have a hangout and for Michael to spend the family fortune, buy friends and create his dilettante image. Still there was no denying the star quality of the group with myself as female figurehead and charismatic Jess magnetizing the local film folk. We looked like some famous rock group -- clothes furnished by local thrift shops -- although Jess stuck more to the purity of Salvation Army. This entourage worked and played in group rhythm, something that was difficult for me to adjust to. These were night people and my psyche was attuned to day. Everyone at the 'studio' except me had a job, or at least their own niche comfortably settled into.

"Hey, turn up the music, I can't hear it over the damn typewriter!" A command came from the loft as Michael edited footage from yesterday's shoot.

"Son of a bitch!"

"What's it now Michael?"

"The damn cigarette fell out of my mouth and burned a hole in the film!"

Jess frantically swept the floor as if preparing to serve dinner on it. Life can't go on unless the stage is clean and that was a full-time job. Busy work was part of his strange abstract being and kept him from facing anything serious.

But with the induced aid of marijuana, a hang-loose attitude permeated the scene. In fact, it was hard not to get stoned just walking into the place -- for smoke hung in the air and I felt like the odd man out having no use for drugs of any kind. My identity once again was linked with my man and the job of making sure dinner was hot on the table when Jess and Company felt need of nurturing and nourishment. Oh, the parade of bizarre dinner guest, rejects of the world, beggar characters Jess found walking the beach boardwalk.

One typical night I remember he walked in the kitchen door as I was bending into the refrigerator trying to improvise dinner from leftovers.

"Mary, I'd like you to meet Henry. He just got off the train. Now, his destination had been San Francisco, but the conductor got sticky about the ticket."

"How do you do Henry? Will you join us for dinner?" Somehow there were remnants of Jake in Jess. In actuality, part of his creative genius was in recognizing magic in the most mundane. There was a particular interest in transvestites, for they allowed Jess a glimpse into the workings of sexual transgression, titillating that deviate part of him where many of his demons lurked. He even had his own woman's wardrobe selected either from sleazy thrift shops or his weekly sojourn through the neighborhood on trash day. He taught me to see it all as an 'Art Piece', a composition orchestrated by the natural rhythm of things. His imagination expanded even more when it came to making love, whether on the beach at sunrise, racing the tide, or inconspicuously giving me head under the chopping block in the kitchen, while preparing a late night snack.

With Jess sex was heightened to an art form and I simultaneously experienced feelings of guilt and ecstasy, almost as if one perversely fed the other. I wondered, is judgment of the rules of the game only in the mind of the creator? Allowing myself to step into the closet with Jess, opened the door which allowed my own sleeping demons escape. God how I wanted to please him, and in doing, fell victim to his needs. Curiously, we acted out reversed roles. Jess was anxious to play the part of victim in our sexual movie -- bound, blindfolded or persecuted. I'd dress him in his feminine frocks and for once, the prodigy played the boss. Smells and tastes were different, sweat from the sun mingled with salt and seaweed, 'fish and fingerpie.' Jess had enough talent and charm to be considered eccentric instead of neurotic, a distinction most women aren't indulged in.

For me he was forbidden fruit; his smile would have tempted Eve herself -- enticement to partake overcame me. Perhaps Biblical figures represent some aspect buried in us, creating a common bond with all archetypes, a little of this one and a little of that. I had played the neurotic mother with Sam, now the prostitute to fulfill another man's fantasy. Mary, Mary, which Mary? The cast of characters came alive, triggered as memory was released in each appropriate circumstance. The stage was certainly set for sexual fantasy to come out of the closet, but it's difficult to appreciate historical perspective in its midst.

In luxury of the purple tiled bathtub, I sank into the bubbles. What a shame not to have a view of the ocean. Someday, I'll put a bathtub surrounded by handpainted screens with pink flamingoes on a stage in the bedroom facing a fireplace and a view. "Oh the telephone's ringing." Marta's out and Jess's playing with the kids. "Why doesn't he answer?" But I knew Jess would never pick up the phone for fear Sam would find out he was a live-in. Of course, Sam and everyone else knew, even my mother-in-law, although she invited Jess to dinner as Michael's friend, not mine. After our separation, I was still included in the family, but non-gendered and so my relationship with Jess was hidden under the rug where everyone felt most comfortable.

Out of breath by the time I reached the phone, "Hello. Oh yes, Sam." I settled into a chair and looked out at the surf.

He wasted no time in making his point. "Mary, I've been hearing a lot of talk about the mouths you're feeding nightly, not to mention the type of characters. You know you're not running a midnight mission and I don't remember volunteering to subsidize it. You'll be getting a few hundred dollars less this month and you can cover your own entertaining bills!"

A declaration had been deemed. He was angry and the Golden purse strings are always their strongest manipulative tool. I just sat stunned. "And if you think it is unfair, well Mary take me to court. We'll let the judge decide!" The phone slammed.

"I'm leaving." Jess shouted from the downstairs; at least there's relief in that -- his energy's so frenetic, small doses are best. I welcomed the peace. Certainly, Jess was not one to look to for support, financially or emotionally; his magic faded when confronted with real-life situations.

The guilt caused by Sam's accusations was penetrating; it never occurred to me that I was entitled to money and could spend it any way I chose. Unconsciously, I gave more power to Sam's position by lack of belief in my own. If only I could have understood the layers of meaning behind this thought and how many times I so subtly would fall back into power traps. I felt scared, not because the monthly budget was being threatened, but my entire sense of security was in jeopardy.

The separation finally hit me below the money belt. My lawyer advised me. "Sam is setting precedence here and if a strong stand is not taken, he could continue cutting your income little by little. The only recourse I see is to let the judge decide."

My first thought was the children and family. My mother-in-law was still my best friend -- as long as our conversation avoided Sam; but could our friendship endure this public exposure? Dirty laundry is something done by the maid in the back room, for the Goldens are very private people. Another no-choice squeeze situation. A court date was set.

Jess had gotten in the habit of coming home very late -- sometimes not at all. This night was especially long; three o'clock in the morning and still no Jess. Sleeping was impossible and I was furious that he hadn't even called. To fantasize mischief Jess could fall victim to was easy. But how could he be so thoughtless on the night before my court appearance? I lay there realizing what an obsession he had become. I wanted him. I wanted to smell him, to touch him. But he could never give me what I needed most. To hold on to him. The eye of the hurricane was necessary to catch and keep him -- caught in the will of the wind.

Anger mixed with jealously produced enough energy to jump out of bed, fill a large glass of water, and with a great deal of pleasure pour it on Jess's side of the bed! At least, the act relieved some tension, but created a new problem, for the liquid knew not the boundary of his side making for a very uncomfortable night. My mother had been a good role model, lying alone in the night, in need, victimized and lonely. Funny, these were the same feelings I had with Sam. Maybe, the answer wasn't in changing partners but in confronting my own feelings . . . And now in the morning, a legal decision would put another nail in the coffin.

The lawyer suggested toning down my avant garde appearance for the judicial proceedings, which meant borrowing an outfit from a schoolteacher friend. No sleep, immutable fear and clothed in borrowed fashion made for dowdy discomfort. I felt like a human impersonator. If I leave a little early, I can stop by Jess' studio and settle my emotions with his arms around me, I thought anxiously. My gloved hand made knocking at the large metal door less painful. I tried to breathe slowly and deeply to quiet my heart.

A young strange girl who worked across the street opened the door. She couldn't be over sixteen. "Jess is in the darkroom." She looked me up and down and walked out. Damn these clothes!

The air was cold and unfriendly walking back through the warehouse-like space used to film in. "Jess" -- my echo came back as Jess sauntered toward me.

"Sorry dear, I worked all night and lost track of the time." His dark circled eyes testified the truth of last night's vigil, but didn't explain his unzipped fly. Thoughts of betrayal and doubts of myself came flooding in. Why does everything begin and end with the genitals?

The bench outside the courtroom was marble-hard and cold like the world. I lit a cigarette, my hand shaking and longed for another cup of coffee, still in shock over Jess and not sure I could handle what was coming. Looking down the long official corridor, the atmosphere heavy with official judgment, it was easy to spot the back of Sam's head; he was in conversation with Zak. Wishing I had brought a friend, even Zak looked good. Squirming in the borrowed clothes, I longed for the security of my own image. I slipped the gloves in my purse.

Sam walked to the stand looking very dapper in the latest

Italian fashion, swearing to tell the truth, at least, his truth. "Judge, I know I have a wealthy father, but how long can you tap into that resource and retain your self-respect? The truth is things have been very rough and you can't squeeze blood out of a turnip, now can you, Judge?"

I had to bite my lip, for I was privy to information that the next day, Sam was taking off for skiing in Switzerland.

Arms outstretched, his head tilted to the side in question. . . . Sam crossing the gorge . . . the black hole . . . flashed before me. His body forming a cross. The image pained me. Now my perfect man was falling into the abyss . . . crucifying our marriage.

"Mary Golden, please take the stand." Walking across the room the memory of a telephone conversation with Jake's friend, Tony, a Mafia-type character I had known since childhood came to me. "Kid don't worry. Just get me the name of the judge and I'll fix everything." Of course, my own sense of morality couldn't accept Tony's offer but squirming in the witness chair, I gave it a second thought as my eye caught Zak sitting at the back of the room smirking. How could life change so much in so short a time? You bastard, Zak, you are still trying to get me, one way or another. And Sam, I wanted to run to Sam, to hit him and hit him again, destroying his cover until underneath it all, I found that sensitive poet I fell in love with. But how then, could he find his 'Rose-in-bloom?' Oh Sam where are we? The hurt came flooding out—my tears preventing answering questions or explaining my position. Sam virtually won by default. Once again, I was my own worst enemy.

The relationship between Jess and me never had a chance to blossom, always being stifled, forced to live in pre-existing form. Now Jess and Company were planning a trip to Egypt to film a documentary. Perhaps this was best, his return might put our relationship on a fresh footing. Both my men were off; one skiing down the Alps, the other filming along the Nile. What exotic place would I choose, but more importantly, how could the luxury of choice be mine? Prisoner of the past.

A long month passed and I wanted to look especially alluring for Jess's return. Spending the entire morning, I prepared my body, anointing it with oils, feeling like an Egyptian queen awaiting her consort. The final touch was ten minutes with electric rollers in my hair, when Alexander screamed, "Jess!" Flashing on his premature entrance the morning we first met, he ran up the stairs with both kids in his arms, catching me frantically trying to disassemble my electric coif.

"Hey, I like your hairdo!" Throwing the kids on the bed, he grabbed my arm and brought me down to his mouth . . . Five days after his return, Jess came down with viral meningitis, a Middle Eastern traveling hazard.

One week later, Sally was visiting for morning coffee when that same Egyptian virus found refuge in my own head. Capturing me so suddenly, I dropped my half-filled cup and let out a blood-curdling scream, clutching my head in hysteria. Demons had gotten inside and were splitting my head apart with a cruel ancient device.

"Oh Sally the pressure's so intense. I think my head's going to explode. Help me!" I cried out.

Sally's face turned white as she pulled my arm and we ran to the car.

"God help me, help me!" My screams continued all the way to the hospital and echoed through its hallways. Impossible to ignore this emergency, the doctors gathered around. With immediate consensus, there in the corridor, one doctor took a long needle filled with Demerol and injected it straight into the base of my skull. The blackness of unconsciousness saved me. My dark night of the soul had begun.

Chapter VI

First, my head in a torture chamber, now my legs in a primitive metal device. Oh dear God, just get it over with . . . Now another hospital, another disease -- only three months ago -- that shot in the base of my skull!

"Already two days in the hospital and they can't put a label on what little monster has decided to call me 'home,' but that certainly doesn't stop them prescribing eight different kinds of medication to cover all the bases!" Jess relayed this insightful medical information in a hospital-to-hospital conversation. "Well I thank the gods for at least one medication -- Demerol. Sometimes, if the pain gets too bad they give me morphine. That's a trip. Now, they're talking spinal tap!"

Quickly, I jumped in, interrupting Jess. "Why? So they can give a name to what we have? They've told me the possibilities and there's not a cure in the lot, so why let them probe your spine to find out they can't help? It's your decision, Darling. I've made mine. Speak to you tomorrow I love you." As I put down the phone, nausea overtook me. Getting up, the room began its circular dance. The intensity of pain in my head was reduced by drugs, but replaced with a gnawing pressure. If only I could drill a hole in my head and let the demons go free.

Where can my family be, two days and not even a call? During visiting hours that evening, the answer came. The door swung open. Walking in looking exhausted, Lenore and Eve appeared. "What's wrong?"

Tears prevented Lenore from answering as she fell in my arms, so fragile. "Mommy I'll be all right! Don't cry. Where's Daddy?"

Eve in her martyred voice, took the lead. "They had to perform an emergency operation. We've been up all night." Taking a deep breath with a shaky exhalation, she continued. "They removed one lung. It's cancer!"

What was left of my insides sank and an empty void housed the numbness. Then my tears for Jake, soon growing to include Sam, the children, Jess and all of life's disappointments and sorrows -- a retching of the soul.

Now my own illness grew heavier with added burden of the vigil for Jake. So many memories, so many regrets. Oh time, I thought you were mine! Now you've run out on me. I realized the backlog of incomplete communications, of all I failed to express and share. At least, there's time now to go over my relationships. None of them had a clean slate unsaid words stood in the way. Where do I start and with whom? What have I not told myself?

After weeks in the hospital I was no better and everyone agreed my own bed would be more conducive to recovery without hospital costs added to my worry. Esther came to take me home but first she stopped by the cashier to pay my bill. I loved her so, not just for bailing me out, but she was the one person I could always count on.

Jake remained in the hospital and speaking to him on the phone was a treat. "They can't keep a good man down Princess. I've got more living to do and so do you!" The words encouraged his 'royal' offspring. If anyone had strength to pull through, it would be Jake, but was my own kingdom worth living for?

"I'm glad you're home Mary. The doctor says I'm O.K., but you won't believe what I've got now -- the big H!" The telephone wire was hushed.

This was another illness Jess and I had in common . . . herpes. Most likely he had company while he was in the hospital. The rat! He can hide behind that cool voice, but not those festering sores on his penis.

I tried to make light. "Maybe karmic lessons come in the form of illness actually carried over from past lives. What a joke all these doctors trying to find the cause of herpes when the source really came from wearing a chastity belt during the Crusades." He laughed and hung up.

Damn him! I thought angrily. Everything's based on his needs, his rules. I can't believe I've allowed myself to be controlled again!

Dear Jess:

> **The written word because of its permanent relationship to paper, can be read and re-read . . . it helps when you don't want to continually repeat yourself.**
>
> **Recently, I told you that finally I was giving up any expectation and had accepted you as you are. Just you, being you. Well, I've really been able to do that. Unfortunately, it leaves our relationship lacking, for the reality is frankly very unsatisfying.**

Tearing the letter into little pieces -- would I spend my life writing the same letter, just to different men? Searching for some mystical perfection memoried in my mind. Was it not them, but me?

Poem to Myself
**I've asked for love a thousand times
Been so close to it too,
But whether it be this one or that,
None of them were you.
What keeps me from you?
Does wanting make it real for me?
Is there more to it than desire?
Is the flame it makes too intimate
That my fear puts out the fire?
Could it be me, can it be true,
That I have been keeping myself from you?**

You can count on local gossip to come through as surely as the mail. Fascinating, to delve into motives and workings of the informant's mind. Michael lit a cigarette and with the same pleasure as the inhale, unleashed his news. "Have you heard the latest scandal?" Placing crossed legs on my desk as he sat back on the swivel chair.

No Michael, but I know you're dying to tell me."

"Jess got out of the hospital and moved in with his latest sexual deviate, a local hooker!"

"That's enough, I don't want to hear it!" I screamed out. Was this the kind of truthful communication that allowed relationships to be in the moment? Now, I added to my list of maladies, a fractured ego and devastated heart.

Memories followed everywhere -- having a life of their own, even more so now at home. I wasn't getting any better and Sally's innovated meanderings discovered a type of chiropractor whose treatment included a more natural approach. My resistance was verging on non-existent, so Sally's idea sparked a ray of hope, She practically had to carry me but our coupled determination got us to Dr. Bradford's office right on time.

In his later thirties, the doctor was a good looking,

healthy endorsement for his way of life. A kind of vigorous vitality made him look like he was perpetually running in place doing a vitamin commercial.

"My method of diagnosis is called iridology -- I look into the pupils of the eyes with a magnifying glass under a bright light." His explanation was fascinating. "In the center of the eye lay the blueprint for the physical history of the body, kind of like the map is buried right in front of your eyes! God's little joke." He laughed.

Why not? Listening to the results of the examination, he gazed into my eyes.

"I'm able to tell every symptom or disease you've ever experienced by the scars left on the pupil." He stopped, rolled back on his stool and looked at me seriously, assuming the pose of *The Thinker*. "Young lady, I'm going to give it to you straight. Your body is so toxic and so weak, that if you continue with your medication, the type of food you eat, cigarettes and alcohol, you haven't long to live. The decision is yours."

Again, there it was. No choice in the guise of choice.

The doctor's prescription was not medication this time quite the contrary. "Fasting, fasting on carrot juice and potato water only -- a purging of the poisons."

In denial I found a new determination, for there was wisdom in this kind of purification, not just for the body, but almost as penance for the soul. Embracing it, I read about it, and made a new commitment to life -- cleansing the slate of my old body. Weekly visits to Dr. Bradford were difficult for fasting weakened me even more. But to be in his presence felt encouraging for his vitality was contagious. First hot wet packs were applied to my back and allowed a twenty-minute penetration, then a deep hard body massage and spinal adjustment. On the third visit his technique changed as he began a slow movement around the outside of my breast. I felt myself wanting more. As if he read my mind, his hands firmly manipulated the entire front of my body -- this I naively, but gratefully considered part of the therapy.

On the next visit the therapy extended to other more sensitive areas. By the following week, I found myself lying on his table hoping his hand would find its way to give a total massage. He was accommodating. The medical profession should investigate this new service for it certainly releases a lot of pent-up energy. After the manipulation, I would get up from the table, say "Thank you, Dr. Bradford," shake his hand, and sign the Blue Cross form to pay the bill. The therapy went on for weeks until . . .

"Did you enjoy the therapy today Mrs. Golden?" The nurse inquired.

"It was exactly what I needed."

"Yes, my husband is really remarkable." . . .

Was this the culmination of ultimate victim-conscious-ness or the beginning of accepting my own power? Sometimes the flip side looks the same -- the distinction lying in the intention, for form often fools. Smiling on the way home, impersonal paid-for sex without all the emotional confusion. But that hypocrite, knowing his wife was in the other room.

Sally was pleased with my efforts of cleansing the physical but now she was after my spirit. "Mary you've got to try T.M., Transcendental Meditation! -- Even the Beatles are doing it. They teach this meditation technique to quiet the mind long enough to listen to the Universe speak. You see, the mind is so preoccupied with questions, the answers are never heard. We don't even know how to be quiet and listen.

Taking all my strength to get above a whisper, I managed, "My God Sally if I get any more quiet, they'll bury me."

Sally paid no attention. "This is a chance Mary, to tap into that energy you touched under LSD, but this time on your own."

Personally, I doubted whether I had strength to reach the

bathroom, let alone the Cosmos, but I agreed the possibility was exciting for I longed to once again feel the 'Light.' I nodded my head and Sally grinned.

Still too weak to go through a ceremony in the Temple, Sally brought the Initiator to my bedside. Incense and candlelight were part of the ritual. "It smells like a mosque on the road to Mecca." I whispered in Sally's ear. We chanted some strange sounds in an attempt to invoke Spirit -- like asking for a direct hookup. Not so different from my old Jewish grandmother hovering over the candles on the Sabbath. Given was a mantra, a sacred word of high vibration, and instructions in the daily twenty minute meditation.

Feeling more than a little foolish, but after six weeks in bed my desperation won demanding inspiration. The only place quiet and childproof enough was the closet . . . so each day, I prepared myself like a priestess and entered my tomb with incense, candle and timer. My clothes took on the smell of the aftermath, but I preferred it to mothballs. For weeks, I commanded myself to sit quietly, but somehow felt pulled in all directions, as though other forces didn't want me to find peace. My own inner voice was the prime offender finding any quiet corner of my mind to invade. But each day I relentlessly continued, determined to exorcise my own closet demons once and for all.

After about the fifth or sixth day of Dr. Bradford's fast I no longer desired food. My body experienced a new weightlessness and my mind felt cleared of the cobwebs. So cooking for the children from the standpoint of abstention wasn't as difficult as coping with nausea from the smells. At least, it got me out of bed three times a day. I forced myself to sit at the table.

"Will you come out on the beach and play Mommy?"

"Soon Darling, very soon." I turned away to wipe the tears.

Jess's recovery was speedier than mine. Once again, my brother-in-law Michael, in his own sadistic way brought me more news of Jess. Still in love with Jess himself, he now treated me like his one-time rival.

"He's finally done it, brought his fantasy down to earth. He's engaged to that prostitute!"

Too weak and dizzy to hold my fragmented heart together, in spite of my arms wrapped around my chest, I managed an indifferent quip. "Male or female?" and slowly climbed the stairs back to bed.

Oh Jess, Jess, what a mess. Jess, Jess, what a mess -- under my breath to the beat of passing telephone poles. How you broke my heart. Funny, in my mad passion for you, I always thought of myself as your whore . . . .

Only once during the two months we were ill was I allowed to see Jake. Sally helped me to the hospital. She could have carried me, my one hundred and fifteen pounds diminished to ninety-five. I stopped to add rouge to a pale face -- no lipstick, Jake always said it made me look trashy. Sally pushed his door open for me and waited outside. I stood unable to move, watching the tubes and machines beating out a mechanical rhythm of life. His eyes were closed, his breath heavy, and his skin a sallow gray, like a shadow passing over. I ran to him and buried my head in his chest, "Oh Daddy, please, please don't go!"

His hand smoothed my hair. "Everything will be all right Princess."

"Daddy listen, this is important. I want you to know I understand why . . . " He was asleep.

When Eve found me in Jake's room, the brunt of her fury unleashed. "Where's your face mask?" she demanded. "Who knows what germs you're still carrying." Eve wouldn't just let her daddy die. She hounded the doctors for any new or outrageous method to save him, even considering freezing his body until a cure could be found. She too, had many incomplete communications with Jake, making letting go very hard.

On the sixteenth day of my fast, Jake died. There was no more room for pain, for it already filled the width and depth of my being. Perhaps to ease her own misery, for Jake, Eve accused me. "It was probably your visit that killed him!"

I wasn't buying, thankful if my germs caused the end to help Jake out of his pain. But I never had the chance to really complete things with him. I'd take a long time to realize that decisions made about my relationships with men were based on my reality of Jake. Unless I forgave my father, would I always sit in judgment of other men?

A cloudy November morning funeral drew five hundred people spilling into the aisles for Jake's untimely death. At fifty-seven, most everyone he knew was still alive. The old ones sat introspectively crying as if mourning for themselves while from behind a thin black veiled curtain, the family watched. The mourners filed past the coffin. They say that the dying have their lives parade before them and now the parade of each friend's face brought memories rushing back. Funny, when I saw Al, who woke me every Sunday morning about his weekly gin game with Jake, then I broke down.

Daddy had adored Sam for he was everything Jake was not. The difference was also seductive for me. Sam's own personal grief over his father-in-law's death also brought compassion for me. Having him next to me behind that black veil somehow made it easier. Physically, he held me during the funeral and gave emotional support in the following days. And my poor babies -- how it broke my heart to watch them grieve. Alexander just stood by the grave, watching and waiting.

He and Jake had a very special connection. Every day since he was born, his grandfather called to check in with him. Here was the son he never had. Later that day, something strange happened, probably not so strange. Alexander was all excited. "Don't cry Mommy, Grandpa came and talked to me. He's gonna watch over us. He told me."

My own suffering blocked out his words. "That's foolish talk. He's gone, Alexander. He won't be talking to you anymore!" He just walked away wounded and misunderstood. Oh my God, could I have been so wrapped up in my own sorrow that I ignored my son's truth?"

The Tuesday clouds brought heavy rain by nightfall. Storming days, I returned home from my stay with Lenore the scene was chaos. The entire kitchen ceiling had collapsed from a leak in the roof. The water then found its way to the basement, flooding it. "No, please, no more! I can't take any more!" I shouted aloud as I managed to maneuver over the fallen debris. Marta walked in. Her smile gone -- she too on overwhelm.

"Could you open the door and let some of this awful mildew smell out?"

"No, Sha-Sha, Sha-Sha, come back!" I screamed as the brakes of a fast moving Porsche screeched. Sha Sha cried out. Running to grab him, I sat in the street rocking him in my arms. Sam had brought the puppy home the day Alexander was born seven years before. He wouldn't bark anymore. Was this God's answer? "Oh, yes -- you can take more!"

Feeling like Pauline in the midst of perils, what next? The pain that so filled the boundaries of my being went beyond pain to empty. A detachment was beginning, an appropriate response for salvation. Perhaps touching bottom is necessary before reaching the top. Emptying the vessel before filling it up. God, I want to be well.

This decision forced change in my life. Now a new wave

gained momentum as I read everything on the market concerning health and nutrition. Next, I ate mostly fruits and vegetables and gave up an addiction to sugar altogether. Before the fast, if the Jamoca Almond Fudge ice cream in the freezer was down to half a gallon, insecurity would insure a prompt visit to Thirty-One Flavors. An extra carton of filtertip Marlboros sitting on the shelf, Sam had considered efficient foresight. With great zeal, I began throwing out all the externals that worked against me: white sugar, white flour, anything with preservatives or chemicals . . . the list went on. To clean up what was going on inside without ingesting more trouble was going to be hard enough. Within weeks, all my weight returned in the proper places and I glowed from unprecedented health.

The phone rang. Walking toward it, I anticipated the adventure of an unknown caller, rather than the dread of ensuing bad news. It was Sam, his message specific. "I thought I would take the kids skiing for a long weekend." A pang of loneliness went through me at the thought. His voice was sensitive and caring. "I know you're not crazy about the sport, but would you like to come with us?"

"Oh Darling, I'd love to. Thank you." He had touched me -- in that moment, no greater gift could I be given.

Did this mean he has forgiven me? Stopping my thought midway . . . forgiven me for what? Must my victim consciousness always take the blame?

The expectancy was magical-intertwining future and past, bringing back memories, the two of us stretched out on the floor with maps and books planning exotic trips to faraway places, relying on the excitement of preparation rather than actuality of the voyage. There had been so many wonderful times. I lay in bed feeling him, smelling him -- soon more than memory.

The three of us sat, packed and waiting for Daddy. He arrived with a special gift for me . . . Sam had shaved his beard, an act proclaiming his vulnerability. I didn't mention it, he knew I was pleased. The nine hour drive was cramped in a small sportscar, but we filled it with singing, playing games and being a family. No one complained. I watched Sam's long tapered fingers tap the wheel as he sang, then I drove a while so he could play the guitar. His voice was strong and helped all of us to stay in tune.

Our cabin was straight out of a Sonya Heine movie with a quaint stone fireplace, dark heavy beams and red gingham curtains. Not sure what Sam had in mind for sleeping arrangements I watched as he tactfully had the porter place the children's suitcase in one bedroom and the parents' in the master suite. An after dinner walk in the snow under the light of the full moon, offered just the right romantic setting and enough fresh air to make two sleepy children.

My nervousness created chatter. "I feel like a bride." Sam was more uneasy than I but as always, took control.

"A honeymoon is better the second time." He took me in his arms tenderly, yet tightly. "I love you Mary." Our first kiss released a message saying how much we both wanted to get inside each other and heal the wounds. Lying in his arms was better than the anticipation. I climbed on his back. I was home.

A lingering smile remained on my face, lazily moving into a morning stretch. Lovingly, I smoothed out Sam's cowlick sticking straight up. He always curses it. Suddenly, I became aware of a tremendous pain in my leg. Sam was still asleep, as I carefully slipped out from our favorite nocturnal embrace into the biting cold morning. My leg was swollen and discolored. "Oh God, give me a break. This can't be happening!" It must be a spider bite was my instant diagnosis. There was no decision to be made. Nothing was going to spoil this trip and I certainly was accustomed to living with pain.

Breakfast seemed endless; the room wouldn't sit still and

my temperature was quickly rising. "Darling why don't the boys ski and us girls will go ice-skating?" My plan attempted some recovery time. Tara, my star, had become an angel disguised in the body of a four year old child with soft brown curls falling around. An exquisite little face dressed in her pink snow outfit. She followed her mother to the front desk.

"Please, is there a doctor here? I think I've been bitten by a spider." Pointing to my leg which was now swollen to distortion and turning blue, the tears couldn't be held back any longer.

"There's a hospital across the quad, but I wouldn't advise walking in your condition." After arguing that I could manage, the desk clerk drove us to the hospital. Tara cried and held on to me desperately.

This gentle giant of a doctor began his medical probe. "Do you take the birth control pill? It's thrombophlebitis, a blood clot in the leg . . . . "

How dare it rain on my parade! I've just begun to enjoy the end of such a long war . . . Can I endure another battle?

And so we've come full circle . . . the end of the beginning.

Life, death and so here I lie on the back seat of a station wagon, reviewing it all. Is it the beginning or the end? Do I look forward or backward, onward or inward? It seems as though we've been driving for an eternity or at least a lifetime. Even by night with this limited view, I can feel and smell the city.

Breaking the silence. "What hospital are you taking me to?"

"We're here." The *Emergency Entrance* was lit up in neon. The realization of which hospital he had chosen hit me.

"This is where my father died six weeks ago. You can't take me in there, never!" Screaming. "I know you hate me, but this is sadistic." My futile struggle ended as they carried the stretcher through swinging doors. "Sam don't leave me! I need you! I swear I didn't mean for this to happen, Sam!" Once more he refused to mount the white horse.

It's the middle of the night. I lay in bed listening to moaning and groaning -- like a floating morgue out at sea in a dense fog. And here I lay on a ship with no captain. **Sam's vulnerability had been brief -- ending with the slam of a metal station wagon door.**

The next two months in bed were intolerable. Effects of stopping birth control pills played havoc on my delicate hormonal balance. Then, two precious areas of my vanity were stricken -- my hair fell out in handfuls forcing me to cut short what was left and a rash developed that would have made measles a blessing. Surely God has fixed it so I would have no need of birth control pills! If Jess had been an interlude that postponed confrontation with myself, now aloneness was my only choice.

Solitude provoked all kinds of fear; but the greater the fear the more I needed to move into that dreaded place and live there a while -- to dissipate the energy with familiarity. Life seems to set the stage for exactly what you need. Maybe I needed to be flat on my back to force me to look up.

Sam was making sure I got what he thought I wanted -- a divorce. The property settlement was complicated -- there was a lot of it. But the Golden strings had to have one final pull. The papers were finally ready to be signed, the legalities ironed out, when Sam called and wanted to see me right away. He determined Zak's office was safe ground to meet, but to me it was more like quicksand. "I'll just be here if you need me." Zak winked at Sam and placed himself in a shadowed corner taking the role of psychological menace.

With his support system intact, Sam began. "Mary, I can't go through with it! This settlement isn't fair. We borrowed a hundred thousand dollars from my father and I think we're both indebted to pay him back -- which means you owe fifty-thousand dollars!"

I sat stunned. Zak watched with pleasure; surely, this was

his idea? A sinister plot! Could he really be this vindictive because I refused to sleep with him? Or was he just too good of a friend? Emotions spilled over my tolerance threshold. "We've been negotiating a settlement for over a year an you've never once mentioned this money. You know perfectly well your father thinks of it as an advance on your inheritance and that's also been your position. Abe's given Rachel and Michael much more than that. You think they'll pay him back? He doesn't expect payment; it's your money, Sam!" My frustration was accentuated by his indifference.

His voice had that arrogant, condescending tone like an annoying pat on the back. "Look Mary, I feel obligated to pay him back, to be responsible and not like my sorrowful siblings." He was covering both ends. If the money were considered an inheritance, it isn't legally shared in the bonds of matrimony. Or if considered simply a loan, he had me caught up in a moral obligation saturated in his own self-righteousness . . . Sam got his fifty thousand dollars -- he kept our house.

I felt like a fighter in the ring, on my last leg, my opponent not waiting for a natural countdown, but delivering that final unnecessary blow. A whisper would have worked. There must be an answer -- Oh shit! What's the question?! Mary, Mary, who's Mary?

Where is peace to be found? Is it like the mind, obscure in location? If pieces of the puzzle are to be put together in a new way, perhaps it's necessary to first disassemble the old game plan. Maybe life is just a series of births and deaths, life after life. The swan is dead . . . Long live the swan.

Part II

"Lord, make me pure, but not just yet!"

St. Augustine

Chapter VII

How do you begin a new puzzle? Start with the most recognizable piece. Silhouettes of figures falling into a master plan--all trying to find their groove, contracting limbs, forcing a fit to satisfy form. But each time I place myself in the game, my piece crumbles. As external support had been stripped from my life, it was now impossible to recognize my own identity by the pieces that held me together. Certainly, I had to work on getting my own innards assembled before I could think of re-entering the game. This Humpty Dumpty was going to put herself together again.

Crystal was an old family friend of the Goldens, her age falling about halfway between Esther and me. Compassion lived in her soft, watery eyes and mellow voice. Her open heart reflected warmth and an extraordinary wisdom that had comfortably settled in. A student of metaphysics and yoga for many years, she had chosen astrology as a tool, tapping into a greater intelligence. On the coffee table at home was her priceless possession, a signed first edition of Manly P. Hall's *Secret Teaching of the Ages*. She told me the tales of Madame Blavatsky, the Theosophical Society and how they had raised Krishnamurti from a child preparing him for Christhood. Her stories enthralled me. She also explained reincarnation and karma as simple truths.

My relationship with Esther was closer than ever. In some curious way, she seemed to replace Sam for me. Esther planned a small dinner party for my twenty-ninth birthday and Crystal prepared an astrological chart for my present. Sam had designed this new family house with two identical wings perfectly balanced and like our beach house, the open space was dramatic. The two of us quietly slipped into the guest room after dinner. We settled on the bed and Crystal began to explain my chart.

"It's God's handwriting on the wall the moment you enter at birth. We choose a specific instant in time that contains the *set-up* with all the props needed for our particular scenario. That's why you're a Scorpio, placed in the seventh house of relationship. Scorpio is the most passionate, sexual sign of the Zodiac. Like Mary Magdalene represents a feminine Scorpio. A cold shiver went through me, standing all the hairs on my arms at attention. It also explains your sensual beauty. So consequently some of your hardest lessons will come through sex. Along with Scorpio in the House of Relationship is Saturn, ruling your karma or past lives. This means relationships will have strong memories of other times, often hard lessons still unlearned which need working out. You should try to let your dreams help you remember. The third planet you have in the seventh house is Mercury -- this is the planet of communication. To sum all this up, you have an intense sexual desire, heavy karma and a strong need for communication, all living together in the House of Relationship. Please my dear, walk softly through life; don't make waves, ride them."

Crystal embraced me, feeling concern for my destiny, then added. "There is a balance shown by Jupiter in Aquarius in the twelfth house and a Cancer nadir which is a powerful Mother aspect. Remember, the lowest level of Scorpio is the scorpion, but it can evolve into the highest level, the eagle, and then, you can soar with the Gods."

All this vernacular though foreign to me, somehow held

within it a recognizable truth. My gaze fell upon a book, isolated on the self. *The Secret Vaults of Time* . . . were they beginning to open? "Tell me Crystal, how does a scorpion become an eagle? Is it like a caterpillar becoming a butterfly?"

"Exactly, or it's like the sun affecting a plant in the process of photosynthesis. Stepping into the *light* will make the change."

"Intensely, I tried to understand. "But how can I find the light?"

She smiled that compassionate mother's smile. "You must first see the river and be so hot that even though you can't swim, you know you're going to jump in."

Yoga would be perfect, combining flow of dance with the depth of meditation. I was ready to put my toe in the water.

"Esther how about taking Crystal's yoga class with me?"

"You know I've always wanted to try yoga and certainly my body could use a little encouragement. But I'm not sure about shutting down my mind long enough to meditate."

Esther was quite a woman, strong, eager and willing to put it on the line for the sake of a good philosophical argument. Our own independent mother-daughter love for one another generated a mutual intrigue in the search for meaning. Surely, our relationship was based on a strong karmic tie; but at this point in the game plan, we had no way of knowing what deep lessons we were to learn from one another.

Walking into the old Masonic Temple, I could feel mystical overtones still hanging heavily in the room. There were at least twenty women, most of them old enough to afford the luxury of a mid-day yoga class. On the carpeted floor were four rows of bright red, orange, yellow and blue mats equal distance from each other -- the large heavily carved chairs moved aside. A stage heightened the drama between student and teacher, the light dimly coming from a high ornate chandelier that looked like an inverted crown. The rhythm of quiet meditative music permeated the temple -- a throne room for a priesthood.

The class began with Crystal on stage dressed in a leotard revealing that side of herself before hidden, now seen -- a voluptuous haunting woman. "Yoga is a secret to youth. The spine, which is the switchboard to the central nervous system, is kept supple and flexible and most importantly, we have to learn how to increase our supply of oxygen to the brain. The breath, or prana, which is our life force . . . " I was startled as Crystal looked directly at me. "Would you mind helping me demonstrate a point?"

"If I can." I tried to accommodate.

She went on. "Take a deep breath." I obliged by sucking up all the air I had in me, causing a deep hollow in my stomach. "This is the way most people breathe; they learn to cut off air supply as they inhale and contract the muscles of the diaphragm. In Yoga, we re-educate to reverse the process and breathe as God intended. Taking in air and expanding the lungs, like blowing up a balloon, and on the exhale, we contract . . . " Crystal nodded her head in approval. "Thank you Mary. Sorry to set you up to be wrong."

"Believe me, now I'll never forget the lesson." I smiled, intrigued with the truth of the way most of us breathe. The very essence of life is nipped in the bud because of a learned process. Our very breath is part of this belief system . . . Crystal was impressive, as multifaceted as her name.

By the closing meditation at the end of class, the whole experience left me somewhere hanging between earth and the nearest cloud. Humpty Dumpty definitely had a smile on her face.

In a matter of months, I began working for Crystal -- first collecting monies, then actually training as a teacher. During one of our frequent intimate talks she mentioned having come from Nebraska. Not only were my parents from the same town, but as a young girl Crystal had worked for my uncle, collecting monies and trained in his business. She called it synchronicity. Whatever, certainly this was a person destiny had deliberately placed in my path.

More than Sally, Crystal was involved in any New Age advance to come along, especially in the field of alternative medicine.

"I've found the most wonderful Doctor, Evarts Loomis . . . considered the father of this whole movement. He was obviously tired of either cutting something out of patients or covering up symptoms with medication. On his ranch near Palm Springs you can be treated as a whole being, not just a body but a connected mind and spirit -- this is holistic medicine, not the fragmented variety." Whether *holistic* stood for whole or holy, I was ready for both.

A week's retreat dedicated to fusing all parts was perfect for my Humpty-Dumpty image. Esther's interest, as usual, was more intellectually based, but however diverse our inclinations we both desired results. We had to wait a month for reservations, which made our arrival early spring.

The ranch was built in the thirties by a movie tycoon as his personal retreat, I think Louis B. Mayer. The moment you entered through the gate, weeping willows -- the compassion tree, began lining the long driveway. It looked like a sleepy little Mexican village with adobe cottages forming a circle around the main house and purple bougainvillea covering each one, tying it all together. How beautifully nature connects things. The temperature had reached ninety degrees and the pool lying beneath terraced paths looked inviting.

After we registered, it didn't take long to get into the swing of the routine. First, a total physical.

"Please don't do that! Is it absolutely necessary?" I protested as the nurse cut a large chunk of hair from the nape of my neck and clipped my longest nail. My hair was just beginning to grow again.

"Sorry, it's the best way we've found to test for vitamin and mineral deficiencies."

Dr. Loomis at sixtyish was stately and gentle, with those same knowing eyes as Crystal. What does it take to get those eyes? What secrets do they know? With complete trust, we listened to his instructions. "The first day you'll begin a water fast, but the rest of the week family style dining will offer an array of homegrown organic foods and freshly baked breads. Cooking classes and recipes will ensure continued use at home." The ranch only took ten guests at a time and our group represented ten totally diverse life styles.

A typical day included Tai Chi, an Oriental movement class, meditation, painting therapy, hot baths, massage and ping pong. My favorite class was intensive journal, where key questions were asked, answered in a kind of James Joyce free flow of consciousness onto paper -- intense was an understatement. In the evening, encounter sessions led by a psychologist probed deeply and caused some sleepless nights. It bothered me that Esther won't really open up to her feelings; how much like my sister Eve she is -- always painting everything rosey.

On long walks alone among orange groves, inhaling their intoxicating scent, the real magic of a safe place penetrated and I allowed myself to confront my feelings. Everything blooming in spring is so vibrant. How could I know this tree wasn't dead if we met in its winter? But now, the blossoms speak of being alive. By week's end, a new surge of optimism filled me that Humpty Dumpty could indeed be put back together again.

Back in the city, I was anxious to re-create that cloistered environment to nurture my own growth. The beach house had been Sam's expression of himself -- all that glass and metal in straight lines; now it was my turn to let imagination run rampant letting curves, circles and colors create my space.

Up and down the streets of Los Angeles, I searched for my dream house to present itself; finally, after many weeks, there it was -- a handmade sign peeking out from an over grown gardenia bush, my favorite flower -- *For Sale by Owner*.

The house was hiding behind a curved wall encircling what looked like an acre of property. Already, I was excited by the mystery the wall created and the eccentricity of a faded aquamarine strip painted around its bottom half -- gay, like tequila had been mixed in with the paint. The front of the house looked like a Mexican jail, bars on windows and a low sloping red tile roof.

Parking quickly, the kids and I peered over the wall. Alexander was growing so fast his eyes just made it and Tara, I lifted up. "Oh Mommy, please can we live here?" Smiling, I noticed the cracks in the wall were fake -- like a giant movie set! A house of illusion. There before us lay a magical garden, huge old trees, roses, fruit hanging from vines . . . a sanctuary with a bizarre touch. A statue of Pancho Villa guarded the entrance to the front patio, while little crooked paths followed a stone creek winding through the garden. Even a wishing well -- it was a fairyland for devas and elementals. Standing on a large rock, I could see an abandoned tennis court. Surely, all this enchantment midst an affluent westside neighborhood was more than my finances could contemplate. Do I believe in miracles? At the children's insistence, I wrote down the owner's number.

After our weekly I Ching class with Khigh Deigh, Esther and I stopped for lunch. "Have you had any luck house hunting?" She always showed an interest.

I'm afraid my aesthetic is not exactly aligned with my budget. I did see an enchanted hacienda that satisfied all my fantasies, but that's all it is -- a fantasy!"

"Now I'm intrigued. Let's go see this magical place, but first let's throw the I Ching to glimpse the outcome . . . "

As the large carved wooden gate opened, the dream-like energy of the garden engulfed us in another world—Mexico with a touch of jungle fever.

The eccentric image of the house was sustained by the residents. The Steins greeted us at the door -- he in his maroon velvet smoking jacket with black satin ascot and a small waxed mustache for which he had a tactile fascination. An artist, he looking as though he had created his own image from a Salvador Dali self-portrait. Many canvases throughout the house testified that his wife was his favorite model.

Mrs. Stein was wearing spiked heels to compensate for her five foot stature and a black, off-the-shoulder cape emphasized her best feature or hid her worst. Insuring the drama a large brimmed straw hat perched on her head. A white powdered face, bright red lips and bleached blond hair completed an effect somewhere between Renoir and Toulouse Lautrec.

The capricious genre excluded no corner of their home. The living room in particular looked like a set from a 1939 movie and smelled as if in moth balls ever since. Leaning over, Mrs. Stein held her bosom and fumbled with an old Victrola; it appeared their act was down pat, a little music to muffle the sounds of late afternoon traffic.

Now Mr. Stein's voice had to project over *Swan Lake*. "We consider it a strong selling point that the house once belonged to Greta Garbo. It's a marvelous place if you vant to be alone." He twisted his moustache, pleased with himself. "Before the house was built the grounds had been a miniature golf course, which explains much of the fantasy. You see this fireplace." Leaning on the mantle, he struck a pose. "I painted Thomas Mann's portrait right in front of it."

They were wasting their time trying to sell me, for I had been sold since my first glimpse of the walled garden. He went on and on as my mind wandered back to those Saturday afternoon matinees as a child . . . The Carthay Circle, that wonderful old art-deco movie theatre. A wet Saturday and *The Enchanted Cottage* was playing with Dorothy McGuire and Robert Young. When these screen lovers were together in their enchanted cottage, everything magically changed, even their crippled unattractive bodies became whole and beautiful, but only to one another. I must do a reality check with Esther, but it seemed she too was under the spell.

Slowly, I walked through the house remembering more of those childhood Saturday afternoons when I explored thoroughly every door off the balcony, finding a network of secret passages and thrilled by their mystery. Now, the floor plan of this house brought back other memories -- underground tunnels, pyramid passageways, catacombs and caverns -- a sense of the unpredictable, unlike less adventurous modern architecture where even blindfolded, one can be assured of finding the bathroom.

This was my house. I knew it. Strangely, the Steins also felt it, but they didn't approach the subject. Their main focus turned to selling Esther a painting. I'm not sure she paid them $700.00 for the *Still Life* or the floorshow. Later we learned that for years, the couple had kept the *For Sale Sign* up in order to lure prospective art patrons into their market place. Now financial distress was forcing them to seriously sell their precious retreat that protected them from the outside.

"Well there's no doubt that house has your name on it." Esther was convinced as we strolled through the garden.

"Of course it's my dream house, but there's no way I can afford it."

"Well I want you to have it and my grandchildren grow up with this incredible beauty around them. So that's settled . . . it's yours!" That was Esther's promise. Continuing on crooked pathways next to the creek, like Dorothy on the Yellow Brick Road -- already having her wish granted -- surely this was the proper setting for a fairy tale or a miracle.

Of course Sam was the obvious person to inspect the property before his mother bought this extravagant gift. Sam and I were establishing a new relationship and as long as I did everything he wanted, it worked.

"God Mary of course the place has charm -- but there's dry rot, termites and general decay. If I were a dentist I'd say pull it and as a builder, I say tear it down and start over!" He'd probably tell Robert Young that Dorothy McGuire wore dentures. For sure Sam wasn't under the spell. "And by the way, in going over this with the lawyers, the best way to handle the purchase until a better plan comes along, is for the house to remain in Mother's name. You will receive a letter of intent, that the first eighty thousand dollars belongs to Alexander and the next eighty thousand to Tara. This amount totals her gift, so whatever's left over if ever sold is yours. Is this something you want to live with? If you want my advice, I think it's a big mistake to get yourself so much in her debt, just when you're in a position to really be independent."

I was hardly listening; once again, there was no choice. The house was already mine on whatever terms I could get.

The Steins were originals! The day they were to move out, they locked themselves in the bedroom and refused to leave, like two children orphaned by the loss of home with nowhere to go, bewildered by reality. My heart broke for them, as I passed food into their manmade cell so they wouldn't starve. Then I tried to figure out ways to adopt them. If the house were bigger I would have. The seige lasted three days; finally, I convinced them they could continue their eccentric lifestyle on a lesser budget in the south of France. Half their possessions remained behind. I think it was their way of holding on.

Now came the real challenge of making our home livable and still maintain all the mystique. Because Sam said it would take at least three months to complete the work, I was determined to do it in thirty days, acting as contractor, designer and by far, the most enthusiastic worker. The flooring in the house was old peeled linoleum, chipped up piece by piece and replaced with terracotta Italian tile.

"Continuity of flooring makes a house flow. Now, how does this sound? Bright yellow coming about a third up the wall and around the doors. Each room a different color accent aquamarine, terracotta, you know, like in Mexico. Nothing like splashes of color to add some fun." My enthusiasm spilled over as I gave Esther my decorating tips while sprawling on the floor sorting dozens of color chips. Esther appreciated my style.

"Take this, Mary, for your remodeling fund. We've got to insure continued quality." Esther handed me a check and not waiting for my reaction, walked out the door. I stared down at the check deposited in my hand -- ten thousand dollars! Jake slipping me a twenty was usual, but this boggled my mind!

Mr. Stein's huge painting studio became a three shades of blue master bedroom. The stage at the far end of the room under a skylight made a perfect sitting area and created a cozier scale to the space; opening directly onto the garden was just the right spot for a tiled jacuzzi . . . now that's a bathtub with a view!

One month later to Sam's amazement and my near demise the children and I moved in, for days just walking around in deep reverence for all our blessings. The first order of business was to put up a basketball hoop.

Ah, the pitfall relating my own identity with my external creation. Did I create it or does it create me? A subtle distinction. Sam was impressed. "Mary you really are a frustrated architect!"

Smiling my retort. "True, if you look at what kind of person you're attracted to you usually find your missing link!"

If that's true, it'll be interesting to see what kind of man would next possess what I needed most in myself.

Sally had fallen in love with a young gorgeous musician half her age. Her missing link? Maybe. She came by to share the news and help me unpack.

"Well he's asked me to marry him and I said yes!"

"Oh Sally dear I'm so happy for you. . . .And the age difference is something you can live with?"

"Hey Mary, he worships every line on my face. Youth isn't afraid of age and he's teaching me. Anyway, I want someone who adores me, instead of a phone call once a week because the guy notices something hard between his legs! All those years in accommodation not relationship. I think I was just jacking off! By the way, I met him at an EST training -- a new human potential thing. We're going to a guest seminar tonight. Come with us?"

Arriving early we sat in the front row. "Sally, are you sure about this? Who writes their script? I can't believe the jargon. It makes it hard to hear what they are trying to say."

"I know it sounds like someone pressed a robot button, but try to get beyond the language." My tolerance threshold needed bolstering. I wanted to knock on the leader's head to see if anyone was home behind all those words and smiles. But somewhere, hidden behind the facade there was substance, something they knew and I didn't that just might be worthy of two weekends and two hundred dollars.

Within a week, I found myself in the midst. The trainer was delicious which made the torture of sitting for hours on my end more bearable. The desperate need to urinate mingled with a heightened sexual desire -- kind of like a kid on a maypole. But after six hours and no break, I was able to separate the impulses. I definitely had to pee.

An excessive amount of badgering and swearing bombarded the senses. A sad commentary on human potential when the best way of learning truth is through a drill sargent's bullying and intimidation, though it seemed to produce results as life-long barriers were being dynamited.

A guided imagery meditation took one back to childhood. Urgently, the trainer paced back and forth across the stage and shouted into the microphone, *"Remember the first time you made a decision about your mother,"* a pause, then, *"your father?"* My hands began to sweat. I shrunk as though on an inner elevator; someone had just pressed my memory button and sharply began the descent.

There we were -- "buy me, give me, take me" -- Jake's

three girls, standing at the entrance to a sleazy downtown bar, on a mission to retrieve Daddy from demons' clutches. There he was sitting at the bar with what from that instant on would be my version of a whore. His wallet was out showing her pictures of Eve and me. Upset and embarrassment had deeply buried the incident, but now for the first time, it became clear. There, in the whiskey-soaked dank air of that bar, I made the decision. Men are never faithful, they love whores, the other woman has more fun, and finally, wives and mothers are victims and weak.

"How does the decision you made then affect your relationships now?" By the booming sound of his voice, the elevator button was painfully pushed to the basement level. With this set up, of course Sam could never have filled my needs. I had to seek out someone like Jess -- faithfully unfaithful. Even trying to be his whore so he'd love me didn't work for underneath the charade was my mother, the weak victim, the wife. That role intensified even more after I became a mother myself. The realization of how these basic decisions had so influenced my very being brought waves of sadness and oceans of tears.

The next order from the stage. "Will the attendant pass Kleenex up and down the aisles?" Giggles suggested there was some humor left in the room for the similarity of the human condition. It didn't seem to matter what particular incident happened to force a decision about life at a very tender age. What irony, the very thing everyone has in common is also the foundation for withdrawal and separateness from each other.

"Quiet! Go deeper, deeper back into your past. *What happened as a child that destroyed your connection to the Source of your being?"* I'm feeling nauseous and sick. Sam was wrong; he always told me I was physically peculiar because I never sweat. Squirming and wet, I wanted to get out of this tight inner space.

There I was on a street corner, holding my sister Eve's

hand, watching traffic go by. Time and space stood still. I
merged into all things, being part of the center -- the same
oneness experienced under LSD. No wonder kids are so
high -- the memory closer, more specific. Surely, the people
are just pretending to be busy and not recognize me. Where
are my maids in waiting? My son Solomon? Everything had
purple and gold overtones. David, David, my soul cried out
as the traffic light turned green, a surge of regal power
coursed through me. A naive five-year-old communicating
this strange phenomenon to an already tainted nine-year-
old brought a strong negative reaction concerning ego. Eve
assured me I was not a queen nor the center of anything, as
she pulled me across the street. For Eve, as most children
will, had already fallen from her connection with memories
of source or past lives and was now teaching her little sister
the confines of earthly reality.

Oh God, what have I done to my children? What decisions
have they already made? What judgment about life and death
did Alexander come to when I denied his truth about Jake?

At two Sunday morning the first weekend finished, but the
roller coaster ride continued. During the week, vivid moments
of enormous clarity were only to be clouded by creeping old
patterns. I phoned Sally twenty times to ask if I'd *gotten it.*

At the close of the second weekend, the trainer quoted a
phrase from their leader, Werner Erhard, who had made no
appearance during our entire training, but for whom reverence
had been established -- "Always ride the horse in the direction
it's going." Everyone but me stood up and cheered. I just sat
there. Of course, if you want to know what you need, take a
look at what you've got. You can always have happiness if you
choose things the way they are. It's all perfect! I had it!
Rushing to write it down before I lost it . . . illusive little devil,
revelation!

Extended seminars continued -- weekly investigations into
whys and wherefores of deep-rooted feelings, running the

gamut from self-image to sex. I chose the latter, an exploration into the forbidden fruit. Within seminar safety, incredible fantasies were revealed -- from flagellation and bondage to sex with animals. My voyeurism heightened, I wondered what Harry did in the bathroom all those hours when he lived with us over the garage? Man is certainly in a sorry state about his own sexuality. Social deviations are as outrageously extreme as the moral order that places them there.

A fond memory brought back a strong impression -- my eye peering through a magnifying glass closely examining Indian Temple sculpture. Stone turned fluid as they began to move into contorted, bizarre sexual positions, all for the sake of religious orgasm -- to arouse the seat of power, the kundalini, coiled and sleeping like a serpent at the base of the spine, commanding it to rise up and connect them to God!

How little patience we have for differences!

Beyond the many decisions made as a child about sex, I realized just how much the abortion disenchanted me with the act and how much anger against Sam I still felt. What takes place under covers of matrimony is not about enjoying, but pleasing. With Jess, a new dimension was made available, but perimeters set by his fantasies, not mine. But there was more, something I couldn't yet get a handle on. Hidden away in some timeless calendar were dark secrets of my own sexuality, a mingling of brothels and coin.

"Close your eyes!" Another meditation was coming. God, I hate these intimate confrontations with myself -- no place to go but inside. *"What is it you would like to experience in sex?"* Not to play the waiting game. What would it be like to have the freedom of the masculine role? The aggressor? The hunter? Sex for its own sake? To call the shots simply to enjoy a stranger.

Certainly, this variety of classroom uniquely offered freedom to verbalize sexual intimacies, but I felt ready to unlock a portion of untapped reservoir through more direct experience.

To free myself from confines of this role-playing pattern passed down from generation to generation or life to life.

Thursday morning, after that Wednesday night, I was on the telephone making reservations for Club MED in Tahiti -- my fantasy of a bacchanal throwback, a virtual playground of sexual availability.

Getting off the plane alone in a strange land, I recognized the freedom that comes with being the prime mover in one's own life. Driving through Tahitian countryside in an open-air bus jolted the senses, each one called upon for maximum use. The air was hot and wet. The dampness carried the smell of coconut palms and the fragrance clung to my skin. I took off my sunglasses as not to distort the perfection of color. By noon, the bus unloaded with the buffet lunch just beginning. Seating in the dining room was family style and by the end of a week one had occasion to break bread with the entire Club's international clientele. Each afternoon at five was a classical music hour in celebration of sunset, on a large veranda jutting out over the sea. But even Bach or Mozart had difficulty capturing all the magic presiding here.

After dinner was a major theatre performance put on by the staff with an amazing level of professionalism from costume to script. Young aspirants of the stage came to teach waterskiing by day and perform in this unusual repertory company by night. The outdoor amphitheatre added to the pagan effect the mood was perpetual revelry.

I remained determined to experience the other side of the coin. After the floor show, the dance began. The mood on the veranda altered from the late afternoon concert. Now the music announced the hunt had begun. Couples drifted across the floor. Jake's voice resonated in my ear. "You're on, Princess." What I had in mind would certainly not win patriarchal approval. Surveying the scene, my eyes narrowed in on the one -- the water ski instructor. No doubt this employee moonlighted as a stud service. His fifties Hawaiian

shirt opened to the waist, exposed a deep bronze tan, while
short sleeves were rolled up to reveal more muscle -- a benefit
of his daytime occupation.

My red and black floral strapless dress spoke my intention, I
waited for an alluring slow dance. The exhale of a full yoga
breath passed through my lips, calming me. Seductively, I
approached my prey. Feeling enveloped in his amazingly
strong arms, the realization came that this classroom under
the stars required very specific homework.

We danced on and on until night turned morning. Finally,
he lifted me in those arms and walked us down to the beach. A
crescent moon left enough room in the sky for a million stars.
Sand, air and water were the same temperature, a left-over
memory of the sun. We spent the remaining night lulled to
sleep by sounds of the surf.

More challenge than one trophy waited for the hunter. Each
night I changed partners for the *dance.* By mid-week, my fifth
partner had enough staying power to last the whole day. He
was a wealthy young German playboy telling stories of antics
in his private jet. Laughing and talking for hours on the beach
reserved for nude sunbathing, then discreetly, two well-oiled
bodies moved into lovemaking under the hot sun. In the minus
ledger, the truth of bright sunlight revealed all the scars of
births and battles, as well as sand sticking to overly lubricated
private parts.

There's no escaping one's femininity. The penetrator and
the penetrated. Only attitudes change -- feeling attacked and
violated by the sword, or infused and fulfilled by the connection.
"Ride the horse in the direction it's going!"

"Come let's go inside. The sun can be brutal to skin as fair as
yours." He offered his hand and kept mine while leading me
into the bathroom, introducing the joys of joint showering . . .
extra preparation went into dressing that evening. I couldn't
stop my mind slipping into fantasies about a more permanent
connection with this man. God, my grandmother would turn

over in her grave -- not only is he not Jewish, but a German.

At dinner I missed seeing him, but on the dance floor he was quite visibly at work setting up his next afternoon. Ironically, he represented a perfect reflection of my own motive for being there; however, he proved to be a more serious hunter. Having won his trophy, he placed it on the mantle to accumulate dust with the rest of his collection and was off again in hot pursuit of prey. I had used just as he -- but my pride was injured. There's danger in the jungle.

But indulgence in my sexual appetite had peaked. Like a child with a sweet tooth let loose in a candy factory, I now suffered from a giant stomach ache.

Time to leave. All these different detached bodies, detached feelings. A whore not a hunter. Instant gratification as an isolated act emphasized my aloneness. For me, sex is an expression of love and passion of the moment part of a continuing growing process.

Chapter VIII

Oh for a sustained beginning. Where do relationships go wrong? Retrospect, was a far safer and more objective position. My thoughts exposed a common thread. My men wanted to be accepted as is. And my almost Christ-like expectation was too high, making them feel inadequate or stretched. Where was it written in my soul this manifesto of perfection? What ghost lurked in this black hole? Was I sentenced to walk the plank over this deep abyss?

The weekend was going to be lonely. Sam came to take the kids giving me a patronizing kiss on the cheek, intentionally leaving the impression of whiskers behind and a little paternal pat on the back which he knew infuriated me. If I'm this lonely on weekends, what must it be like for Sam during the week? Sam my darling, I'm so sorry if I hurt you. I'm so sorry that you hurt me. I'd have the pain surgically removed if I could. How self-centered we are existing in our own tormented cocoons thinking we're the only ones in pain, so isolated in suffering. The duel of relationship is always played with a double-edged sword.

Alone with all those hours of day and seemingly slower ones at night? Finally, I understood, relationship is not going to make me whole. For certainly, it's too precarious and changeable, being within someone else's power to call the shots. Even the perfect man can't make me complete.

Another Saturday night alone. I lay in bed thinking a way to be free from sexual dependence, well aware of how strong an influence my physical needs play in luring me into unwanted relationships -- my mind probing the question as my hand unconsciously explored between my legs. Damp and excited! Here was freedom! I don't even have to dress up or down. But orgasm didn't come easily. Lying alone in the dark, I experienced how before climax the sensation causes a tightening up cutting off, and holding on. The energy confined to lower levels. Instead of opening the door and welcoming it, I put up a barrier that only an explosion could penetrate. Fascinating how these observations reflected clearly many areas of my relationships. I had to laugh -- masturbation, one of the great teachers!

With the aid of a vibrator, I trained my involuntary sexual habits. At the moment the fuse ignites, I surrender, allowing the energy freedom to soar up body to the top of my head, experiencing release through every pore. The ecstasy was far removed from the twisted sexual suppression I had been morally confined to. Orgasm is truly one of God's greatest gifts to experience a real connection to Source. My Indian stone friends would be proud.

The internal mechanics began to pay off. At first, I merely desired liberation of sexual expression but like osmosis, or a fine sifting process, womanhood seeped slowly into who I was.

Not waiting to be taken, I went alone to a holistic medical conference in San Diego. The speakers ran the gamut from mediocre to inspired -- the latter in the presentation of an older woman psychiatrist, Elizabeth Kubler-Ross, whose life is dedicated to understanding death and easing transition for the dying. She's a small, fragile framed woman, whose mellow voice was without great emotion -- the mark of Europe during the war years still about her. She spoke not trying to convince, but with power of her own conviction.

"Each of us has spirit guides, never far away. They protect and help direct our lives." She shared personal experience when her own guides made themselves physically known to her, how they helped the dying cross over. The silence was powerful. One thousand professionals, all medically related, sat spellbound as though their own guides had put a hold on rational thought. Exposing her truth touched a deep place in each memory bank, creating a group closeness, as if we shared a precious key gaining membership into a secret society. Dissolving of my own fear of death was initiated through understanding the transition.

The buffet line for lunch was almost long enough to come to no choice in eating.

"It looks discouraging for a hungry appetite," said a low male voice with a twinge of New York in it. "There's a lovely little Indian restaurant around the corner. I'd love your company." His name tag introduced him as Mark von Holt, a free lance writer and psychic researcher. Possessing a wonderful sense of humor with a spiritual bent, he quipped, "People tend to be so heavy about the *light*". He adjusted his heavily rimmed glasses that disproportionately took up space on his face. He was rather adorably ingratiating.

Over chapatis and curry, Mark explained. "I'm intensely involved in the *Course of Miracles*, a book supposedly written by spirit guides, through a very credible atheistic Eastern college professor. She simply wrote down what she was instructed, in midnight sessions. The result is an extraordinary work of a rarified quality. It speaks truth that affects you at an experiential level." Mark made a gift of the *miracle* book to me.

The course consisted of three hundred and sixty-five lessons -- one for each day of the year. His sincerity although a little preachy, touched me, and I promised to begin the course and a fascinating friendship with Mark.

Crystal was presenting Yoga to the conference as a means of stress reduction. Over a cup of herbal tea, we chatted. "What's the latest inner intrigue on the consciousness circuit?"

"Don't you ever get enough Mary? Well the inside scoop on the best workshop is *Set Your Own Stage for a Play Called Life*, put together by a young Englishman, the boy wonder of the human potential movement, Sydney Davidson."

"Why not go for overflow? An injection of Mr. Davidson's positive thought shot straight into the adrenals? God Crystal, my only fear of overdose is being labeled a workshop junkie; it's so in. Maybe I can do it before the kids come back from camp."

The timing was just right. Arriving the first night, I sensed something special about to happen and the Biltmore was an appropriate setting. I settled into my front row seat, a reward for early workshop arrivals and enjoyed the elegant old Baroque architecture in all its eclectic grandeur. The audience seemed an imposition to that moment in time. The sculptured cherubs appeared to be spewing out love directly into the room. Deep regal reds and blues of woven wool in rich Oriental carpets made the entire room demand attention. But there lingered more here than simply visual stimulation, of course, . . . I remember reading that Yogananda had performed *samadhi* in this very room.

Just then Sydney Davidson walked on stage. Joining in the applause at his appearance, I wondered if everyone could see the light emanating from him. My heart responded involuntarily, stunned by powerful recognition of this man. Now here could be my missing link.

Although on the short side of medium, he wore a dark pinstriped suit with distinction of a diplomat. I'm certain his deep red tie was chosen to match the regality of carpet; he appeared immaculate to that kind of detail. His greying black hair was obviously premature for the boyish face framed.

The mysterious depth of a mystic prevailed and expressed his extraordinary charisma while, his authority made it easy for participants in the workshop to temporarily entrust their power to him, as they would do to a doctor or teacher in order to be healed or learn.

"What a teacher and workshop do is force people to reveal themselves to themselves in the presence of others. Having exposed an unworkable plot before an audience, you are compelled to assume responsibility for resetting *your own stage for a play called life.*"

Apparently, this was a more loving and supportive episode in the workshop saga. Sydney seemed to possess amazing psychic powers, enabling him to tune into someone's act and force them to leave it behind, like a fur coat on a hot day. The exchange occurred between the person on stage and Sydney, acting as their alter ego. Sitting on a stool at the back of the center aisle acting like a mirror, imaging instant replay with his slingshot retort. It was better than video!

My turn to go on stage, fearing my heartbeat would be heard over the microphone. Sydney was just finishing a thought to the group. "Anytime we're not expanding, we're depressing."

Instantly thinking of a yoga breathing parallel, I retorted as sudden revelation. "So depression comes from a lack of growth!" It was a good beginning. Sydney impressed by my lack of intimidation to his strength, acknowledged his admiration in eye contact.

Once begun, I found it actually fun to be on stage . . . "I made an important discovery in realizing how unsatisfactory it was merely to collect and possess. I began to turn inward to wake up that part of me that's been asleep. Slowly, I'm beginning to understand my mind is my servant, not my master. And if I see darkness, it's my own inability to turn on the switch." . . . I continued to allow an inner exposure.

As I left the platform, Sydney commented. "Well, if that's an act, it's a damn good one!"

Odd how events seem to be always on cue, as though the director in the sky is following a well-written script. For years, Sydney had been involved in work and play with a very powerful lady, Anne. They had just bought a magnificent new house together and were considered the sweethearts of the movement. By some strange quirk of destiny this particular weekend, she seriously sought romance elsewhere and immediately telephoned Sydney with the news. She must have known this would devastate him, especially in the middle of a workshop.

Surprisingly, he didn't try to hide his feelings. With great tenderness he shared his pain with the group and gratefully accepted our support, although admitting his difficulty in continuing. While Sydney was vulnerable, he had no fear of exposing his feminine side -- this balance enriched his power. Sometimes, I turned and caught a glimpse of him sitting on his stool at the back of the room staring off into space with a sadness beyond the personal, more for the whole human predicament -- like a king mourning his flock. Still, his marvelous wit aided by an English accent, peeked through the gloom bringing his own version of sunshine back into our midst.

Close friends were instantly made for in our deep sharing the thread wove a common cloak. Over dinner that night with two women psychologists, we wondered. "I can't figure out why Anne would cheat on a man like Sydney and announce it so cruelly?"

Thor, a young handsome tennis pro joined us and added some masculine input. "Hey, some broads are just ball breakers!"

I couldn't let that go by. "You put your foot in your mouth with that one. You must like to live dangerously."

He smiled slyly. Thor and I began to spend our breaks together.

With the long three day weekend behind us everyone felt reluctance to leave. A reunion of the group and guests, mid-week was routine to share reviews of our new play on the stage of the streets. Thor and I had dinner before the Wednesday meeting.

"You want to drive?"

He was quick to accept. "Sure maybe I'll be able to afford a Jaguar someday when I teach my own version of the Zen of Sports!" He pulled into the hotel parking lot. "Oh ho, look who's in front of us. It's Mr. Sydney in a very classy car," referring to a black and white Mercedes. "Who do you suppose the red head is?"

I knew it was Anne. "What a team; she must be a consumate fuck-up and he a devout forgiver!"

Sydney hastily made his way to a side entrance with Anne on his arm -- a public display of forgiveness and a happy-ever-after front for the world of consciousness.

At least three hundred people, guests and graduates mingled all properly name-tagged and if you couldn't distinguish those who just completed the workshop by their smiling faces, we were insured acknowledgement by a big red star. Sydney being the brightest star, awkwardly moved through the crowd, but he skillfully stage-managed an introduction of Anne to me. The maneuver not difficult to detect, I felt like a pawn in his game -- though I then presented my own knight -- "You know Thor, of course!"

No one could question Anne's beauty. Those devilish green eyes invited challenge though you wouldn't feel safe resting there long. Her red hair pulled back in a tight bun transformed the 'girl next door' into a sophisticated lady -- and it worked! It looked like a contest between her and Sydney to determine who was more expensively dressed and meticulously groomed. Tonight, she won. Wearing a black gabardine Givenchy suit and white satin blouse tied in a floppy bow at the neck -- the shine of the fabric reflected in her face. There was no doubt of the market they were after. Given all that, Anne acting as hostess, would still be more suited to leading cheers at a football game. She certainly brought out the kicker in Sydney. Far more attractive to me was that side of him wanting to sit on the bench and watch the flowers grow. Anne was very much aware of my potential to manicure his garden.

Her conversation kept to the offense, as an intimidating strategy, demonstrating that a controlling nature isn't confined to a man. Then I learned from her not only was the *Set Your Own Stage* office in a building that Sam had designed, but Sydney kept a beach house in Los Angeles, amazingly in one of the apartments that Sam and I still owned.

"I'm Sydney's landlady? Which apartment?"

"Two-O-four."

My mouth opened in astonishment. "If this were a movie no one would believe it. My ex-husband moved into that very apartment when we separated!"

Anne's retort was quick. "You know what Sydney's theory is -- there's only your basic two hundred people on the planet and they keep bumping into each other."

Extending the thought ". . . and perhaps reincarnating together!" I sensed the enormity of what we had to learn together -- which turned out a mere understatement.

Common knowledge was that Anne and Sydney's relationship extended into the public eye, for she shared a T.V. talk show that he hosted. Everyone remained uncertain as to the status of their romantic involvement after her weekend escapade. Thor, not oblivious to the intrigue, was more than aware of the precarious nature of his own role.

The telephone rang early the next morning. "Sydney!"

"I'm just sitting here in Apartment Two-O-Four -- trying to work on my book. But I keep staring out at the ocean and the same question persists in my head." He wasted no time in getting to the heart of his call. "Mary, I'd like to explore the possibilities of having a relationship with you. What are your feelings about that?"

Showing no hesitation or doubt, "I think the possibility is definitely worthy of investigation."

He was leaving for New York that day. We set up our meeting for the night of his return. Beginnings are best for they haven't yet a past, nor are they lured by promises of future. But how quickly the now of a beginning disintegrates into anticipation of tomorrows.

As Sydney walked through my enchanted garden for the first time he felt bewitched -- a spell was cast. Here was the ideal setting to sit and smell the roses. He greeted the statue of Pancho Villa guarding the front courtyard entry as I opened the door.

"You have magnificently managed to *set your stage* in style. And I can see you also believe in magic." The week's wait seemed to have cemented the connection between us. Taking the lead in our dance, he intentionally brought his mouth to mine, sealing the inevitable.

"I knew it would be like this. Can we take a jacuzzi now?"

Once again I managed no shock in my response, but agreed to the perfect next step. We stood facing each other undressing, sharing only anticipation but no words. Smiling as he folded everything neatly, I thought of Sam.

Excited vibrations echoed in the sound of bubbling hot waters. The steam formed a mist enclosing us from the rest of the night. There in the water he penetrated my body as he had already left his mark on my heart from the moment I first saw him. And on my soul, where and when I knew not.

"Ouch! I've sat on a bee and it's stung my bottom." The spell was punctuated. Were the Gods laughing?

Lying in bed excited by the newness and oldness of it, we spoke of our expectation in relationships, revealing similarities and differences in our individual needs. "I married Helen at nineteen, my childhood sweetheart. She was my friend and mentor for fifteen years. We came to this country together and when she found the need to explore life on her own immediately I found Anne, leaving no time to be alone. . . . Well, really, I found Anne before Helen left. That's why she went. But Anne was an exciting temptress. She taught me how to play. Sexually I woke up from a long sleep. So my dear, my romantic scope has been quite limited. Now, I've girls offering me head for a snack during a workshop break, but I've never been in the position to taste the fruit!"

"We're unequivocally at different places in the romantic process. I've tasted enough fruit to raise anyone's blood sugar. I'm ready for a committed relationship. By the sound of it you still need a chance to eat a banana or two!"

But here we were, smitten. The stardust not yet settled. First, we agreed about our desire to have a relationship and our committment to making it work, but most important, without ever being unfaithful to our own needs. Sydney laid out the ceremonial words.

"This relationship will establish a new form and it may just work!"

"Do you know one of the great secrets of healing? You must care more about the other person than yourself. It's the same when you love to care enough about their growth to encourage what you feel their process calls for. Jealousy and fear are left behind."

All my feelings surfaced expressing pitfalls and resolves I'd come to. "Most demands in relationship are based on the expectation of your partner performing exactly as you would. Our psyches understand and demand mirror image. Prisoners of our own experience. Let's not go on automatic pilot when you've done something I would never do, simply because we have different needs. If we could find a higher common denominator based on love and trust, committed to each other's well being, now that would be quite a role model!"

Here is a man I can finally talk to. He'll never fall into the black hole between my expectation and his reality . . . "men and women are meant to be different. It's merging of male and female principles that has to take place. Man's penetrated focus is directed toward his work. Whereas women have this diffused awareness embracing relationship. Unfortunately, the dichotomy creates the main conflict between men and women." I paused digesting what I had said, my tone softening. "How very sad, when really it's a perfectly incredible combination for meshing the gears in the romantic wheel -- the penis and vagina, in a phallic mystery dance!"

Sounding like I was writing a text book for the Human Potential Movement, Sydney could only quiet my monologue by rolling on top of me. He held me closely. "I can feel all the love you have just waiting to be unleashed. Now, you've found a safe place." . . .

"That feels so good!"

"O.K., we've set the stage, now let's begin the play." Having learned independently the joy of surrendering to the energy of orgasm, with Sydney the dynamic squared itself.

One great pitfall of unveiling the skins of consciousness, is trying to sell each new technique from the exalted height of a soap box. Sam, always at the top of my conversion list, most often would simply patronizingly pat me on the back, telling his child to go off and play with her new toy. Well aware his condescending attitude infuriated me, but he also noticed, I responded less and less to his bait. Somehow this time, perhaps out of curiosity to watch my new lover in action or maybe even out of a growing respect for me, he consented to take Sydney's workshop.

Sydney knew my enthusiasm about Sam's possibilities, so at each break he phoned with a progress report. For Sam it was easier to cleverly manipulate conversation into attack than allow someone inside to view his inner workings and most assuredly, it wasn't going to be my lover.

By the second day Sam decided he was ready to share. His confidence accompanied him on stage . . . or better put, his arrogance preceeded him. "I'm convinced the social dynamic of a group creates energy which can be used for healing. But I think a lot of these baby gurus bank the energy instead, by not telling the group that they're responsible for creating the power, not him. The student is left no way to re-light the candle, for the teacher keeps blowing it out to retain control. Hey, a teacher can't teach without a student." Sam was proud of this insightful exposure. And tossed the ball to Sydney sitting on his stool in the back of the room.

Loading his slingshot with marshmallows, "Is this attack a ploy to avoid any personal sharing, or to create a defensive position for me?" With ease Sydney turned it around. "I agree with your analysis in many cases and I promise not to blow your candle out until you yell fire."

The weekend developed a mutual respect between the two men, with Sam conceding Sydney's mastery on his own turf. The results were less than lasting however. The only technique Sam relied on to rekindle his flame was a match to light up a joint.

To carry on a successful relationship with Sydney meant I had to attend his various sessions, for his work schedule was grueling. Coming up was a special one-day class devoted to the investigation of relationships. Sydney approached me as tactfully as possible, his salesman and 'mystic' in perpetual conflict. "Darling, could you be careful about spreading the word of our involvement. You know the public T.V. image of Anne and me is still marketable and we have to keep up a front."

Slapped in the face with reality, shock triggered another memory of a relationship -- long ago and secret, too vague to recognize. Had once another love been held captive unto its own passion? Concealed from public view? This is certainly an interesting test -- of putting my partner's needs first. I had imagined his wants of a more physical nature, which would be easier to be brave about. This compromise felt humiliating, but determination to my commitment soothed my wounded pride.

The day began. "Turn your chairs and face the person behind you. Look directly into their eyes. Now, take turns in asking of your partner this question: *What is your idea of a perfect relationship?* Please begin."

Sitting across from me was an impish young man with enthusiasm written from grin to body language. My partner went first as he adjusted his glasses. "That's easy. My model for a perfect relationship is Sydney and Anne . . . "

I wanted to storm the stage and announce the truth over the P.A. system. How could he perpetuate such an image?! Instead, I moved the pain inward questioning my own hurt and worth.

What unconscious motivation prompted my choice of a man still involved with another woman? Learning to assume responsibility for these kinds of decisions demanded an understanding of why. Was it possibly my identity with Lenore or perhaps a deeper desire to experience the role of Jake's other women? At the least, here was an opportunity to gain compassion for the other side of the coin.

At that moment, a new decision was made. If you want something in relationship, don't ask for it, give it! Always it will come back to you. If not now, later. Life is not tit for tat. The giant scoreboard in the sky computes on individual deed, not retaliation.

Each night the telephone rang long after sleep came, but the intrusion was welcomed. "Hello darling, how did your day go? I've missed you very much. I wish I could be next to you in bed right now." Sydney always began this way. His phone calls sustained our relationship. He knew how to fill the spaces between our time together with a seductive power as strong as presence. Having a man around all the time was unnecessary or even undesirable. My solitude was coveted, but I cherished the support system, knowing somewhere, someone truly cared about my well-being.

Smiling, I now understood the story our old Jewish landlady had told me when Sam and I first married.

"Tilly, who's that man who walks up and down the street smiling everyday?"

"That's the happiest man I know."

"Why Tilly?"

"Because he lives here and his wife lives down the street!"

Our relationship could be a fascinating and workable new model for marriage -- a part-time live-in. But our lives were definitely run on Sydney's time schedule. This really wasn't a problem for Alexander and Tara were with Sam on weekends and holiday vacations. Teaching my yoga classes on schedule required some maneuvering, but somehow it all worked out— in fact, my life was 'golden.' A New York workshop was coming up the next weekend and Sydney invited me to join him.

The rain on the tile roof made wonderful sounds as I sat in the cozy window seat watching drops land on the slanted, leaded glass overlooking the garden. The smell of logs burning in the fireplace mingled with the aroma of bisque soup simmering on the stove. Sydney was expected soon and night was coming, then candles -- all the right sounds, smells, lighting -- like a painting or dance, a living art form.

Slowly turning the pages of *New Realities* magazine, I came upon a piece about the *Course of Miracles*' written by Mark von Holt. The article was a moving account of his own experience doing the lessons and the effect on his life. Catching my eye was a full-page photograph of Judith Skutch, the woman responsible for publishing and promoting the book. I sat staring at her picture. That same light I first saw in Sydney encircled her face, as though they belonged to the same brotherhood.

The phone interrupted my concentration. "Mark, this is amazing! Can you believe I'm sitting here reading your fascinating article on the *Course of Miracles*? Are you calling from New York? I'll be there with Sydney next week."

"That's right, I heard you were going with 'the Mr. Davidson.' And yes, I'm in New York. You must meet Judy Skutch when you're here; I'll set it up for you. Have you been doing the course?"

"Yes, but I've stopped for awhile. It got a little too heavy into Jesus for my taste. You must remember, I'm just a nice Jewish girl under all this liberal thought."

"Listen, He started that way too!" Came the retort.

Electric New York, walking down the street was an adventure heightened by expectations of muggings or miracles. Definitely, in a miracle mood, I stopped in a flower shop to buy gardenias, an added aphrodisiac to place next to our bed.

Sydney kept an apartment in the Mayfair Regent, a spectacular old hotel, a renovation in art deco. The doorman called me by name as I came in loaded with packages; somehow his greeting elevated my self-esteem. Entering the lobby, I half expected Ginger Rogers and Fred Astaire to come dancing through the turning glass doors. This must be a little bit of heaven. Remaining in the clouds, I dressed for the workshop. The occasion called for something extra feminine -- my hand-embroidered Romanian wedding blouse.

New York brought a different kind of workshop attendee more spirited vitality, fewer *do-it-for-me* or *I've already done it* blase attitudes of the West Coast. But there was a harder intellectual shell to crack here and Sydney had his hands full.

As each person introduced themselves, the group had opportunity of individual appraisal. "My name is Mark von Holt; I'm a freelance writer." Amazed, when does coincidence stop and miracle begin? That rascal, he knew I was going to be here.

At the break Mark explained. "I thought I'd surprise you. I'm doing research for an article on your beau and his *Stage of Life*."

"Well I hope it's as incredible as your article on the 'Course of Miracles.' Glimpsing your psyche brought out all my voyeurism. That kind of sharing takes courage. My congratulations."

"Thanks Mary. Hey, I'm planning to fit dinner in at the break tomorrow night with Judy Skutch, would you join us?"

The elevator opened directly into the foyer of Judith's spacious apartment covering the entire seventh floor. Immediately, I was aware of a very special energy bombarding me. A presence not limited by confines of physical matter, permeated my very being--a spiritual welcoming committee. And it was true, Judith carried with her all the light the magazine photograph had captured.

The apartment maintained its elegance while being warm and lived in. We gathered in the library. Judith asked her secretary to hold all calls -- whatever was before her consumed all attention, making everyone around feel important. When she focused the power of a lazer beam was hers. She unfolded the tale of the woman who had channeled the *Course of Miracles*.

"Can you imagine being an atheist psychologist all your life, then suddenly being prompted and prodded by spirit to write every day for a year, woken up in the middle of the night to get the job done. Two volumes of information on how to bring God and miracles into your life, however reluctantly were written. You can imagine she's still confused about her own shattered belief system!"

Judith stopped and looked at me carefully. Sitting serenely allowing that light energy to wash over me, I knew if anyone could actually see it, she could. "I've been looking for someone to spend time with Mrs. H. to help her through this confusion.

Somehow I feel you would be just the person! Do you have the time Mary?"

Not a compliment, but a statement, a soul recognition, one that I understood. It spoke to a new me and an old me -- a new beginning and a completion. Perfect that I spend time with this lady of miracles.

Arriving back to the workshop late, Sydney noticed Mark and I take our seats. Mark's intellectual impishness and nonchalant assurance provoked Sydney's sting. With a slight misuse of power, instigated by a twinge of spite, he called me to the stage for my turn to share. Efficient timing, for I was still infused with the spirit of Judith's welcoming committee.

Taking the stage with a calm command, I began telling of the extraordinary woman I had just met. Sydney interrupted; he was anxious for everyone to see the magic he saw in me much like waking baby to show it off -- to share where I came from and who I was now. To me in this moment, the past seemed quite irrelevant and who I'd become was changing so quickly that the best way to capture it was just to be -- rather than talk about it. I didn't succumb to his guided direction.

I on stage, he seated on his stool in the center aisle. The dialogue between us became heated. But only on Sydney's side. Each action, instead of creating reaction in me, I gently handed back to him. Most of the group were unaware of our intimate relationship. My compassion for Sydney's frustration finally slipped out -- "Darling why are you doing this?" Laughter lightened the mood. Applause from the female contingent accompanied me off stage, while frustration infected the males, having something to do with lack of control.

In closing, one hundred participants held hands and sang together creating a powerful presence. Something very dramatic happened inside of me, as though the spirit of the welcoming committee and the healing energy generated by the group had literally pried open my heart. A tremendous sense of being bathed in love engulfed me . . . Not personal, but the golden thread of love that connects all hearts, woven together by deep sharing into a tapestry of brotherhood. This kind of love could end human conflict. Where it came from I cared not. This was the glue that would cement Humpty Dumpty together again.

That night in the hotel room Sydney apologized. "I'm sorry Darling. I just wanted everyone to see what an extraordinary woman you are."

"Hey, if I'm so extraordinary, trust me a little more!"

"I do trust you Mary, more than anyone I've ever known."

We began to settle into physical reconfirmation of our connection when the telephone rang . . . Anne, right on cue. As usual she had a problem that couldn't wait until morning. For the next hour he plugged into her intrigue. Sydney needed to be needed. The hook was to create a problem and you could be sure of his attention.

At a subliminal level, Anne's point injected the right amount of guilt to activate his proper memory bank. Sydney's father had deserted his mother and growing up there was constant reminder. No way would Sydney ever totally leave a woman and Anne had his number. He and his mother struggled financially, so identifying personal worth with his bank account was understandable and because of their business entanglements, Anne knew well how to threaten his pocketbook.

Finally he hung up the receiver. An almost involuntary evaluation came forth. "If you keep putting yourself in the role of teacher in relationships, the universe will continue sending you students. You reward her problems by giving them so much time."

"That's my business isn't it?" He accentuated his English accent when making a point.

"Sometimes I'm tolerant verging on stupid! Right now I feel like telling you to fuck off but long ago I made an oath never to make a decision before *that time of the month.*'" I looked in the mirror, "and my skin is confirming my period's due."

Sydney retorted. "That's not a period; it's an exclamation point!"

My support of creating a safe harbor or docking at one, wasn't reaping the rewards I'd hoped for. During those victim years, arriving at *no choice* felt suffocating, like being pushed against a wall. Now, at last, *no choice* was like a green light, a simple move forward in the game.

I began the *Course of Miracles* again—after all, he was Jewish.

Chapter IX

That long New York weekend, strained our relationship and dictated a respite. Nine months of operating on someone else's frequency was enough. Time was needed to mend my own life, to find my place on the stage. Funny, it wasn't seeing Sydney I would miss the most, but rather his tender phone calls in the night.

A letter from Jacqueline arrived. Ten years had passed since our trip to Europe -- the same ten years since Sam and I stood, not in each other's shadow, in front of a window overlooking Central Park. She now lived in Paris. Adopted French ways permeated her detailed description of the tres chic apartment near the Eiffel Tower, but less about tne man she shared it with. He was simple Rene, a wealthy French-Moroccan businessman. She invited me to come taste another side of Parisian life quite different from what we had experienced on our maiden voyage.

Her timing was perfect. The children were planning their Christmas holiday a skiing trip with Sam and I wasn't looking forward to an empty holiday house. I didn't even know where Sydney was. Anne probably scheduled him in East Afghanistan. Writing Jacqueline a grateful acceptance, I bought a ticket to Paris that very day.

Bright shiny red lips moved in perfect synchronization with
scarlet fingers pointing to stored life vests and showing what to
do in an emergency. Feeling myself tuning out slipping off, my
eyes closed. Preparation had been hectic and events to come
still unknown.

To close your eyes in public is like pulling down the shade on
the shop's front door, with a sign 'Out to Lunch'. More
difficult was putting my mind to sleep as thoughts flooded
through in random form. Daydreams became vague and
finally merged into dreams somewhere halfway between the
two. . .

> **I found myself driving narrow mountain roads
> following the rugged coastline to Big Sur. I had
> been invited to teach yoga at Esalen.**
>
> **Music of a carrousel came from the radio as I
> drove round and round up the mountain. Quite
> suddenly, the coastline below disappeared into
> a dense fog bank. What had revealed a breath-
> taking view from high on a mountain road
> seconds before was now hidden. Mother Nature
> had abruptly pulled down her shade. I switched
> off the carrousel. My body sent out its distress
> signal soaked in sweat as fear immobilized me.
> Rigidity took over my limbs, inhibiting my
> hand from leaving the wheel to wipe tears
> streaming down my face.**
>
> **Only moments ago on the left was a sheer
> cliff with a drop straight-down to the ocean; on
> the right, had been a curving solid mountain
> wall. Surely they must still be there behind the
> fog but where? Impossible to go on -- fear had
> taken over. The car slowed to a stop.**
>
> **Tightly clutching the wheel, dialogue with
> myself began over sounds of my heart. If I sit
> here in the road, a lost car behind me, could**

push me over the edge! Dear God, what's
causing this paralyzing fear?

The answer came with the swiftness of revelation. *The unknown.* I'm afraid of what I don't
know. The next step is filled with fear if I'm not
sure where the road will take me. The only way
to go forward is to have faith that the road was
there and still is. The center white line reveals
itself inch by inch and if I follow slowly,
carefully, it will lead me to where I'm going. I
had received the gold ring.

My shoulder was being tapped. Opening my eyes, the two
red lips were moving at me. "Your fortunate, we've just gone
through a terrible storm and you've slept right through it.
Would you like dinner now?"

The leaves were gone from the trees, but winter couldn't
strip Paris of her beauty. Jacqueline was transformed--a
round girl now a voluptuous woman. Her blond hair still long
was released from its pony tail confinement. Sophistication
smelled in French perfume and new sensuality became her.
Rene was short but adorable. Conscious of his receding
hairline, he would place his rimless glasses atop. His excitement
about the arrival of their American houseguest was genuine.
The apartment, just as the letter described, obviously had
maid service from what I remembered of my friend's fastidious-
ness. The guest room small but charming. Shutters and heavy
draperies offered total protection from the invasion of morning's
arrival, a necessity considering the lifestyle.

Rene was rich and charming enough to have an entourage of
at least ten or fifteen friends who accompanied them to dinner
and dance at least six nights a week. My simple vegetarian diet
an enigma to French mentality, but our common ground was
dancing!

The morning after the first night on the town we slept until noon. Over two or three cups of strong French coffee, we reminisced.

"You always knew I was really in love with Sam, but honestly, having the lens cap on at your wedding was an accident."

"Truly, my intellect was never sure, but my instinct was convinced of both." It was good to laugh.

"But now that you're free, we'll find you a Frenchman."

"I'm not yet enamored by continental charm. From the conversation last night, it seems they're only interested in food and sex, in that order."

Jacqueline's response was packaged as retaliation. "I once went out with this gorgeous American actor; after a few dates, we spent the night together. Lying in bed we watched one of his old movies on television. He played the American dream, a physical Adonis, abounding with masculine virility. Well, the illusion proved better than the performance; in my bed, he couldn't even get it up. But I promise you, a Frenchman produces what's advertised."

"Truthfully Jacqueline, I'm not here for fun and games. Absurd as it may seem, my interests these days are far more involved in spiritual growth than physical pleasure."

Having environmentally acquired more of a French mentality, my words went unheard. "Come on. Let's dress. I want you to meet my lover."

The taxi scurried through traffic, crossing over the Seine. I could see *Sacre Coeur* on the hill as we entered Montmarte. His apartment was a garret copied directly from a stage set of *La Boheme*. He fancied himself a painter/lover or lover/painter, whose tastes would have been more indigenous to turn-of-the-century living. Jacqueline had at least fifteen years more experience than he. Seemingly unaware of my presence, he embraced her, slowly undressed her, and dramatically made love to her. My eyes waivered between closing in embarrassment and staying open to voyeur. After their initial passion was released, they asked me to join them. Declining, I timidly suggested, "I think I'll just take a taxi to the Louvre."

"No, no, no -- five minutes. I'll be right with you. We just stopped to say hello, ca va!"

The museum was alive with the past. Each period revealed its own war or peace. Two thousand years and as many interpretations of how Jesus looked . . . but only a few managed to lock that inspired gaze within the confines of canvas and capture who He was. I came upon Him for I would know Him anywhere. A deep breath carried me into the painting next to Him, feeling His arms holding me and peace wash over. Standing still as timed traveled.

After the Louvre we stopped for espresso at a sidewalk cafe and people-watched for a while; unfortunately, this time of year glass enclosed the outdoor section. The coffee didn't help much, I was exhausted when we arrived home.

"Rene's invited a special friend for you."

"I've got to take a bath and lie down before they arrive."

"That's a good idea Mary; it'll be another late night."

Coming out of the bath, I heard voices. Jacqueline called to me, "Come meet Pierre."

Wrapping Rene's terry robe around me, I went to greet my escort. "Enchante Pierre."

His skin was rough and his bushy mustache tickled as he kissed my hand. What could Rene have been thinking of? He had that animal look in his eye, having spotted his prey walk into the room, his lust a definable emotion.

"Pierre doesn't speak English and you just blew your entire French repetoire in the introduction. The others won't be here for a while. We'll have cocktails, you take a rest."

Oh well, he's just a dinner companion. Even a short rest was welcome. Lying in bed, on the verge of succumbing to exhaustion, suddenly the door opened. Turning over, I expected Jacqueline. The room was dark. Looking like a huge bear, still wearing his fur coat and Russian Cossack hat, Pierre walked in and closed the door. Dialogue began to pour out of him like a waterfall of French champagne.

"I don't understand a word you're saying, but leave this room now!" I demanded. Paying no attention, he came on like an animal in heat, pulling away my blanket, laying his clothed body directly on top of me. His breath hot from drink. Drops of his sweat fell on my breast. I could hardly breathe, but managed to scream, "Jacqueline , Jacqueline!" She never came.

Oh my God, I'm being raped! White terrycloth covered my eyes. The struggle only exhausted me and my resistance finally submitted. Maybe my efforts were provoking him more, so I simply lay there without emotion, playing dead in a pool of perspiration. When he finished, he walked out and closed the door still wearing his coat and hat. For a long time, I just lay there in disbelief, knowing I had to leave, to get home out of this madness. But I felt paralysed. I wanted to wash -- wash away all the misuses of the body -- the disconnected passions. Jacqueline came in.

"Calm down. I know you're upset, but it was harmless and there was nothing I could do. He would have just had both of us. His wife's in the hospital having a baby and obviously it's affected his sex life."

"Oh my God, maybe I should just hang out in a maternity ward and make some extra money!" My voice was loud but shaky.

"Please Mary, don't tell Rene. He doesn't trust me as it is. Somehow he'll manage to twist it around and think I'm involved. You're beginning to get a fast education in understanding the mind of a Frenchman. He didn't mean any harm. Get dressed now. We'll have a lovely dinner . . . just think of it as a minor cultural intrusion."

As long as hot water lasted, I stood under the shower, cleansing my body, my soul. Longing to be back at the Louvre, with Him, I needed to bathe in His forgiveness, rocked in His arms. Dressing in a daze, bewildered by this perverted continental mentality, I took a deep breath and walked into the salon. Rene had arrived and greeted me with an embrace.

"Mary, I vant you to meet mon ami. He's so so crazee, flying planes and always in trouble."

Pierre extended his hand, smiling coyly. "Enchante mademoiselle."

Dinner was bizarre. Under the table, Pierre tried to continue another kind of communication. Difficult enough not to be violent, just continuing the charade was barely possible.

The next day was Sunday. At breakfast, Rene cooly acted out his anger at my overt rudeness to his friend, "In my opinion, I present you with a verre virile specimen. A reeel Frenchman. What are you looking for anyway?"

Rene was a peculiar dichotomy. On the one hand, he vicariously wanted to procure for me; on the other, he was protective, almost proud of my refusal.

Jacqueline and Rene were both determined to try again, this time with a more eligible bachelor. Henri was a young lawyer with a quiet serious strength and sly smile. Paris became more seductive with my new tall, black-eyed guide. Things moved quickly on foreign soil and after all, I was on vacation. Again, the entire entourage danced until three . . . I watched Rene gratefully unlatch the apartment door. He always seemed relieved when his duties as ringmaster were over.

"Bon soir, mon ami, merci beaucoup. By the way, Henri invited me to the country for the weekend and I've accepted." Even exhausted, Rene played his role.

"Now, you'll enjoy a reeel Frenchman!" But beneath verbal approval were traces of disappointment.

Smiling, I remembered French country roads with Jacqueline in our wonderful Citroen 2CV that looked like a tin can. Now, I was sitting next to a handsome exciting Frenchman driving a Ferarri enroute to a country estate instead of a youth hostel. What an adventure life is!

The poetry of new snow left its memory over French countryside -- sycamores and cottonwoods hibernating till spring. Still, an expensive automobile didn't ensure a trouble free trip; halfway, the heater went out and with it romance of the winter scene. Henri turned and looked at me, his black sorrowful eyes filled with apology.

"I'm so sorree, ma cheri." Charles Boyer could not have been more touching. We stopped and insulated ourselves with layers of heavy sweaters and thick socks, though the winter chill knew no bounds.

Following the long driveway of the estate was like entering a picture postcard. A hunting lodge of a diplomat to France from an African country -- rambled as though added room by room according to need over the past hundred years. The house was made of old grey stone -- taken from the creek bottom which ran along side the road. Smoke drifted out of many different chimneys and aroma from the kitchen mingled soups and souffles.

Half frozen, our first impulse was survival as we ran to warm ourselves in front of the fire. Backlit by flames, we greeted our host.

"Enchante Alain." This was the Diplomat's son, his skin light brown with eyes bright blue and hair handsomely compromised between a blonde mother and negro father. His English carried the status of an Oxford education and his manners that of diplomacy. Introductions began. There were two other young men -- a dentist and a history professor from the Sorbonne.

The men spoke some version of English. Two shopgirls from the local village who couldn't be over seventeen, spoke none. Unclear as to who was with whom, since there was a shortage of females, I was vaguely uncomfortable.

A wonderful old provincial Frenchman with round balding but bereted head and pink cheeks on a weather-beaten face came in to announce dinner. Pascal and his wife, Marie watched over the estate and the needs of the young heir. Dinner was a culinary wonder.

"Pascal shot this duck not three hours ago, which accounts for it's flavor and tenderness." Pinching the meat, "you see it still has some spring."

"And the sauce suberb." Henri delightedly threw a kiss in the air with his fingers.

The dentist antiseptic breath went down my neck as he asked to have dessert passed. Throughout dinner conversation, as usual, centered around food and sex, between me and the four men. The girls simply giggled.

Stuffed beyond capacity, we leisurely moved into the salon for espresso; two men lit up cigars -- the aroma stirring memories of Jake. Alain selected some romantic mood music from *A Man and a Woman* and invited me to dance. He lost no time in holding me exceptionally close and pressed his mouth against my cheek. Pulling away, I excused myself and went over to Henri who appeared to be perfectly comfortable with the situation. Rejected but not discouraged, Alain walked over to stoke the fire. Then joining the others in a seductive slow motion dance, they began to arouse one another, no partners -- a group adagio. Totally flabbergasted, I demanded of Henri, "What's going on here?"

"Whatever you like; it's harmless, but if you disapprove, we can always go to our room."

Having made the decision not to participate, Henri became very protective for I passed his test separating good girls from the bad. His European morality carried equal amounts of hypocrisy and judgement, not unlike Rene -- guilty until proven innocent.

Our room was typically country French, including a hand-quilted multicolored eiderdown made of fragments of fabric as old as the house and almost a foot thick with goose feathers. You could see your reflection in the high glossed wood floors only partially covered by a hand hooked oval rug. Against the wall stood a turn-of-the-century hand-carved armoire and in the corner a French necessity, a bidet.

We read and talked but noise from downstairs continued to intrude. "Being a voyeur rather than a participant could be intriguing." I offered casually.

Henri was quick to take me up on my wish. "Come then, let's go watch."

Our silence began as he led me into the dimly-lit corridor; from there we got down on our knees and crept slowly toward the landing which overlooked the salon below, taking our mission very seriously. Overtook by a *deja-vu* feeling back to the dirty pictures I found as a child in Jake's drawer hidden under his sweat pants. Now they came to life in a full blown orgy! Keeping back a giggle was impossible. Henri impulsively put a hand over the mouth of his accomplice . . . but it was too late. The play stopped short and the characters looked up to the rafters. They didn't appreciate becoming a spectator sport and in native tongue agreed "Let's get 'em!'

A few seconds passed before it penetrated, we were under attack! Lying flat on our stomachs, I turned to Henri with my mouth open, he realizing before me the need for a hasty retreat. Grabbing my hand he pulled me down the hallway back to our room, slamming the door and holding it closed with the weight of our bodies. Boldly, the strength of five won the struggle forcing the door open, crashing it into the wall. The light was abruptly switched off. The girls continued their dialogue of laughter. Layers of sweaters from the journey had been keeping me warm; now, swiftly, they were removed by hands coming from all directions. I was forced down on the bed, the eiderdown swallowing me up as a female hand slipped under my bra and touched my breast. A mouth came down hard on my own. From below, my stockings were pulled down. My panties reached my knees when I felt a head lodge between my legs. My hand was placed around an enormous erection. I can't believe this is happening! Now, I suddenly realized those sensual glances at dinner interpreted as girlish coyness, were quite real, with specific intent. Old furry Pierre was beginning to look like a schoolboy in heat. But this was beyond succumbing to invasion, for it surpassed my limits and I was terrified. My panic and screams were in sharp contrast to their rowdy playfulness.

"Henri stop them! Please, I beg you!"

He responded. I'd just passed the next phase of his test trying to prove all women are whores until they demonstrate they're good enough to be mothers. I wondered what decisions he had made as a child. Were my decisions meshing with his like gears in a wheel, feeding each other's needs?

"That's enough!," he commanded and like spoiled children being sent to bed without dessert, they turned and left.

The brightness of morning allowed the night before to slip into memory. There was virgin snow settling into the landscape in a photogenic freeze frame. Anxious to make my own impression on it, I dressed quietly so as not to awaken Henri.

Morning smells hastened my pace down the stairs. On the long wood table were hot croissants, homemade jam and cafe au lait. Marie arrived with a steaming platter of bacon and eggs on my American behalf. Indulging with zeal were the young men . . . their maidens still asleep. Rising as I entered, they diplomatically ignored any reference to the night before. Alain was especially charming simultaneously combining an aloofness and come-hither look -- an appealing dichotomy. Definite chemistry did exist between us.

Sacrifice to the flame of desire was easy to recognize. Indulging didn't satisfy permanently, for one desire perpetually replaces another -- constantly pursuing detours. A sense of control accompanied my understanding, a strength, which was even more seductive to my over-stimulated companions.

Preparing myself for a winter's walk, the others followed suit. Alain spoke for three. "May we accompany you mademoiselle? Fi and Fi will only walk with beautiful ladies." I laughed, he referred to his two groomed golden retrievers. Any apprehension was quieted by the apparent wholesomeness of the scene.

We walked through forest, bright sun jumping in and out of spaces between branches and dogs chasing shadows. Shadows, can you ever be free of your own? The dogs made their peace with them and ran ahead. Alain and I strolled a few paces behind, talking and blowing smoke rings with vapor our words formed in the cold air. Abruptly he clapped his hands, obviously planned, for the rest of the party ran into the forest.

Then suddenly, Alain impulsively turned and embraced me, pulling me down into the snow. His icy hands slipped under my jacket. "You've got to be kidding! This is absurd! Stop it now!" My words had no effect. I needed a direct plea to this bizarre cultural morality. "Please Alain, I find you very attractive, but I'm afraid Henri has already won my heart and I know he feels the same way about me. If he finds out about this he will be very upset!"

Somehow, my words formed the right combination to unlock his distorted sense of chivalry. He stood up, brushed me off respectfully and offered his arm for the remainder of our morning promenade.

Henri had the Ferrari heater repaired -- all that cold and it was only a fuse. Silence in the car was once again my companion. My leg was getting stiff and I thought of Sam. Now a new question filtered through my mind like chasing a shadow. Why am I always confronted with this paradox as if there were two Marys -- one a passionate, sexual woman and the other, who longed to know God? My mind drifted wondering of another two Marys. Did not Christ see goodness in Mary Magdalene and through His forgiveness, did she not become the pure expression of commitment? Was not the mother Mary filled with compassion, not judgement? Perhaps, these were terms for my own acceptance of self -- taking conflict out of paradox. Shadows, can you ever be free of your own -- like the dark side of yourself.

Jacqueline and Rene waited like watchful but lenient parents, vicariously curious, wanting to know all that happened. My adventures told well, but it was time to go home. Although often blinded by anatomy, biology is not my destiny. Had I put Humpty Dumpty together again with only basting thread, not pure gold?

Chapter X

The magic turning point of a Jewish boy . . . his thirteenth birthday. Invited by the rabbi to read from the ancient Hebrew Torah, during a ritualistic ceremony, he is mystically initiated across the threshold into manhood . . . the Bar Mitzvah. Years studying Hebrew and the Torah at temple school is usual procedure but Alexander flatly refused. To sense bureaucracy in the temple hierarchy wasn't difficult and somehow offended him. Even the language was only taught phonetically, while he wanted to learn to speak Hebrew correctly and study the cultural heritage of his people. So, in an unorthodox fashion, Alexander's Bar Mitzvah preparation was instructed in private tutelage by an Israeli college student.

As time for the ceremony approached, the problem to find a temple and rabbi to perform the rites was an impossible task! Even Esther, as one of the community's leading Zionists, couldn't move this mountain.

"Why not have the ceremony and celebration at home?"

Alexander perked up at my suggestion.

"Such a revolutionary prospect will cause quite a search for a rabbi. Seems I remember hearing about a New Age guitar playing rabbi who held high holiday service on the Malibu cliffs overlooking the ocean."

"Hey Mom, that sounds like the guy!" Alexander responded anxiously.

"Supposedly, it's more mystical cabalistic teaching and Jewish culture, avoiding the mire of dogma."

"Let's go for it !"

After difficult inquiry, success came. I dialed the number. "Hello, my name is Mary Golden. May I speak to Rabbi Stein?"

A soft, clear voice answered. "You are."

"Rabbi, the reason I'm calling is my son is preparing for Bar Mitzvah with a private tutor. Since we belong to no synagogue it seems no one will have us. The temple bureaucracy appears impenetrable. My thought is to have the ceremony at home. Do you find that a sacrilege?"

"My dear Mary, what so you think they did thousands of years ago if a village had no church? Life's journey is too precarious for one not to create his own temple and carry it with him. I'm sure even Jesus did that."

A strange reference for a rabbi, but in his words, I heard the depth of meaning he intended. This was the man to lead my son through the mystic veil. "Will you come to meet us? Tea on Tuesday?"

Giving the address, at first he acted startled, then simply surrendering to destiny, he commented. "You bought the house from an older, somewhat eccentric couple, the Stein's." He paused and almost apologetically stated. "They're my parents. Not only was I brought up in that very house, but my own Bar Mitzvah celebration was on the tennis court. This is divine perfection at work!"

Sydney's basic 200 -- the coincidence brought me to awe; there must be a strange and wonderful plan working far beyond our seeming world of choice. Sam decided to pay the price for a real sendoff into manhood and gave me an opportunity to put on a truly creative production, to honor our son.

Preparations demanded a great deal of time and I hadn't seen Sydney since my return from Paris. Tonight was to be our reunion. Embarrassed by first date feelings as I opened the door. He stood there, a box of gardenias in his hands. The first moments allowed melting in each other and after came the physical connection.

"I've missed you so much darling." Then with that serious naivete and not really wanting to know the answer, he asked. "Tell me, are Frenchmen overrated?" Not waiting for a reply, he walked into the bedroom and pleasurably inhaled the familiar aroma of incense.

"I'm glad you're seduced by the smell; it helps turn a house into a temple."

Savoring the entire aesthetic impact he thoughtfully examined the room as if for the first time. "Mary darling the smell may hit the senses first, but your poetry is expressed in every detail." Touching an art deco bookend of a lady I'd bought on Portabella Road in London, "did you ever realize how many of these wonderful little gems you have around are *women*?" He continued, picking up a bronze ink well from my desk with a sculptured nude woman lying across the lid. "It's all so you Mary, Aphrodite herself -- the ultimate feminine principle, and that extends to your mothering as well. Sometimes, I think I'd rather be your son than your lover. Or perhaps a little incest, hey?"

He winked at me as he began to take off his clothes continuing his visual tour of the room. "What's this? You've put out a photograph of yourself?"

"Your influence, my love. This is my official statement and reminder of self-acceptance. For the first time in my life, I see my own beauty, beyond the image." I didn't mention the circumstances surrounding this particular picture, a legacy of that day in the library many years before. Also a warning to be careful -- considering the herpes it left me with.

We made love, laughed, took a long walk and had dinner in

bed on a lovely wicker tray . . . the gardenias on the side. "I need your intuitive hit on a collaboration with a new producer for my TV series. You know how much I respect your opinion. In fact, if you ever want a job as my personal manager, it's yours! . . . His name is Sy Goldstein and he'll be in town for only one day. I'll be finishing up a workshop and I thought you could meet him alone, kind of feel him out. Sorry darling, it's the day before the Bar Mitzvah, but you can relax for lunch with him at the Beverly Hills Hotel. Not too shabby."

There they were, beautiful bronzed physiques intermingled with white pudgy bodies laying around the Beverly Hills Hotel pool. Smells of Bain de Soleil mixed with chicken salad, green and white striped tented cabanas added to the affluent theatrical flavor. You got the feeling if Los Angeles went into the ocean, surely, it wouldn't dare affect those in the Polo Lounge. I heard my page for Mr. Goldstein and stood on the steps, watching for an acknowledgement. Dressed in a 1940's cut-on-the-bias thrift shop special, I was very chic and shaded from the sun by a large brimmed hat -- my Gene Tierney look.

"Hello, are you looking for someone?"

"Yes, are you Mr. Goldstein?"

"I'll be anyone you like my dear." It was a natural mistake and he definitely looked like a Mr. Goldstein.

"Come use the telephone at my cabana for another page." Pushing me in as he removed his hat to wipe the perspiration from his bald head. Making the inevitable move on me, I declined graciously, but offered my card if his preference might turn to yoga.

"Please excuse me, I must be going. My son's Bar Mitzvah is tomorrow and I have a hundred and fifty people coming to dinner. Needless to say, my mind is preoccupied," succumbing to the temptation of a proud Jewish mother.

"Well my fair lady, you must have been a child bride. Now if you had just one wish for yourself this minute, what would it be?"

Letting go of a long breath, I admitted my passion and need for a deep body massage, hoping he wouldn't take it personally and make an offer. The real Mr. Goldstein came forward and we left.

Early the next morning, the doorbell rang; a hefty lady in uniform stood at the door. With a professional attitude, she presented her card announcing she was the masseuse from the Beverly Hills Hotel. The card was signed, "may all your wishes come true!" That funny little man must have been the good fairy trapped in a Jewish body!

Months of preparation had been crammed into two. The result was a tent over the tennis court, decorated as fantasy, an atmosphere that might well bring to mind the question -- what is this magic of mystic veils that turns a young boy into a man? ... White moving into soft gradations of blue balloons filled the tent's top; with indirect lighting they appeared as tufts of clouds. Huge real lilac trees created a fragrant purple forest and ground covered in green, pretending grass. A breath-taking illusion carried you directly into make-believe -- a setting for the initiation of a poet or king.

Programs were made to follow the ceremony. The cover a Maxfield Parrish drawing of a young boy day-dreaming, seated on a mountain top blowing bubbles. On his head very subtly added was the skull cap and his hand held the proverbial fountain pen.

That sunset on the eve of Easter seemed in preparation for resurrection of the morning sun. Warm April air lingered still as the colors of evening sky welcomed arriving guests. Approaching through the magic garden prepared the way for the fantasy of the tent where a chamber music ensemble was playing *Summer* of *The Four Seasons* as white wine was served.

The tent was arranged as a temple with an altar for the ceremony. Alexander's antique carved armoire was used as a backdrop, its mirrored front panels reflecting lilacs onto the stage. Alexander dressed in a three piece white suit appeared calm, and in command, and with a deep sense of humility captivated the audience. I watched his presence on stage; Sam was only three years older when we met. How much he looks like Sam, with traces around the mouth of Jake. An angelic aura emanated from him as he expressed his personal thoughts and feelings about the responsibility of becoming a man. Chanting and reading from the Torah, those ancient words resounded the vibration in our make-believe temple. In closing, each one given a candle to light and hold -- chanting and swaying together. The forest glowed everyone touched by the magic of a spiritual union. My tears were tender as I looked at my son, so very proud. Then like an old wound opening, my heart was pained at the thought of ever losing him. Why did this thought so haunt me? The cobwebs in my mind silenced as the celebration began.

Cavier-stuffed bellinins and champagne were served in the house, as a crew transformed the temple into a dinner dance extravaganza. Pheasant under glass and rack-of-lamb were indulged in as part of the opulent feast. Before dessert, the strobe light whirling atop center stage announced the disco had begun. Round tables encircled the dance floor. Sam and his current lady shared the table with Sydney, Helen and I. Sam and Suzenna made a stunning couple. She was tall, statuesque with large almond eyes needing no makeup and high well-defined cheek bones. Her black dress draped in front now revealed a bare back as Sam led his partner to the floor. He never once asked me to dance.

For weeks I had shopped looking for just the right thing to wear, with an internal battle between the seductress and the mother. A layered white matte jersey elegantly covered was ultimately chosen satisfying my maternal instinct while I relied on a gardenia in my hair for seduction.

The early morning hours left a few stragglers who finally succumbed to the inevitable. Quiet was welcomed--by two in the morning almost everyone had gone. Tara my baby, who still looked like a pink fairy princess and a very tired 'little man' went home with Esther. Only Sydney, Helen and I were left. Legally they were still married. Ever since they parted for the 'Anne' years, she had been living up North. The pain and humiliation of that episode left its mark, though Helen carried with her a quiet dignity and wisdom. Sydney always recognized her role as his mentor . . . Helen, now saw me taking that meaning even further. No reason to feel threatened by me for Sydney didn't exclude her from his life; they simply created new roles for one another.

Sydney unbuttoned my dress. "Well that was one hell of a production. I'm incredibly impressed and proud of you Darling. By the way, did you meet with Mr. Goldstein yesterday?"

Smiling I remembered the good fairy. "Yes and I think you can trust him to do the job, but keep in mind he's only in it for the money."

"Oh Mary, I do wish you had more time to handle my life."

"Would you settle on handling your body? Arranging the covers, I slid in next to him.

Troubled he whispered, "Sweetheart, I feel really badly, Helen sleeping alone down the hall while we're all cuddled together in here." He paused, then looking straight at me with his boyish charm, asked, "How would you feel if I asked her to join us?" A strange request by most, but somehow I was touched by his sensitivity. This was the kind of group love I could accept, bridging separateness, real caring -- like extended family. Exhausted the three of us slept peacefully together.

The day after, the lilac forest looked as if Red Riding Hood had lost out to the wolf after prolonged battle. Easter Sunday and a luncheon was planned for out of town guests at the Bel-Air Hotel. By night, I longed to be alone and indulge in that sumptuous feeling of a tired but contented body, slipping into my old funky oversized white robe and cozy slippers, filling a plate of exotic leftovers. More perfection could only be reached if television programming were accommodating. This must be a reward for being good, a TV Easter special was on -- a Zefferelli production of *Jesus of Nazareth*, a proper way to end this weekend!

Magic of the night before still permeated the house leaving its mystical overlay. The performance now expanded this sense into a real presence of divine spirit. Growing in intensity the story unfolded and reached a heightened pitch when Mary was touched and impregnated by God. I lay in bed watching and weeping with the joy and pain of it. My soul was magnetized, pulled out of a deep sleep. A vague stirring but somehow, somewhere, my own fear of losing a son was connected here. I wanted a strong wind to blow away the cobwebs of my mind.

The scene of the Bar Mitzvah of Jesus was not unlike yesterday's. What would that ceremony be like if Jesus were alive today? Wouldn't he still rebel against church bureaucracy? How deeply one can accept legend when expressed in such human form. We don't need to deify our Saints keeping them separate from us, but rather humanize them with our compassion. Allow them to be daring enough to be different.

That night, this dream . . . .

> **White washed rounded houses -- an ancient village. A beautiful young woman with dark red hair, bare foot and frantic. Running from door to door arousing everyone with an urgent message . . . Now she's alone in a deserted road crying, grief breaking her heart in two. Suddenly an older woman appears. The younger runs to her comforting arms. The shawled woman rocks her, holds her and makes her a promise.**
>
> **"What you have done for my son, I am eternally grateful -- I will be with you always."**

Awake the pain lingered, but the protection of her promise remained. Who were these women I know not, but a new relationship with old events was awakened in me that night. The next day I began again my study in the *Course of Miracles*.

Although Anne was invited to the festivities, she declined. For virtually one year, I attempted to heal our relationship before we could even have one. Like a threatened queen bee willing to die for the sake of the hive, her sting was potent. Her strategy now waivered and she invited me to dinner.

At a chic restaurant, Anne proposed a toast with V-8 juice to powerful women. I carried on, "You know it's a fascinating dynamic when two women have interest in the same man. Usually, they'll find a similar charisma or magnetism in each other. Underneath the intrigue there can be genuine attraction, if we can let go of the fear of losing out."

"An interesting theory and it's true I'm beginning to feel a definite appreciation of you." Dinner was full of the excitement of two strong women coming together. Anne began to relax.

"Believe me it hasn't been easy maintaining an image once you've made it. It's still a man's market at the top."

"Yes but the great gift a woman has to give is her compassion. Somewhere in this struggle for independence, I think it's been undermined. Changing her job isn't as important as changing her attitude and embracing who she really is."

For hours we went on. The following day two dozen red roses arrived with a card.

"You epitomize all that a woman should be.
It's time the world had a taste of you. Whenever you're ready to get your feet wet our
organization will be there to support the
effort.

Sincerely, Anne"

Being acknowledged so dramatically by someone who represented the ideal woman for so many moved me. Love isn't something that needs to be rationed. The supply inevitably meets demand and on this day, in this time, my cup runneth over.

Sydney was amazed but pleased, having greater visions of one big happy family. Anne graciously arranged his calendar so he could take off the next weekend with me. I wanted us to share a very special seminar together without Sydney being on stage.

Sydney was so happy to have time off, I could have taken him anywhere. "Look for the sign. It's someplace here, 'Sky Hi' ranch or retreat. The man in charge is a medical doctor, Brugh Joy. He was terminally ill, had a profound transformational experience -- and in the process, cured his disease. If our culture used vernacular of the ancients, this man would be definitely referred to as a high priest."

"It's all right Mary, as long as I don't have to go to church!"

Brugh was a manifestation of polarity, strong yet gentle, intricate but simple, masculine and feminine. All these extremes reached a pivotal balance in his being and expressed themselves in eloquent clarity.

The first instruction for the weekend, "I'm going to request couples refrain from sexual activity." The doctor explained, "I feel as many spiritual teachers do, that sexual energy comes from the same source generated in spiritual experience. At the base of the spine sits the kundalini. Provoked by man in sex or spirit in meditation is individual choice." My little stone Indian friends flashed before me as the doctor went on. "But for this weekend, dissipating the energy at a level of physical phenomenon and emotional expression would be counterproductive." Sydney was definitely pissed off, but reluctantly promised to conform.

That night walking down the narrow path to our cabin under a canopy of stars, Sydney navigated as I gazed up at the sky. "A three-quarter moon. Is it becoming all that it can be, a full moon? Or on its way out? Interesting, travelling in a circle, it looks the same -- or maybe one side is just reflecting the memory of the other."

"That's why there's a man in the moon; he keeps track!"

Our cabin was sparsely decorated, meeting only the simplest needs. "Well its certainly conducive to monastic life," but Sydney wasn't deterred.

"I've checked for bugging -- didn't find a thing. I promise I won't tell if you won't."

Disgusted and shocked by his basic single-mindedness, were his desires so uncontrollable? "Sydney your whole show is based on results. It's a basic argument I have with you. Life is about integrity to the route not only the destination. Each step in the journey is a mini-arrival. Each moment has value. It's not just emphasizing some future event without caring how you get there."

"Darling my reality operates at ground level and it's too late to be so lofty. Goodnight!"

How many woman would break any rule to lie in bed with so rich and famous a leader? Lying there beside Sydney, I wondered if the small double bed was just another test.

Up before the sun, we rushed out to watch it rise from the desert floor giving promise of a warm day. The breeze carried healing smells of herbs in bloom -- rosemary and sage. I felt brought back home as the desert stirred ancient feelings, a mirage of memory -- caravans and camels.

After breakfast the doctor gave a group assignment. "Go into the desert and find a teacher -- confine it to the vegetable or mineral world. There's a lot of space out there. Go alone. If you choose to go naked that's great, but don't forget your shoes!"

Already the sun was hot, a hat would be needed. Image-ing this white creature with long dark hair wearing only a hat and shoes, I decided rather to meet my *teacher* wearing a bathing suit.

Having limited sense of direction, I sighted some landmark before venturing out. Walking entails some sort of balance between looking down to watch where I'm stepping and looking up to see where I'm going. After the first hour of up and down the rhythm made me aware of the larger perspective above, then I lowered my head to a smaller dimension below. What a tremendous teaching in this! The macrocosm merged into microcosm and microcosm blended back into the macro cosm. Every little rock tells the story of the mountain it came from! In the veins of each leaf is written the map of the tree! I sat down on an old tree stump that had met its destiny in a stroke of lightning. Only missing was a river for my personal Siddartha image. Did God recognize Siddartha because he was wearing robes? Perhaps a bathing suit presented too gross a vibration? . . . What an extraordinary place to be clear, quiet and listen. Each small thing tells the whole story. Every step along the way is filled with the secret of its destination. Surely, if there is a God it follows He lives in each of us!

Walking back, I carried with me inner peace that comes from keeping your connection open with nature -- a conduit to spirit. If in fact your soul chooses parents before entering this life, as the doctor suggested, why had I chosen mine? Now for the first time, I appreciated their extraordinary gift to me, unconditional love. They never hung their love on any rules; love simply was given -- without reward or retaliation. What a precious treasure this inheritance. And I worried about frayed towels and stale cigar smoke!

"Well you've come a long way baby! You seem very happy." Crystal acknowledged me, giving a hug. She came not to teach yoga, but to be part of the group. We sat together in the shade of a big willow tree. Smiling at her observation, "I'm truly blessed, my health, two wonderful children, a magical home all paid for, teaching yoga for pleasure and a marvelous relationship with a leader of the 'New Age'. I'm in the driver's seat for the first time in my life." My eyes closed, my own words filling me with deep gratitude.

"We've even talked about my moving to New York and being Sydney's personal manager. Quite a compliment considering the offer came from this master of logistics and efficiency. But somehow my power put to use supporting his seems a deviation from my own destiny."

Sydney's weekend was less productive than mine and a gap emerged with my emphasis increasing on inner spiritual experience and his own outward oriented-results -- funny, not unlike the crossroad Sam and I reached after LSD. Patterns, patterns tying us up in their perpetual knots.

Esther and Michael had both taken Sydney's workshop. The son was written off as a hopeless dilettante, while Esther became smitten with the handsome English leader and he with her. For the first time since my divorce she acknowledged me as gendered and capable of relationship. Family dinners depended on the ambiance created by Sydney's charm and he was treated like a prestigious son-in-law.

One of Sydney's basic fears emerged over that desert weekend; a woman depending on him for financial support. Understanding the obvious source, a dependent mother all his life, didn't change the emotion. Letting go of his fear would take solving more of his own puzzle, but far easier for him to attempt solving mine. There was no hiding anxiety in his voice. "Mary darling I'm really concerned that your house is not legally in your name. From the information Sam's giving you his brother has been devouring the family fortune like a ravenous pig -- subsidizing his dilettante habits." True I shared his apprehension.

"Sam has a similar fear. In fact, he admitted he wouldn't put it past his mother's devotion to mortgage my house if Michael needed the money."

Now Sam and Sydney had a common enemy: Michael, and a common interest: me, which was a mixture of protecting

Mary and covering themselves. An independently wealthy woman is more attractive to an ex-husband as well as potential one. Esther's excuse for keeping the house in her name was for estate reasons, so we looked for the answer. For weeks, both men researched. Accountants were consulted, but the final brainstorm was Sam's. Even Sydney admitted his ingenuity. Now a tactful demonstration of the plan's effectiveness had to be presented to Esther.

The opportunity presented itself. Esther invited the children and me to dinner. She was going to a concert and I would play cards with Abe who was more often than not in a state of senile bliss. My heart broke to see him like this, sitting on his leather throne just watching , a smile on his face. Sometimes in the middle of our game, the cards would slip from his fingers while he closed his eyes and dozed off. I'd wipe away my tears remembering the dynamic man that once built an empire. Tara nudged her Grandpa to wake up and play the game.

In years of closeness somehow calling her Mother or Esther was uncomfortable; one to familiar, the other, not enough. At two when Alexander began using Nanny, I conveniently adopted the name solving the problem.

After dinner, I walked into the bathroom where Esther was preparing herself for her evening out. "Nanny, I want to talk to you about our house. I know you've been concerned about the estate, but Sam has . . ."

Esther cut me off in her rushed sweep-it-under-the rug fashion, "Mary I'm so glad you brought it up. I did a stupid thing five years ago. Never realizing that giving Alexander and Tara eighty thousand dollars a piece meant I would someday have to do the same thing for all my grandchildren. Right now I simply can't afford that, but more important, my first duty is to my children, not their children. Michael and Rachel need my help and I know you're about to get some money due from the beach apartments, so I thought you could pay me back the hundred and sixty thousand dollars." She continued dressing avoiding my eyes, her irresponsible tone deliberately non-chalant.

My own reflection in the mirror looked as though struck by lightening. My voice shaky, "The money I'm getting is nowhere near that amount and I need to re-invest it to live on!" Typically avoiding anything uncomfortable Esther walked out of the room leaving words trailing behind . . . .

"We'll work something out. I must go. I'll be late for the overture."

Left alone standing in front of the bathroom mirror, I half expected it to shatter from the icy wind that had passed through. Trying to keep my tears quiet from the children, I locked my emotions behind the door. Oh God the shock of what Esther had done, the repercussions to come! But the pain penetrated by suggesting that her children were more important, meaning she was excluding me from that position. Although not my birthright, the role had been mine more than the others over the past twenty years. I felt all the separateness of an abandoned child.

The children wanted to spend the night. By rote, I went through the movements of putting everyone to bed and drove home alone. Thinking the tears were under control, I dialed Sam's number. The sound of his voice offered safe harbor reactivating my feelings.

"Oh no, what happened?"

Between tears the story tumbled out.

"I hate to say I told you so. My mother is one of those people who gives her love to the weak. She creates dependency, then supports it. The ultimate in maternal manipulation . . . often referred to as love."

No wonder Sam had so much trouble after we had children, then I became 'Mother'. My bruised mind briefly scanned thoughts of Sydney. Was his support of problems manipulative as well? What does he win? Certainly, it helps to define roles, the needed and the needy.

Sam's voice interrupted my thought. "You and my mother created each other as perfect role models. You just got a little too strong. Calm down and tomorrow I'll have a talk with her, so go to sleep."

I placed the receiver back in the cradle just in time for a ring. "Mary darling what happened? Did you tell Esther the solution?" Sydney was calling from New York. Once again, my unleashed emotions told the tale provoking his own anger leaving no room to take a philosophical position as Sam had.

"That bitch, indulging that twerp of a son at your expense!"

"Please Sydney, I know you just want to defend me and I love you for it, but please don't get involved. I know I can work it out with her." What Sydney and Sam both needed to protect was their reality rooted in past pictures and personal financial stake.

Sleep was a stranger this night. All the voices in my head were working double shift. Well aware of reflecting who I was through my house but had the house become who I was? For the past five years our identities so intertwined the thought of separation seemed impossible. And what of my identity as a Golden, as a daughter? How could she do this? Drifting off, I convinced myself daylight would bring a solution.

Morning never fails -- it always comes. Strong coffee first, then Esther. I prayed for the right words to come. "Hello Nanny."

The response was totally unexpected; her voice brutally cold. "I have nothing to say to you! You'll hear from my lawyer!" With the force of vented anger, the receiver slammed down. I felt as though a brick wall had fallen on me. What could have happened between her last words of 'We'll work something out,' and this?

The explanation came through Sam. "It appears after your conversation with Sydney, he took it upon himself to be a one-man crusade against tyranny, waging a long distance campaign. I'm afraid profanity ran rampant from East coast to West."

Sweeping accusations and judgements from Sydney could be more than brutal -- lethal and this outbreak carried that kiss of death.

Unfortunately, I was to inherit the result of his rage, instant excommunication from the family! All rights of an ingratiated ex-in-law were stripped away. A letter soon arrived from Esther's lawyer expressing her legal and moral obligation of five years prior, but legal title to the house to remain in Esther Golden's name. Reference was made to the brutal verbal attack by my consort, which Mrs. Golden was still suffering from. And a postscript, "Mrs. Golden feels it's time that you take full responsibility for the support of your own mother, Mrs. Rosenbloom. The monthly checks to her will terminate as of now." Since Jake's death and enormous hospital costs, Abe supplemented Lenore's small income. Sam became especially incensed over this act of revenge against Lenore. Over the years he had grown to appreciate his mother-in-law's goodness, for living simultaneously with her fears and frailities was a pure giving heart. To keep this from Lenore, Sam worked out a plan with Abe's secretary to continue the checks without interruption and he would personally cover them. Ironically, Sam's fear of further financial dependency came instantly true -- thoughts are powerful. He became the second casualty of Sydney's telephone tirade.

Sam's protection didn't stop there. For the first time in the years since that fateful station wagon trip, he really stepped forward. God how I cherished his support. We agreed continuing to live in the house under her conditions was impossible. Since I couldn't afford to buy it, Sam offered a solution. He would buy it from his mother at the original price, but for personal reasons keep it in his name. An internal chuckle -- out of the frying pan into the fire. Maybe the need to control wasn't just a maternal condition, but a hereditary affliction.

"Thank you Sam, I do appreciate and love you for your

support, but it's time to be independent. I'm tired of putting myself in the position where someone else can pull the strings, even if I have to sell the house." Once again -- choice reduced to none.

Tremendous frustration built in not being able to communicate with Esther directly while watching this storybook family fall apart. In desperation I wrote a letter, a personal plea to have Rachel and Michael see what their expensive habits and indulgences had forced their mother to do. At least, in knowing the facts, they would never be able to excuse the issue for ignorance of it.

How incredibly naive of me to think that truth could put out the fire between Rachel and myself. Now the written word simply fanned the flames. Feelings toward me were based on her distorted reality years in the making. Only a month before at a family party in her usual aided-by-alcohol state, she finally unleashed pent up jealousy towards me in a physical attack and quickly the incident was placed in the family closet. Funny, I really always did love Rachel. I always did love them all. No response came from my letter.

I pleaded with Sydney, "Please apologize, or at least explain to Esther I had nothing to do with your tirade against her." But anger wouldn't allow it, his voice exploded.

"Now after all she's done, if I hear her voice, I'll simply do it again."

Oh my God what of forgiveness? I thought of Gandhi. "An eye for an eye only makes the whole world blind."

Sam helped me take out a loan and I paid Esther back her gift, plus at her request the ten thousand dollars she slipped me to pad my decorating style. The house was finally in my name, but the cost was much too high -- The *For Sale* went back up behind the gardenia bush. My external identity as mistress of the enchanted cottage was being stripped away and in the process, I lost my family. There was a hole in the egg. Time to let go. Time to surrender to the energy that was changing my life.

The swan is dead. Long live the swan.

Part III

"For that which has remained
unknown to all men for an aeon
may be disclosed to one man in
but a moment."

Kahlil Gibran

Chapter XI

A piece of my heart remained behind and life went on. So hard for me to remember what I thought I knew so well, *that nothing's personal* -- then why did I take it so very personally? Now that Esther removed herself from my life, Crystal with her maternal wisdom helped to fill the painful void. Once again she discovered the latest star on the 'New Age' stage Peter Samuels.

Peter who predicted July 7, 1977 as the first day of the Age of Aquarius (curiously it was also his birthday) discovered his psychic gifts as a lark. As a means to stop smoking, he and a friend dabbled in hypnosis and when Peter went into deep trance another entity began to speak through him. Astonished, his friend's fear quickly moved into excitement taping the channeled *voice* to prove to Peter the phenomenon had truly taken place.

Peter's upbringing had been as a strict Baptist and at one point he verged on the ministry, but ultimately chose to marry a woman instead of God. When the woman ran off, God was forsaken in total. Deep depression set in, slipping to the bottom -- lost years -- as his dark night of the soul ensued. This *voice* was the first light showing him the way back.

Skepticism had stubbornly settled into his fiber and proof of the *voice's* powers was demanded. He sought the answer to the perfect question that no living man knew. The hypnotic session began. Peter an easy subject, instantly fell into a deep sleeping trance.

The conductor of the experiment addressed the *voice*. "If you are from another dimension, you must have powers beyond that which we know. Peter's grandfather died before revealing where he had buried his life's savings. Can you tell us where to find the treasure?"

A large, rounded *voice* filled the space coming from Peter, but not his own. "Yes, we have those records. The one known as Joseph Samuels who has already crossed over the threshold of light buried his worldly treasure under the ground in a tin box. It still lies amongst the flowers in his garden."

This meant a trip back to Georgia and there they found under the winter's ice, where before had bloomed flowers, the tin box. Peter Samuels experienced instant conversion and a confirmed belief in hypnosis. Revealed to him by the *Source* was a past life as the Apostle Paul and once again he was to be a prophet in his own time. Then came seven years of preparation turning him into an extraordinary teacher of spirit and a powerful psychic channel able in hypnotic state to tap into the Akashic Records. These etheric files catalogue all that has been or ever will be -- the metaphysical conglomerate of the Hall of Records and the Library of Congress . . . recording the soul's journey through all its incarnations.

Sensational intrigue of this kind is not easily ignored. Crystal his sponsor and hostess, invited me for a personal meeting. Peter stood at the door as I walked in. At once I knew I was in the presence of fire. Nodding his greeting, I was thankful, for his power demanded the impersonal, making touch unnecessary. Though captivating his mystique was a little frightening. We sat around the kitchen table while tea was served. The wife of a famous television talk-show host, a wise fox camouflaged with Gracie Allen dialogue heightened the patter before deeper waters were tread.

"Sometimes I feel such trememdous hypocrisy in this so-called New Age movement. People espouse higher conscious-ness but are the living antithesis -- eating junk food or still smoking. Perhaps if they were truly evolved they could transmute the negative but . . . " I was interrupted by Peter's voice, steady, clear and authoritative, not condescending just explaining.

"You limit your own understanding by setting up so many rules and then sitting in judgment on them. Form can fool. You must learn a new language, a sensitivity and discernment to vibration rather than form. Therein lies a higher truth. Many things can look the same but be totally different." Looking up he motioned to Crystal, "Could I bother you for a piece of that delicious chocolate cake hiding in the box over there?" He was pleased at the paradox he had set up.

His ethnic looks seemed from another time. I watched his deep dark eyes; they told an ancient story, all the secrets of ages appeared stored within them. My questions went on -- his responses satisfying and stimulating a deep memory bank within me. "On the way the path is up, on the return the path is down; it's the same path. The profound is often nothing more than the confusion of the obvious." My soul had lain dormant waiting for our meeting.

The part of teacher in my life was finally cast. Reluctantly leaving I turned for one more glance, such an extraordinary enigma he was uncomfortably housed in a body and culture no way matching the magnitude of spirit and strength of commitment to his mission. He looked like Merlin the Magician pacing back and forth—stroking his dark beard streaked with silver as if a magic device. His power tried to escape confines of this physical dimension, while remaining within him a deep brooding endured. Whatever spell he wove, I was now under.

His organization, *The Brotherhood of Light*, offered an advanced workshop. In two weeks at Paradise Ranch in northern California, Peter would conduct the retreat. The prerequisite was an introductory course teaching his very distinctive techniques in meditation, journal writing, dream interpretation and the mystery school called life -- all very specific and powerful tools taught to Peter through the entity he called *The Source.*

Something inside me went way beyond just taking another course -- a sense of being right on my own destined path. And nothing could stop me -- as if I were born just to be there. Accompanying this inner demand was a strong instinct, almost an urgency, to get Sydney and Peter together as a team. They felt karmically comfortable. To teach first street level consciousness, then elevating that teaching to spirit. Also apparent if this plan was to work it best be Anne's idea. Sydney's career was her domain.

"It's like he's scratched a deep itch in my soul." My exuberance was not withheld as I shared my tale of Peter. "Darling I just know you'll feel the same about him. It might take getting beyond his polyester edifice, but trust me, there's a pure silk interior." Consciously omitting that he wore the fabric twice too many times before a trip to the cleaners I realized, I shouldn't have mentioned polyester at all for it offended my own aesthetic sense and Sydney was far more impeccable. A linen suit that had a crease in it was dismissed.

Sydney listened dubiously with a touch of jealousy disguised under a pose of curiosity and asked, "Does he preach reincarnation? Is he a disciple incarnate or the Messiah himself? And who does he say you are or excuse me, were? Be careful, Mary, he may be after your soul by way of your pocketbook!"

Conveniently, Sydney was planning a trip to England with Helen to sell off their belongings left behind. This would leave three weeks to follow instinct without interfering with our personal time together or being influenced by his negative rhetoric about Peter.

The introductory night was the first of ten evenings of the

prerequisite course before the advanced retreat. One of my favorite 'two hundred' appeared. Mark von Holt the writer. For some reason he brought out all my maternal instincts. I hadn't seen him since New York. Having already completed the course he was there to write an article. Mark carried an aura of awe from constant changes and strange coincidences taking place in his life combined with an intellectual cynicism -- a peculiar duality. Perhaps his doubt made the miracles more astounding. "Here we are again, another mini-miracle. Believe me this is not your basic spiritual business as usual. There's something more powerful going on here. Peter is . . . well, Peter, but the course is fantastic!"

Occasionally in groups, I find someone who offers a special magnetism. This night, both John and I felt the pull. He was a young, delicate guitar playing singer with a well defined halo effect. A warm friendship began. A freeing idea scanned my mind, the possibility to be turned on and not physically compelled to act it out. Oh thank you, thank you, thank you!

We planned to meet the next night for dinner before class at the Aware Inn on Sunset. But early in the afternoon John called with a change of plans. "Hey sorry. I was really looking forward to dinner with you, but Peter asked me to pick up Rama at the airport. He's kinda Peter's right hand holy man ya know. He's coming in to teach the rest of the course."

As a postscript John added the need to scout out lodgings for Rama and my hostess instinct spoke out before my practical side offering shelter.

The bell rang. There he stood, robed in splendid Indian garb, setting off his regalness, not merely a king, but a sage. He was the three wise men rolled up in one. What star had brought him to me? Instant recognition flashed between us. Definitely he was in the top few of my 'two hundred.' His slender dark fingers held my hand, nobility in his touch. Then his full attention went to rearranging a misplaced fold in his fine cotton garment.

Rama had been a wealthy aristocrat and political leader in India, much on the indulgent side with expensive tastes that took him to Paris on buying trips for cashmere sweaters. But after a potent spiritual awakening, he abandoned his worldly possessions and position and went off in search of a teacher. At an ashram in the Himalayas, he found him.

"I've come here to learn." Proudly adding, "I have renounced the material world and have given away everything I owned." He stood waiting, erectly superior.

"How then do you anticipate eating or sleeping? Do you expect me to keep you and teach you as well" - asked the guru. "If you are to be my student first you must earn two years' keep and then we can talk!" His confronting tone had Rama groveling for equal opportunity, which he contained in a startled gaze. Surprised but full of enterprise, Rama considered the challenge. He went to New Delhi, checked into the most expensive hotel and began to play capitalist from memory and nerve. In three months he returned with a dowry and began his training and so learned an important lesson -- both worlds must operate simultaneously, as above so below. And as he put it, "God is not a bellboy!"

The pace quickened. After class each night, I stayed awake and alert for hours listening to Rama's stories. Like the old cabalistic rabbis, he taught through tales of folklore. Often John joined us and after a late night would sleep in his camper in the driveway.

The hour was late, delicious for Rama to tell a tale. Curled up in front of the fire like a child I awaited my spiritual bedtime story.

"In the beginning of Creation, eternity expressed herself as three beautiful sisters -- Past, Present, and Future. Past wore black robes and in her eyes dwelled all life's mysteries. Past was adept in illusionary charm. Things seemingly insignificant in the hands of Present, became infatuation when viewed through the realms of memory of Past.

Future dwelt on the other side of the mountain in the land of hope. She was inspiration for those tormented by Past. She always offered only a glimpse, leaving much in the shadows. Her promise of a bed of roses would not make mention of thorns. But she had nothing to offer that wasn't a gift of her sister Present.

Present was so beautiful that once beheld, one would never be inclined to another. But unless the enchantment of Past and Future was overcome, it was not possible for anyone to embrace Present and wed her.

Then came a pursuer who perceived the traps of Past and Future and courageously held the hands of Present and felt the depth of her wonder. He was transformed, his conscious-ness expanded to infinite measure. He saw Past and Future merge in her and gazed into the eyes of Eternity."*

Spellbound in the presence of parable his audience sat still. Another time during the telling of a tale, I interrupted Rama with an opinion. Fire and strength soared through his peace when provoked. "I beg your pardon Madame. You are not only wrong, but impertinent." Instantly my ego succumbed to the truth in his attack -- I didn't take it personally. This gift of Sydney's teaching had finally taken effect. Rama was impressed and amazed by my acceptance of such confrontation without need to react.

"Mary dear a wise man once said, 'one is allowed to use the sword only if he knows how to heal the wound,' and you my dear, have aided in your own healing." This appreciation ingratiated us one to another and also clearly established who was the teacher.

Not long after, I was visited in the night by a vivid technicolor dream. . . .

The spaciousness of my blue bedroom became even more grand. In the center stood the brass bed, all alone. Nude and vulnerable I sat on the

**satin quilt waiting, uncertain as to why. When
suddenly, the door flew open and Rama came
charging at me. His body was dwarfed making
his head appear enormous. Arms outstretched,
dark eyes bulging, he ran toward my bed. Fear
of a woman under attack coursed through me ..
but I knew it was not my body he wanted. No,
he was after my soul!**

The morning light brought Rama back into proportion.
Ours was a kinship of ancient origin. It even smelled of
another time. Like those feelings in the desert of caravans and
camels, Rama was my oasis — or my conscience! These ten
days spent together were more consuming than any I ever
knew. Breakfast was rushed, but I took those few extra
moments to care... how the strawberries lay next to the kiwi ..
that roses from the garden were in full bloom exposing their
openness to a spray of morning dew, for nothing went
unnoticed or unappreciated by Rama's discerning eye.

Walking into the kitchen, he handed me a gift -- a picture
wrapped and framed by his own hand in an expession of love.
"How very sweet. Thank you my dear. And from Elephanta,
my favorite cave temple! It took me weeks to write a paper on
this very carving of Shiva."

His amazed look preceeded his words, "And I thought you
were a primitive!" I realized only then he really knew nothing
about me. In all this time, not a word was spoken of my past,
nor thoughts expressed of the future. Rama was about being in
the moment and spending time with him demanded that of
everyone. He was the pursuer who courageously held the hand
of present. A new vitality and aliveness came with each
moment when I gave it my full attention. No room left for
deviation, being present created power and focus of a laser
beam. No wonder I've tried all my life to escape the intensity of
now. I thought of Sam, of drugs.

How quickly ten days passed, so rich and full. The

prerequisite was complete. Alive and expanded, my awareness stretched. All the techniques needed to tap into another dimension were now ready for experiment. The next morning we set out for Northern California and Paradise Ranch another ten intense days, this time with Peter.

What began only months ago on that Easter night watching *Jesus of Nazareth* grew and expanded as if my soul were being resurrected. A deepening sense of altered states became my constant companion. And continuing this night, I lie in bed waiting for sleep to come, wondering who would be dancing in my dreams . . . ?

> **Joan of Arc. A courtroom scene. Her male armor now gone, making vulnerable her maiden's heart. The entire trial reenacted -- living out its torment and judgment. Her feeling of abandonment in prison I experience. "Oh dear God, why did you choose me only to forget me now?" And then an enormous resurgence of faith. "Forgive me, it is not you who have denied -- it is me denying you!"**
>
> **Then that final walk, hands tied, blindfolded and stumbling. Laughter. Ridicule. Anticipation of the smell of burning flesh. Waking just before the sentence is carried out.**

Startled and confused, I sat up in bed. What dream interpretation could I give? Was this a remembrance of something I had once lived or a more universal memory? How could my subconscious have known all this specific detailed information? Somehow, I sensed my experience lay in the need to understand the *courage* and *commitment* of Joan of Arc, that her qualities would be necessary for something that was about to happen in my own life. But what could happen? Why would I need such courage and commitment? I stood poised on the brink at the mercy of the Gods.

Rama, John, myself and a few others from the classs flew to San Francisco and were picked up in a large van for the trip to Paradise Ranch. The van overflowed with hope, laughter and singing. One of Peter's teachings was to maintain a high level of expectancy. "We get exactly what we ask for. Our prayers are saying 'win' but our hearts are anticipating defeat. Expect a miracle!"

Crossing over the Golden Gate Bridge, we pulled aside to rest and enjoy the view. My legs were grateful for the stretch; since that station wagon ride they were quick to protest a confined space. But if my soul's dark night brought me to this moment, I'm deeply grateful.

Rama and I walked toward the cliff's edge and looked back at the majesty of the bridge leading to the city -- or away from it. *Suddenly*, I felt a strong unnatural *energy* pervade the air around me, go through me, ignoring matter, a total shift in reality. Mystic veils holding time in abeyance, lifted. There before me as on a giant movie screen, enacted for my eyes only, in broad daylight, I gazed spellbound as the entire metropolis of San Francisco came crashing down. Buildings crumbled. Echoing reverberation. Explosions of light and dark -- flashes of a city lay waste. I could smell the total devastation. Whether earthquake, bombing, I knew not why; only the result was revealed. My knees gave way; the experience taking with it, my very breath. Rama caught me as I fell. "Oh my God, my God." The only words I could say. He asked no questions, knowing not the content of the experience, though understanding that something vast and unspeakable had touched me. Gently, firmly, he told me to keep repeating the 23rd Psalm. "Yea though I walk through the valley of the shadow of death . . . "

Not unlike all great seers and prophets of the past, Peter's psychic readings were filled with prophecy. He spoke of hard times to come and of earth changes. But in literally being shown this disaster was I witnessing something yet to come? What spiritual Pandora's Box was opening for me?

By the time we entered the gates of the ranch, I was calm but bewildered. Adam and Eve would have felt at home in the lushness of this paradise, a true retreat, with a direct command from nature -- be healed! The whole aesthetic was home to me -- a real Mexican ranch house (not unlike the one I was about to lose), rustic cabins which sprawled in and out the landscape hiding in overgrown nooks, swimming pool, tennis court and winding trails which upon investigation brought one to a bath house. Tucked in among the trees, outside, though under shelter was a redwood hot tub; in the little house were the rest of the accoutrements, a sauna and massage table. Paradise was well endowed!

My plan to get Sydney and Peter to work together first included Anne experiencing this retreat with Peter. Anne was a master magician, but my strategy here was more altruistic. To get Anne to Paradise was no easy task, but somehow fate aided my persuasive powers. "Mary I think you just sold ice to an Eskimo!"

"But Anne dear, I wouldn't even try except for the thaw."

Hierarchy being acknowledged, Anne and her entourage, a staff of three, were given entry without prerequisite. Sustaining her celebrity image at a retreat took extra energy, somehow defeating the purity of purpose.

Everyone gathered in the spacious heavily beamed living room after dinner, ready for the first session. Large comfortable sofas lined the room and bright colored pillows softened the blow between hardwood and a Navajo rug for those sitting on the floor. Peter was late due to car trouble. Funny to think of Peter at the mercy of the mundane. John brought out his guitar and singing began heightening the expectation level. Peter walked in with Anne at his side. She must have given him a ride. Everyone applauded and a slight twinge of jealousy flashed across my sensibilities. Was this such a good idea? The enthusiasm of my heart often spoke before my mind had an opportunity to compute the outcome.

Already Peter was picking up techniques of the trade from Sydney as Anne suggested we begin by each person introducing themselves. Thirty of us from many parts of the country were there, even two from Europe -- searching for answers to life, asking questions similar to those that had burned so in my heart all these years. Ancient human questions. Where did I come from and why am I here? How do I get from here to there? Does the soul ever die? There were healers and those who needed healing. One young girl had cancer; her skin was whitish gray and all too close to the bone -- death stalked her. My arms wanted to hold her and make it all right. A wonderful older couple from England -- she a Baroness with steel gray hair braided in a crown on top of her head; he a painter, always smiling. Both involved for eons in metaphysics. Another couple brought their two-year-old Downs Syndrome child, sharing with us a psychic reading Peter had given them, telling of intertwined karma of the three carried over from a past life. This new understanding brought them a sense of peace and they were ready to let go of the past to heal their child. Peter told how the 'Law of Grace' can end karma, the law of cause and effect . . . Oh what the medical profession could do with the 'Psychology of Karma.' Karma here, karma there, karma karma everywhere! And of course there was the staff -- Peter's blood line, all young, possessing 'Mona Lisa' like smiles, seemingly lost in their connection.

Wrapped in a new talcumed naivete, I felt anxious to open myself to God -- the feeling clean and pure like having bathed in a fresh mountain stream. The agenda for the first morning was full; a sunrise meditation on the hill, yoga in a salutation to the dawn, breakfast in the stone-walled patio under yellow umbrellas and finally, a group meeting with Peter under a large oak tree on the grass. At breakfast, I received my first reprimand from Rama for wearing my very low Romanian wedding blouse. I changed.

Peter sat cross-legged in a Buddha fashion, difficult because of his large stomach, having given up women for food. The oak's umbrella effect created a majestic backdrop and refuge from the August sun . . . Thoughts of Sam and wedding vows under oaks that stand not in each other's shadow . . . Peter gave a brief review from the introductory course in use of a personal journal, then asked us to write a list of the most important people in our lives and what made them so. To search for meaning in the connection -- kind of why and wherefore list of Sidney's basic two hundred.

My head facing up the slope, I lay flat on the grass, my body cooled by the earth. The green blades tickled. I watched a lady bug crawl into Peter's beard and scratched for both of us. My diary was electric blue with embossed red satin. Etched in the center was a drawing of an ancient temple. Opening to the first page, I began the list. A cool breeze went past . . . more than a breeze. *Suddenly*, sucked up by the very ground beneath me, like being caught in the eye of a hurricane, *the energy* surged through me -- becoming me, traveling down my arm and compelling my hand to write. Not destructive energy, but creative force. My brain had ceased command. I stared transfixed as the words gave birth out of my control. On pure white paper, the script issued shakily. *Virgin Mother, Earth Mother.* Having written, *the energy* moved on.

Breathless, I sat. Obviously I had heard of the phenomenon of automatic writing but was in no way prepared for the reality or impact of it. Looking around me, all was calm, each person intently involved in their own two hundred. Not only had I been praying for these last two weeks to make contact with God, but increasingly, I knew it was possible. Now this experience dwarfed my imagination. Oh dear God, what am I supposed to do? And why the Mother?

After the session ended, bewildered I waited for the crowd to leave Peter. As he walked along the winding path up the hill, I approached him. Surely he would be able to explain everything. My mouth was left parched from the whirlwind that had traveled through. Stimulating the saliva before I spoke, I began to tell him what happened containing my excitement by guising my voice in calmness; but he sharply cut me off. He must know, and not want the words exposed to the light of day. He merely suggested I enjoy the beauty of the tree he pointed to and left. Confused by his abruptness, my gaze fell on the tree. The tall trunk shot up the center with its head in a slight mournful bow. Two branches reached out from either side taking the burden of weight, appearing as arms from a body. Mother Nature had sculpted her own cross and upon it placed the Son I smiled warmly; he must know!

An old iron merry-go-round sat on the lawn, beckoning as I walked by. Stepping on with one foot and using the other to put it in motion, I could hear the music. The momentum built as it went round and round. My old childhood dream flashed before me, music of the carrousel. How does one ever get off? Turning, turning . . . life after life, endless cycles, always the next turn. Gong! The lunch bell rang jolting me. The answer came. So simple. If you want off, take responsibility for the courage to jump. The speed picked up by a push from a passerby, I took the leap!

At the end of a crooked path was my log cabin shared with two roommates. One was a lovely young flower child with dark full wavy hair. If I were a primitive, Rama would definitely consider her a prehistoric. The other was an older woman — slight, but hearty, spent a lifetime in the search but still didn't get it. She was full of questions and hard of hearing when it came to answers. Kindly, I suggested a game, instead of shouting, we would whisper and perhaps learn a new way to listen. It worked.

Last to shower before dinner, my roommates were dressed and out as I sat on the edge of the bed putting on my shoes. Then something in the air changed . . . a density, a manifestation.

My eyes darted to all corners, in search of what? *Suddenly,* announcing an awesome presence the room began to shake as though hit by a violent earthquake, shaking, shoving its reality into me. Holding onto the bed, I sat terrifed and stunned. This time the saliva vanished, my mouth left dry beyond rescue. Trembling, I reached for a glass of water losing half in the attempt. Unsure whether my voice would accommodate, but electrically charged, "I'm not afraid; I welcome you." I sat shaking.

Silence, then abruptly a response came. A *voice* otherworldly, outside of myself -- low, monotone and fluid, without human personality to hide behind. Entering my left ear, it went through my head like a ticker tape. I was spellbound. The *voice* disclosed the nature of the universe, the hour life began on this planet and then spoke of the meaning of the Immaculate Conception. It explained that "Jesus and Mary are the same soul. This soul then gave birth to itself first as Mary, immaculately conceived as well so that Christ could virtually enter through Himself." No hesitation, the monotone went on . . . clearly, lovingly, though without emotion.

Mysteries, sacred mysteries were revealed allowing me entry behind the veils, as I sat motionless on the edge of the bed. The only thought that crossed my mind was how would I remember all this information coming so fast? At that instant, the *voice* picked up my thought telepathically and said, "There is no need to worry about remembering. I will be back. The most important thing you must know is to take one step at a time. The person who is one step ahead of you is your teacher, the person one step behind, you are the teacher for. Do it with love, compassion and humility." Life, like following the white line in the road in a dense fog.

The energy left the room as abruptly as it entered. For an undetermined time, I resonated in the aftermath, feeling physically transformed; my own vibratory rate had been altered, slowed down. Bathed in calmness; tranquility becoming a part of me. On my knees next to the bed I knelt like a child saying prayers. "Oh God, I feel like a vessel being prepared for fine wine, so blessed. But what do you expect of me now? What does it all mean?"

The meal passed in silence. My hunger was gone, no need for food. Over ten years had gone by since that LSD experience which opened so many doors but leaving me empty, a gnawing bottomless pit in my stomach. Now I was finally full. After dinner we gathered in the large beamed living room. A fire danced in the huge stone hearth as we prepared for the evening session. The young girl with cancer had admired my Romanian wedding blouse. That night I gave it to her. She ran to put it on. The color of her face changed.

Over the years Peter perfected his ability to channel. No longer was it necessary to go into a sleeping trance. As he began to speak, I could almost hear a click to automatic pilot leaving himself behind like shedding skin. His words became biblical and commanded the power and truth of a prophet. Guiding us in mythical meditation, a journey up the mountain, through seven multicolored terraces, painting magical pictures of fragrant lush gardens, each level reached a new challenge to leave behind the old and begin anew. A potent hypnotic effect was powerfully transmitted through his voice vibration.

"You're in the red garden -- smell the roses. See bougainvillea winding around pillars. This is the terrace of expectancy. Something is about to happen! Feel yourself merge into the red -- expect it, accept it, as you move up the mountain." I listened, visualized, expected -- believed! Then as *suddenly* as before, *the energy* abruptly entered and fused my body with its mystique. There was no fighting or fear, I welcomed and trusted. My head was firmly pulled back by unseen hands and my mouth steadfastly opened. Something was planted on my tongue. Somehow, I understood. It was a seed . . . an annunciation, a visitation . . . I was seeded with *the energy*.

Then, its mission complete for the time, it left. A deep breath helped to settle back in my body, newly empowered.

With the group still in soundless meditation, I continued my own silence for I knew not if I was to share. *The energy* had implanted a seed and I had accepted it.

All week the time-space frame shifted in and out, like being caught in a surreal time warp. Paradise Ranch became an Essene village of two thousand years ago. Covering my head with a shawl, I roamed the crooked paths, feeling like a holy woman shrouded in slow motion -- more alive as illusion and reality reversed themselves. My consciousness listened to its own memory, transported into another dimension, another time, another place.

The energy knew not the limitations of sleep or awake. In dream that night Joan of Arc returned. The sentence was to be carried out! Joan walked bravely toward the hot red flames. They jumped out at me as I woke in a pool of sweat. Oh God, am I now to go through fire -- transmuting base metal into gold?

For three days now everyone had been on an apple fast. All desire for food had left me, even bodily functions closed down. My body less dense, almost weightless, I needed consciously to grip my steps to the ground. All illusions and masks of earthly reality were of little importance. I wore no makeup and dressed simply. That same feeling as a child crossing the street with Eve returned -- everyone there was an extra in my movie, but none of us knew the script.

By mid-week a well-known teacher, Kay Ortman, joined the group to share her creative methods in dance and crafts. The sun shone hot in clear skies; everyone was eager to dance and gathered on the grass around her. The wind played havoc with dozens of scarves Kay threw into the air. Silk scarves of all seven colors of the mountain meditation circulated in the wind. A red scarf floated down into my lap. Red, the color of expectancy, the first garden terrace up the mountain. The music began — my favorite, Pachebel's Canon — a quality and combination of sounds that turned the key to open the heart. Free flowing gestures, the bodies moved in adagio across the lawn and around the pool. Blues, yellows, reds, greens . . . the colored scarves trailed, mocking each movement and changing hands -- a passerby becoming the temporary owner of a new color.

As I let go of the red silk, a bright orange one took its place and with it, I felt *the energy* begin to shift upward into the next garden terrace. Once more something was about to happen. This time, I maintained an awareness of two realities operating simultaneously, one above, one below. My body carried out its horizontal dance as each color in proper sequence reached my hands pushing my spirit further up the mountain. Orange, dying to the old. A pirouette into yellow, rebirth! Green, where I opened my heart and met my teacher. I choreographed a low bow. Blue lifting me into the cosmos beyond the void. Violet brought me to commitment as I lay myself down on the altar. The music stopped short -- the dancers caught in a freeze frame. Someone slipped the white silk scarf around my shoulder. White -- the top of the mountain!

That small part of me still operating at street level was already embarrassed by the thought, but I knew what the end of the music would bring. Slowly, I stepped down into the pool. The water met the white silk draped over my shoulders and floated it on the surface. This was my initiation, a ceremony of baptism. My eyes closed and my head bowed in the water three times. The sun warmed my smile as I gazed upward. The seemingly undirected ceremony went on as if repeating a ritual known deep in my soul, a mystical marriage, a union with God. This was the gold ring I had waited for all my life. The rabbi's promise at another ceremony -- the veils of the bride lifted and now kissed gently on the mouth. Spirit had spoken.

Only Kay noticed this strange event and came to help me out of the pool. Still wearing the white scarf, the water made it transparent and clinging. Feeling like a bride longing to share my joyous news, I surveyed the scene, but everyone was busily involved with painting and sculpture. So filled with wonder I never stopped to ask what marrying God meant. Aware of an obvious lack of synchronicity between myself and others, I dwelled in a place where they were not allowed entry. With gentle touch Kay guided me to a seat, dried me and placed a large piece of clay in my hand. Holding my face, she knowingly confronted those faraway eyes. "Allow that energy to help you create."

The lump of clay rested on the table, slowly I placed my hands around its sides. With only a touch, once again *the energy* engulfed me. By magic the clay began to mold and take shape without moving my hands. Within seconds it formed itself into a perfectly sculptured mountain. Sitting in awe at the creation, I recognized the shape -- Mount Sinai! Where Moses met God!

Kay came out and stood behind me. "That's extraordinary, you didn't mention you could sculpt and with such speed!" She once again tried to make contact with my eyes, but now they were further away than ever.

Later that afternoon a loud sigh escaped as I slipped into the therapeutic waters of the hot tub. "Ah, this is an outrageous earthly ecstasy." John echoed with a sigh of his own. "I know I've been appearing perhaps a bit on the strange side, but so many things are happening . . . "

"Best you don't dissipate the energy by talking. Keep in the experience."

Disappointed, I wanted so much to share -- but I took his comments as a sign to remain silent.

"At least let me do a reality check. What do the others think?"

"Well, there's this talk of sending you off to a funny farm. I even heard that older couple from Texas say you must be on drugs."

"Oh no. I did take LSD once which started me on this seeker's journey but I've never taken anything since. This week is infinitely deeper into another dimension and I not only didn't use drugs, but no food. They aren't the answer, but I can definitely see where the entire drug culture was an important link in preparation for miracles. At least, with drugs something else is responsible for the experience and that softens the blow. An honest to goodness *miracle* doesn't have a cushion."

"Watch it Mary, we have company. It's Anne and entourage. She has such lovely red hair, I wonder why she dyes the roots black."

"John stop it!"

Borrowing the Pachebel tape and small recorder from Kay, I walked to the top of the hill where the sunrise meditation took place. In the pasture everything appeared silhouetted against the clarity of open sky. The tall green grass mingled with wild flowers swaying in the breeze and stirred leaves on the large oak tree setting the swing hanging from its sturdy branch into motion. I breathed in the scent of it all. Alone and safe, I yearned to pay homage. My movements were slow, ritualistic, as I took off my clothes, wanting to be caressed by the sun on my body. I switched on the music and began to dance, with closed eyes the strong memory of a pagan rite, a temple dance of a high priestess. In and around the pillars the trees -- the pillars -- the trees. My soul merged with music, movement and time, my body able to do things that I had only done in my choreographed daydreams as a child -- long leaps and precise pirouettes. As I took a low bow the music came to an end. The sound of applause from a one-man audience shattered the mood. I opened my eyes; there stood a man from the group, his intentions obviously amorous. Simply and deliberately I put on my clothes and dismissed him as though not there.

After dinner I changed into the white caftan John had given me as a gift for the mornings of breakfast after nights of Rama stories. The bodice was white on white distinguished by a heavier silk thread used in a hand embroidered Indian pattern. Saving it for something special, tonight was that rare occasion it awaited. Passing Peter as I walked into the evening session, my affection and gratitude spilled over in a hug. Always I felt the barrier of some emotion expressed in his body with rigidity. Was I to take it personally -- or was it his attempt to remain impersonal? Rumor did have it that after his wife left him, he had trouble with women. Trying to ease the mood, I joked, "What's on the cosmic agenda tonight?" -- as if he were privy to the programming. He didn't laugh.

The mountain meditation began. Red, expectation, I knew something was about to happen. By the second orange plateau, the terrace of death to the old, I saw my body being left behind under a tree and the weightlessness of my spirit ascend. Through the yellow rebirth of the third level.

"Now climb up the mountain to the fourth terraced lush green garden -- the garden of the heart. Amongst the shadows of the trees, listen for footsteps. For here you will meet your teacher."

And then it happened! *The energy* not only went through me but transported me no longer earth-bound into another time-space dimension, where existed a different mode of language -- beyond word or form. Experiencing all communication as a pulsating vibration of energy and light, there was no doubt as to when and where I was taken for I understood the language. This was the frequency my physical body was being prepared to receive. Telepathy in its raw state is like electricity without wires or telephones without receivers. The time was two thousand years ago -- the place at the foot of the cross. I clutched the legs of Jesus in my arms. In His final moments, His blood mingled with my tears. I screamed with His agony as my own, as if He were my flesh, my soul in ultimate compassion. Pierced by the excruciating pain of my heart breaking in two from depth of grief beyond anything I thought mortally possible.

Screams unlocked from eternity. The sound of my sorrow traveled the space-time barrier, abruptly breaking into the silence of the room. My body fell to the floor as the life force returned. I knew not for how long I lay there.

Then Peter's voice. "Don't you all want to touch her?" Yes, please touch me. Now in a state of ecstasy, I felt an intense white light radiating out from me, and I wanted to share its healing powers with everyone -- the girl with cancer, the mongoloid child. To heal all wounds and judgments. Warm hands came down, covering my closed eyes, blanketing my body, sharing the light. Finally, a helping gesture brought me upright. Gradually the room came into focus; Anne was the first I cast my glance upon. She turned away. Peter observed it all as a detached third party. As I scanned the room, each embarrassed face withdrew from my gaze. Only one young girl knowingly smiled back. She too had a light around her. I didn't understand.

Surely being in the same room at the same time, they must have experienced Him too. Did they not speak the language? Was I sprinkled with ruby dust and they saw only red sand? In the flash of revelation a great lesson was burned into my soul. We're like little computers, programmed in our DNA of what we know and who we are. Individual truth is the reality to a particular moment in time, perceived through singular con-sciousness and therefore as we grow, always in a state of change. How fickle truth! We're all drowning in our own knowingness. But if we come from so many different realities, so many different truths, how do we ever communicate? Can we bridge the gap to avoid inadequate and impoverished views of reality?

Peter asked Jonah, his personal aide to help me back to my cabin. The night air was fresh, Jonah's arm reassuring. "Do you see that?" Excitedly I pointed to a **red light** that was blinking on and off quite near us in the sky, then a **blue** light. But his reality of that moment saw no red or blue light: he simply held my hand tighter, leading me up the path to the bath house. Sense of the surreal surrounded me as a dog walked by caressing my leg. As I looked down and placed my hand on his coat to return the affection, before my eyes and to my touch, he became a lamb. Slowly beginning to understand the need to protect my credibility, I didn't mention it to Jonah for this was my movie, a private showing.

"Leave your clothes on the chair and lie on your back." He pointed to the massage table and tried to show a professional care in his voice. Disoriented, he helped me undress. Uncertain as to his intention, I thought it must be fine since Peter instructed him. Still in a much altered state, I followed by rote. Jonah's strong healing hands kneaded my body and urged the soul to return to its temple. Using a tantra yoga technique, he began to simulate my sexual parts in an attempt to raise the energy upward, totally impersonally, simply as an accommodation to assist me. Before my closed eyes passed a blurred image of those contorted Indian stone figures. They understood the connection of sex and spirit. I responded, the energy building as it traveled up the spine until the point of release. At that moment, my entire body turned rigid. Re-entry had occurred.

It was a deep sleep this night, although I have no recollection of how I got into my bed. . .only a feeling of **missing time**. But somewhere in that heavy slumber was a vague dream that had haunted me as a child. But why did it reoccur this night?

> **Terrified I go into the closet to hide. I climb through a trap door in the floor and follow a tunnel down into the bowels of the earth. At the bottom is a tank, I get inside, not breathing. . .finally I'm safe. . .from what I do not know.**

Avoiding the morning activities, I wandered through the gardens. An early morning summer rain surfaced all the smells. I inhaled the odor of wet redwood. Yet a tremendous sadness burdened me, for this connection to a higher dimension was at great expense, feeling cut off and separate from the others.

On a bench placed inconspicuously under a tree off the path, I sat alone. Rama came and rested beside me after drying a spot. He smelled of frankincense and myrrh. His strength brought out my weakness and the tears came.

"I feel so isolated. I don't understand. All of us came here in anticipation of a spiritual experience and I've definitely been touched. Not only is it unrecognized, but I'm treated as though I've had a psychotic breakdown!"

Rama, cloaked in his Indian wisdom, answered with a quote from Kahil Gibran. "For that which has remained unknown to all men for an aeon may be disclosed to one man in but a moment." Thank God for Rama. Night brought with it yet another portentous dream.

> I'm high on a hill, but can't get down. The Mountain has turned to mud; it's everywhere. I ask Sam what to do -- "You'll never get down through this mess!" I turn to Sydney. "Let's see, logistically it might be best to stay where you are!" "Peter, what do you think?" "What mud?" . . .I'm left holding onto the down side of up.

On the last day at Paradise Ranch, I said my goodbyes. When I approached Peter he casually turned and walked away. Why would he do that? How could he let me go without explaining everything? I felt crushed -- surely, this was his mystery lesson, teaching me not to give away my power -- not even to him. Reassured by my understanding of his reality, I walked the grounds giving a silent prayer of thanks for all I received. *Suddenly, the energy* began to subtly shift, as though coming to say goodbye. This time not audibly as the *voice* had been not another space-time frame, but now, thoughts simply made their impression telepathically, through vibration and light of wind passing between trees giving them speech. I was being opened even more. Veils that stand between the known and unknown limiting conscious thought were lifted giving me sight to wisdom. Everything is but a reflection of a reflection. The Universe is but a mirror. This is how your own thoughts create your own reality. Like throwing a rock in a clear pool of water, the ripples tell the tale. And having thrown you must be responsible for the wake the rock creates. And so, if everything is a reflection of a reflection, then the prudent way to change things around you is 'to be' and reflect who you are and 'never be concerned with or seek to control the effects of your influence.'

Our beliefs are the tempest in the storm, simply reinforcing themselves with themselves.

I stood in the wind, looking up at the sky. "Why me God? Why not a superstar like Barbra Streisand? She's Jewish too. Or better yet, Mother Teresa? Oh well, I guess God can cast his own story. But who am I supposed to be? What am I to do? Why was I chosen with all of my faults?"

Deep down, something inside me knew, for I understood the purity of my own heart. My life's adventures stirred up the muddy waters, but couldn't hide the gold beneath. . . We are forgiven by our ability to forgive. What we can't forgive, we become! So the first must be self, else we project our own judgment.

Chapter XII

Forever changed by *the energy* that touched my soul, there was no going back, never to deny what I now knew. A vital expectation exceeded my former faith, now etched by experience. This altered state had thrust me beyond the threshold, from the misty into the mystic.

Radiating light and feeling weightless, no longer earthbound, I left Paradise for New York to meet Sydney on his return from England. Peter left Los Angeles where Anne had scheduled him as a guest speaker. He and Anne had become confidants -- she mesmerized by his enormous power, he smitten by her upfront charm. But far more important to him was her influence in the New Age arena and the hundred thousand people Sydney had trained.

Men who work for God don't usually have the luxury of living in affluence, so I invited Peter and staff as houseguests. Thinking of Peter getting his stomach behind the wheel of my white Jaguar provoked a laugh.

Sydney's New York hotel apartment looked more charming than ever to new eyes. Even frenetic vibrations of the city didn't penetrate the protective shield that seemed to engulf me, as though in a womb. The afternoon gave time to arrange for Sydney's night arrival. Everywhere, I placed gardenias, nature's

aphrodisiac. Inhaling a gardenia is a way to make a blind man
see the sunset.

Sydney would be the first person to tell about my experience,
I lay waiting. All my deepest thoughts of life and relationship,
I had shared with him. Often I went beyond my own
knowledge as if a greater force were feeding me profound
wisdom just to fill him. Usually, the next time I would hear
him speak publicly, my words would have become his own,
affecting so many. Of course he was the perfect one to tell
about Paradise -- probably through Sydney, it would be
shared with the world!

The hour was late when I finally heard the key turn in the
latch. Stretching to arouse my body from light sleep I had
fallen into, I called out, "Darling is that you?"

"Hello Mary!" His voice wasn't simply cold, but carried
disturbance mingled with doubt. As enormously sophisticated
as he was, his boyish qualities made hiding his feelings
impossible. His training not only encouraged expressing but
confronting issues. "I stopped by the office on the way from
the airport and had a long talk with Anne on the telephone."
Like a dam that burst his voice flooded with emotion. "What
happened Mary? Do you know that Anne and Peter think
you're crazy?"

Pierced by betrayal, certainly Peter can't believe that,
assuring myself it must be a type of mystery school teaching he
set up to put me through a few loops. Peter could make us all
dance orchestrating chaos to promote growth. Quickly the
drama thickened. Not to get caught up in it was a forced
conscious decision. A better seat for the performance was
certainly from rafters looking down -- the perspective less
limited than being a performer on stage.

I switched on the light. Sydney's clothes were wrinkled and a
grey shadow covered his face -- emotion had taken him beyond
caring about the perfection of form.

"Mary, you look different, more beautiful than ever." he

said wonderingly. "I rediscover you each time I look in your eyes." Then he buried his face in my lap and revealed the source of a deeper hurt. "Anne also said you were having an affair with some young guitar player."

My mind instantly replayed Anne and entourage approaching the hot tub -- John and I bathing nude. All of her telephone calls . . . they were reports to London! Only three weeks had passed since Anne sent me roses endorsing my credibility! Hanging out in the rafters without a script wouldn't be easy.

Sharing Sydney's personal pain, I put comforting arms around him. "Darling, what happened to me has nothing to do with anything mortal." My words went unheard offering no immediate sense of relief to his suffering for whether man or God -- something had come between us.

"Please let me tell you what happened, though I realize it may be difficult to understand." Pausing, I said a silent prayer. "Mostly you call on memory of experience to relate to something, but if you never heard a sound, how could you understand the majesty of a Bach fugue?" My voice carried a personal plea. "Please my dearest try to rise above what it is you think you know, to possibilities of other dimensions." Slowly unfolding my extraordinary tale, I formed the words, grounding the energy for the first time.

He sat stricken. Any cosmic spiritual talk had been always considered 'airy-fairy' -- now his pragmatic, horizontal reality was precariously jeopardized because of his love and trust of me. He tried to pull himself together. After all, I was still the same person he had asked to manage his life. "Don't worry Mary, it'll all work out."

I felt Jake patting my head in the hospital telling me, "It'll all work out." Then he died. And Esther's last words as she walked out the bathroom, "It'll all work out," before her final slam of the door. How will this work itself out?

Sitting on the bed, he used his body to maneuver a lying position, assuming that making love could heal all wounds. I still deeply loved him, but had not the need to express it personally. With compassion reserved for the most delicate situations and clarity of delivery, I explained my feelings. "This union with God is so new and full, I'd feel like an adultress having a physical relationship with a man." Saying these words, I realized the impact and separation they created. Sydney pierced by the sharp edge of my words began to weep as we lay in each other's arms, our tears flowing into one another.

Reality of the morning rang out loudly. Anne was reporting, spreading more tales of me and also that she was scheduling a series of guest seminars for Peter. "You could have asked me first! That's like putting Dracula in charge of the blood bank!" He slammed the receiver down. Before tea this was too much, fury set in. I watched him, his hand always a dead giveaway as it made a fist so tight his knuckles turned white. "Is everyone being mesmerized by this spiritual Svengali? Just who the hell is Peter Samuels anyway to have such influence over you and now Anne?"

How could I explain that Peter was my conduit to Spirit. The bridge connecting Sydney and me weakened and tears washed it away. It would be difficult to continue on together through so much pain of letting go -- or was the pain from trying to hold on. The intensity seemed to increase in proportion to the resistance against it.

That night we accepted a dinner invitation aboard a lovely yacht, including an after-dinner cruise of New York harbor. Among the guests was John Irvin, an associate of Manly Hall's. With an odd professional dichotomy, he was a distinguished lawyer and knowledgeable metaphysician. He took my hand in greeting momentarily ignoring all others and with knowing eyes smiled, as if acknowledging a brother in a secret fraternity. Had my initiation allowed entry?

We talked only briefly, but he promised to send a poem he

had written that reminded him of me. I felt reassured -- there must be others out there who understand.

Stars, moon and warm summer breezes added to my romance with a higher dimension, but left Sydney even more frustrated and abandoned. Seeking refuge from the after-dinner smoke, I carefully maneuvered on deck hearing Sam's voice in my memory, "hold on to the stanchion." -- The time we spent memorizing *Royce's Manual* to learn all the sailing jargon. My smile turned questioning, what will Sam think of all this? Sitting alone on the bow, I surveyed the skyline parading by. A shift of density in the air occurred. *Suddenly without warning, the energy* was back, once again infusing my being. The black night created an astonishingly dramatic backdrop for tall skyscrapers and thousands of sparkling lights. Just as San Francisco had been brought to its knees, now New York's destiny too was devastation. Was the city acting out its own fate in front of my eyes? Present and future mingled together? Streaking terror in the night, I watched as it came crumbling to the ground, in soundless fury, uncertain if created by a freak of nature or mistake of man -- like an earthquake setting off a nuclear reactor. My mind unable to fathom the depth of horror. Time stood still waiting for me to catch my breath . . . Thankful for being alone, I remained on the bow until I could manage the precarious journey back to the cabin, using the Twenty-third Psalm as my crutch. No need to tell Sydney for he couldn't hear it -- a lesson I was to learn well. No need to wonder who to tell, if they're not to know, their computers simply reject.

Feelings of isolation worsened -- time to go home and begin a new life. Peter left Los Angeles before I returned to investigate land in Kentucky to father a new community. A special place, like unto an Essene community of two thousand years past -- a place of peace and love where a Christed being could be born and nurtured. Each time I listened to Peter speak my heart longed for such a place.

I seemed as a stranger in my own home, everything so grand. A diminished sense of ownership, less personal attachment pervaded me, similar to my new feelings about Sydney. Even my own precious children were now more God's children. No matter how uncomfortable I knew I had to tell Sam. As a good Jew it would be difficult for him to accept an experience of Christ as anything short of blasphemy. He would never allow a Christmas tree in the house and now maybe not even the mother of his children.

"I'll spare you the specifics other than referring to them as extraordinary mystical experiences. Now, I need to go out in the world and be of service."

Sam was uneasy, lighting a cigarette gave him time to think. He twisted his moustache. Now lined and heavy, his handsome face turned white computing the information as to how his own life might be affected. I held my breath; he was still able to manipulate the purse strings since alimony and child support provided considerable padding to my financial security. After calculating the information, "I think it would be good for you Mary, really good to explore your talents publicly . . . "

The rest was easy to read. The time was convenient for him to take the children for a year, being in between relationships and lonely. "I think we'll live out of the city for a year, in the country somewhere. I could even buy a horse, great private schools, skiing . . . they'd love it!"

Part of me wanted to go with them. Personal life, personal questions. Now that I was in the pot, someone began stirring the stew! Alexander and Tara may be God's children, but a mother's womb never forgets. Sam was more heavily into drugs than ever. Could he really take care of them? Or maybe it was their turn to take care of him? A weekend father all those years -- perhaps reversing roles could be a key to understanding each other's joys and pains and lay to rest having to punish one another. Peter's words echoed in my mind, "you must place everything personal on the altar." But dear God my children?

And so it was a time of letting go of my personal life, with everything moving so quickly I gave no thought to the wake left behind. Word spread like an infection. Even my family thought the devil had its due -- a Jew for Jesus! How they package their narrow understanding! Particularly incensed, Eve's reality was threatened and needing defending. "A Jewish mother would never abandon her children!" Was her righteous cry a way to manipulate the situation through my guilt? My action gave her opportunity to have a common enemy with Sam, a neurotic mixture of hostility and compassion. Esther who wasn't speaking to me anyway, now had extra ammunition to build up her arsenal, if only to be used in further retreat.

Staff from the fellowship shared my house as I put my organizational skills to work -- an operation to promote the prophet in Peter, while Peter reaped the profit. Rama returned home with exciting news; Peter had found the perfect land in the Blue Mountains of Kentucky. That night after dinner Rama spoke passionately of our community. "Peter is a great prophet with a special mission in our own time. This is not just another spiritual community. It is a commission from God!" His voice commanded authority. "A Christed being will be born and this will be his home. It's part of Divine Plan! But we must have seed money to begin. We need wisdom to understand this mission along with tremendous courage to carry it out!"

Rama's fiery words burned through me. Surely this must be the seeding of my experience -- to help give birth to this community. "How much do we need to put down on the land?"

"At least twenty-five thousand dollars."

Excited at the rightness of financial sacrifice for the altar, here was a way to externalize my commitment. This must be why I needed courage. My heart responded. "I'd feel blessed to give the seed money for the community."

Rama agreed. "My dear Mary you must be blessed, it is you who have received the gift. For to be allowed to mother this community is a sacred task!"

"I'll have to take out a second mortgage until my house sells. My one request is that the donation be kept secret." The reason had dual meaning, expressing my understanding of humility at the time, as well as fear of Sam finding out. "It may be morally backward, but our affluent society, especially in this city of illusion can easily accept twenty-five thousand being spent on drugs, travel or any other indulgence in desire, but give it away or try to create a better world, surely would be cause to have somebody lock me up." Rama acknowledged with a smile this sad state of humankind and agreed to keep my secret.

Contact with Sydney was confined to the telephone making letting go easier. All wasn't heavy. Even Sydney saw a lighter side and called to tell me. "You must go see the movie, 'Oh God!' You and John Denver have a similar problem."

Too intrigued to wait, that night Rama and I went to take in Hollywood's version of the mystic . . . The crowd large enough to run into old friends and dense enough to get lost in if you chose not to. There was Jess still with a camera around his neck. The years brought a few extra pounds. His new lady clung to him as if each woman in the crowd were his prospective lover. Our eyes met for a long second, in the release both acknowledged no need for more. Five years with his demons provoking mine were enough. I said a silent prayer of thanks for release from that life.

"Hollywood" managed again to move tongue in cheek with creative ease. Driving home my enthusiasm overflowed. "What a joy to find a movie maker actually putting truth into a form people can hear, laugh with and begin to ask questions about. Humor's such a wonderful healing and non-threatening way to learn." Laughter brought me to thoughtfulness. "He was so funny going to a newspaper trying to convince them that God spoke to him."

Benevolently, Rama injected. ". . . Positively diminishes one's credibility factor."

"Of course, in a movie, the audience is easily on the hero's side being a voyeur to his experience. It's quite another matter when you're the only one privy to it. How can you convince anyone else?"

Rama's wisdom surfaced without effort. "What foolishness to try! It's presumptuous and egotistical! If your reality is more expanded it is you who must be more responsible and speak to their understanding and subtly inject a new idea into their frame of reference." He smoothed the folds in his sand colored shawl.

We drove in silence. Turning into the driveway, I postscripted the last thought for the evening. "No wonder ignorance is bliss. You don't have to be responsible for what you don't know!" We walked the yellow brick road to the house.

With each day that passed, I longed to make contact once again with *the energy*, to deepen my understanding of what it all meant and what I should do next. One thing was certain even in Hollywood you don't go to the newspapers. I was convinced that only Peter in a state of trance, could tap into *the energy* again and explain what happened to me. Peter was my conduit. But unfortunately for now, he had gone off to Europe raising donations for the land.

My need was immediate. Two years before at Crystal's insistence, I visited a psychic named Maria Pappas. Beyond her gypsy fortune teller appearance there lay unique powers. UCLA's parapsychology department rated her abilities as high as any Russian counterpart. Certainly, in two past readings she had given me many predictions already came to pass, including meeting Sydney and details about my house situation. Concerning my spiritual life her channeling was always specifically vague, saying that my body was being prepared for something. Cells were being rebuilt and altered, but I was not yet ready to understand. Perhaps now I was.

Driving up in front of Maria Pappas' house, I reminded myself not to tell anything of my experience allowing only her input. Her's was an unpretentious home on the exterior, but the inside -- adorned with enough paraphernalia to expose her flamboyant Greek nature and deep religious beliefs.

Introspectively, I waited in a small dark room until she entered. Then spending no time whatsoever in personal greeting, she sat down to face her subject. Behind her on the wall hung a photograph, the white marble *Pieta*. My mind flashed back to St. Peter's Cathedral where I first saw The Mother holding her Son's broken body. Somewhere in the archives of eternity was written my understanding of the pain of it. Oh God, it's all unfolding! She asked for some personal object; I took off one diamond stud earring I always wear, a present from Jake and Lenore on my twenty-first birthday. Long brightly painted red nails reached out, gently rubbing the object between thumb and index finger, eyes closed as if answers were contained within the diamond. Turning the tape recorder on, she began with a prayer. I silently added my own -- that *the energy* use Maria Pappas to speak the truth and help me understand.

"The Mother energy has been trying to reach you. I can see her holding you, your dark red hair against her white shawl. She's making a promise to you. 'What you have done for my Son, Mary, I am eternally grateful. I will be with you always.'"

I was overwhelmed . . . My dream on that Easter night . . . the Bar Mitzvah . . . *Jesus of Nazareth.*

Moments passed, her eyes remaining closed, then she spoke. "I can't grasp what it is they're trying to tell me." She sat for another minute listening, her head shaking as if the message were beyond comprehension. "This is what they say on the other side. '*You're pregnant!*'" Her voice slowed down in a reverent tone, her head still shaking in disbelief with a question, "*Pregnant by immaculate conception . . .?*" She repeated, this time the doubt had vanished. "Pregnant by immaculate conception!"

Struck by the vibration in the room that had become so

intense, my skin tingled, the hairs on my arms standing upright. "No, no, it can't be. You don't understand. I had some extraordinary mystical experiences, but the pregnancy is only symbolic. It has to do with my seeding a community!"

"No my dear, it is you who do not understand. There is to be a physical manifestation! They have been preparing you from the other side for a long time. I've told you this before. The cells have been altered, the DNA restructured."

After the reading which lasted an hour, Maria Pappas walked me to the door. I was in a state of shock. Obviously the channel misinterpreted the reading. I couldn't be pregnant. Using all the gypsy in her soul, she penetrated my eyes. "I feel very blessed that spirit used me to give you this message. God bless you my dear!"

Driving home was difficult. The jolt had numbed my body. My hand moved over my stomach as thoughts poured in. Listening intensely, I replayed the tape of the reading again and again. Yes it was true, the Mother energy had definitely touched me, but what was she trying to tell me? First, with the automatic writing, *Virgin Mary, Earth Mother.* Then the meaning of the Immaculate Conception told by the *voice* in my ear, after that a seed was placed on my tongue, an annunciation, a visitation, a mystical marriage. Finally, I experienced the pain of a son dying on the cross. But now, this was too much; it couldn't be possible! Could it be possible? Oh my God!

Once again, there was no one I could tell. Never have I been in such an alone place-isolated with my knowing. Conversations back and forth with myself continued to clutter my mind. A small voice inside kept gnawing at me. "Yes, it must be true." Instantly repudiating the answer. "What colossal presumption!" My mind conjectured what Mary the mother of Jesus felt, most assuredly it was humility, not presumption. Would anyone believe me?

Total confusion set in . . . a week of inner turmoil passed.

Another friend brought a well-known psychic healer to town. An expert in herbology, Stewart Wheelwright had lived all over the world with primitive tribes, learning intuitive and mystic healing techniques passed on by folklore. I had an appointment for a private health reading made weeks before.

The large room was full, the audience acknowledging his introduction as I arrived. In the telling of his background he shared having lived with lamas in the Tibetan Himalayas. "Like a fine instrument their highly tuned awareness announced when a High Lama was to be born. The mother was always looked after lovingly. Each day she would receive a massage, carefully stimulating every energy point in her body and after the baby was born, he too, received the same care. These nurtured infants grew into their birthright with never an IQ under two hundred." The body, mind and spirit inspired through loving touch -- incredible! With all the subjects he could choose, why was he talking so specifically about mothers of destiny's children?

After his talk the group thinned out and private interviews began. Interestingly all of us waiting to see him were allowed to observe the others. His unusual and fascinating techniques enthralled me. This type of unorthodox medicine was so often a last resort, with many very sick children brought by anxious parents hushed by his compassion. The children's reactions were the most obvious; their pain impossible to hide . . . their healing so joyously expressed.

My turn. This large lumbering man with such a gentle touch took my hand. His kind face broke into an easy grin and I felt assured. First he examined my eyes with a light and magnifying glass, as the chiropractor had so many years before. Then something unheard of to me, he studied the soles of my feet. "You have pretty feet my dear." Sam always called them little peasant feet next to his superior long tapered ones. "It's not so strange that feet give the map of life's entire journey. This sole simply tells the story of the other soul. Kind of *the down side of up*, you know -- the microcosm of the macrocosm."

His words sent shivers through me; I just stared at him transfixed. My own discovery in the up and down search for a teacher in the desert! And so similar to those words given me through wind and trees on my final morning at Paradise. Each time my understanding crossed a new threshold. Did he know? Or was *the energy* speaking through him to me that I might recognize the truth in what he said? What else did he know or transmit, this unusual man? The others in the room, as if watching a magic show were totally left out of what came next. Leaning over, he embraced me and whispered in my ear.

"You know my dear that you're pregnant and it's very, very special!"

I went limp in his arms, with a whisper, "It's not possible!"

He smiled and lightly kissed my cheek. "God bless you dear one."

All alone, every second filled with memories of Paradise and now a new dimension exploded in my thoughts. Could these experiences have produced a result other than spiritual? Was it really possible that the seed actualized into physical manifestation? It's impossible! Well, if man had learned the technique of artificial insemination -- certainly God knew. I checked the calendar. Things moved so fast these last few weeks, I forgot to mark my monthly cycles, but positive my period had come at least once since I'd been with Sydney last. My practical side wasn't totally malfunctioning, although it appeared on a slight sabbatical.

Still not willing to confide in anyone at this point, I searched the Yellow Pages for a women's clinic. An appointment was set, the first available that afternoon. During the drive there, I played the tape of Maria Pappas' reading over and over. A battle waged between those two parts of me -- the one who knew the truth, and the other who preferred not to know. I arrived feeling war-torn.

The lab test was immediate. Science bridged the gap into the mystic. I was indeed carrying a child!

Chapter XIII

The puzzle gained a few new pieces, but empty parts were still blatantly missing. The wake created in letting go of the personal was a ripple compared to the tidal wave that my new physical condition would create. Eve had been especially upset about the house and children, spreading her persuasion to waiting ears. She was just trying to protect me, she said -- maybe so. Her sensitivities found some truth in the new me creating a touch of conflict, but an old sense of righteousness easily won. Rama tried to reason with her, but Eve interrupted.

"Whatever's going on here doesn't look right. Something's got a hold on my sister. I don't like to say this, but either she needs intense therapy or commitment!"

The gossip came full circle when Eve's best friend telephoned in a cascade of accusation. "How could you abandon those gorgeous children? But maybe it's better than raising them as Christians!" Defense was unnecessary for the receiver slammed down as a gavel . . . the indictment also final judgment. For any mother to love her children more than I was inconceivable to me. To be so misunderstood pained me deeply. The news spread like unwanted testimony thanks to family and friends. Now what would they do with this new information should they ever find out?

My diary seemed the only place to pour out my heart . . .
"Oh God why have you blessed me so then placed me in
the misdst of shadow? Do all people wear blindfolds? Even
those who go one step beyond, is their sight still bound?
Perhaps life gives them a taste of experience widening their
perspective. Ah-ha! Now they think they see; they understand!
What grand presumption is this? Sometimes, our view
expands to one hundred eighty degrees, then we become
even more dangerous. Knowing everything before us in our
sighted domain. Many teachers settle in at this way-station.
But oh Blessed One, you have tapped me on the shoulder
and turned me around, so I see the horizon continues, that
on the other side of one hundred eighty degrees is its
reflection creating a full circle. We mortals so limited by our
knowing, see only *the down side of up*. I fall to my knees in
humility at the awesomeness of this universe. Stripped of
my knowingness, I feel as a child. This is the beginning."

People constantly came through the house on the pretext of
being potential buyers, but mostly to get a glimpse of what
mystery lay behind the cracked garden wall. Now I faced an
enormous complication. Rama listened to my problem.

"How can I get a second trust deed to cover the twenty-five
thousand dollars pledged to the community without Sam
finding out? I didn't realize he co-signed my loan to buy the
house from Esther, which means they'll surely notify him
about a second. All this covering up is so distasteful."

My humble attempt to be the driver halted by controls still
manipulated from the back seat. The loan finally came from a
small mortgage company that didn't ask questions, but the
payments were enormous and pressure to sell was closing in.

'West Coast Coordinator' was my title, whose pomp didn't
match the circumstance. The meager pay barely covered
feeding and housing my new comrades. Thrilled to work in
service for God, I projected a visionary but practical plan to
expand and promote Peter. With each giant step, others saw

me as increasingly more controlling; for accustomed to tiny steps, they were now being forced to run. Misunderstood again.

The drama intensified. Each night prayers asked morning to bring some supporting piece to fill in my puzzle. Let clarity come over me like a soothing hand and courage be injected directly into my soul. Not just for me, but how could I protect my loved ones from their own misunderstanding? The first question of course would be, who is the father? Everyone would assume Sydney. Smiling at the irony for I set the fire that burned that bridge. And my mother -- the news of a fatherless child would kill Lenore! Worst of all, how could I explain it to Sam and the children? I lay holding my stomach to protect it from all negative thought.

All my life has been the perfect result of the world of form; now form reversed itself playing havoc with me. Reminding myself over and over what the *Course of Miracles* taught—this material world is all an illusion. "Everything I see has only the meaning I give it." How can I have one meaning and everyone around me another? How can I make them see the ruby dust?

Conflict between meaning of what my soul knew as truth and mortal fuss it would create began to act out in my body. Now, I was caught in the abyss. What irony! High fever and vomiting plagued me. I attempted to hide under cover and make the world go away. What was I doing to myself? Surely, conflict is man-made like smog. Longing to return to that dimension where fear and struggle had no existence, I pleaded, take me. Death had no threat for me, the other side was truly heaven -- just waiting in the wings.

Maria Pappas' final words had been repressed, now the memory of them replayed through my mind. "If you're not ready, it will be taken away!" A knock at the bedroom door brought me back. Jonah had been staying at the house nursing his hostess, but the homeopathic remedy he prescribed worsened my condition. Belladonna, a toxin, was administered in infinitesimal doses -- a poison to kill a poison was the theory behind homeopathy. An odd mystery lesson here. I continued my own remedy, gallons of chicken soup to quench the fever and maybe, a little to remind my body it was still Jewish.

The rain beat heavily on the skylight. While sitting on the edge of my bed, Jonah began to massage my hand. He, like many who follow a teacher, seemed to be missing that part of himself laid at the foot of the guru. At least, the role of healer had a humanizing effect on that robot quality.

"Oh that feels sooo good." My words elongated as they melted with his touch.

His gaze distanced. "Paradise Ranch seems so long ago."

"Not when the memory is a constant companion. My faith knows that even though I can't feel or see *the energy,* it's still there, like electricity in a wire, waiting for the switch to be turned on."

Jonah continued the massage as I took a leg out from under warm cover when the telephone intruded loudly. "To be continued," he promised as he left the room. This was the call I dreaded. Picking up the receiver I silently prayed that he would really hear me.

Sydney's tender voice exposed that wonderfully vulnerable part of him. "How's everything going Darling? Are you all right?"

"When you call me darling like that everything turns warm. I've something very important to tell you." I hesitated. "Remember in New York when I shared my experiences with you, I said that it would require stepping beyond what you knew, into the possibilities of another dimension? Now my dear one, I'm going to ask you to stretch your imagination even further." I paused and took a deep breath. "Sydney, I'm pregnant -- pregnant by Immaculate Conception . . . "

He didn't hear. I could feel his knuckles clenching over the wires pushing hysterical energy up and out through his voice. "Jesus Mary, my TV show is previewing next month. I'm scheduled for Johnny Carson. The first thing he'll ask me about is my illegitimate son!"

Strange thing human nature, it always surfaces the survivor when put to the test. Each creates his own little play and boos the villain who comes to threaten his production.

"Oh Mary what have they done to you?"

You can trust the world to make any truth wrong if it doesn't fit the script. "Try to understand Sydney. You are not the father! All I ask is your support as a friend." I promptly changed the words around to make certain he didn't mistake my plea as a financial request. This was too sensitive a button. He managed a temporary calm. "Please Sydney, don't tell anyone. We both need time to think."

My mind drifted in and out, fickle with my thoughts. How can anyone feel so blessed and so confused at the same time? I must speak to Peter. Passionately desperate to reach him and running into bureaucracy, I tracked Rama down. He was on a lecture tour in the Midwest and my telephone attempts finally succeeded. Sharing specific details of my experience never seemed to matter with Rama, his senses went beyond form in which words were cast. "Rama, something has happened. Peter is the only person in the world who can help me. I must get a reading from him." My voice carried frantic urgency.

"My dear Peter is somewhere in Europe. It's quite impossible. If you feel it's that important and can't wait, I am traveling with Joshua, a young man who has been training with Peter for several years, perfecting his own channeling abilities. He goes into hypnotic trance and can tap into the Akashic Records."

"But we're two thousand miles apart. Can he give me a reading long distance?"

"Mary, we're speaking of another dimension that knows not earth bounds. You must thoughtfully prepare your questions and when that's done, call me back. I will personally conduct the reading while he is in trance." A new calmness in my voice disclosed my thanks and a sense of relief at the thought of making contact again.

If I could speak directly to God and expect a response, what would I ask? What is my soul purpose in this life? What is the meaning of this pregnancy and how does it serve the Divine Plan? Who is the father of this child? What is my relationship with the Mother Mary and Mary Magdalene and why do I feel such a powerful connection to both? Rama took the questions without adding any of his own. The afternoon seemed endless, spending hours in meditation and prayer. I silenced any projection of outcome, while somewhere in the center of the country, my destiny was being revealed.

My hand rested on the phone prompting it to ring. Rama's voice with that proud Indian accent always made me think of a quiet pond, each word like a pebble cast creating clear-cut ripples. "I cannot speak of these things over the telephone. I will come to Los Angeles next week and bring you the tape recording of your reading." His voice became reverent. "All you need know is you truly are the most blessed woman on this planet." Placing the phone down, absorbed by the awesomeness of it all, I wept tears of humility and thanks.

The fever continued to plague my body, but my spirit was infused with new determination and support. Sleep would be easier this night. Clearing some confusion from my mind allowed a vivid dream to come . . .

> **A simple yet strong message explaining my emotional plight -- A cross. The vertical pole stands upright and firmly rooted, while the horizontal member seeks out its balance, tottering back and forth -- trying to come to terms with its center.**

Startled, I sat up in bed -- the night was still in the making. Of course, this is the meaning of the cross. The horizontal, material world must be in balance with the vertical divine reality or there's conflict. Somehow I knew survival depended on learning to live in that pivotal point in the center.

Endless week, snail-paced days . . . Sydney called sometimes twice each day wanting to know what I was going to do. Had I made a decision? But patiently, impatiently, I waited for Rama. My heart stopped as the doorbell rang remembering the first time this wise man entered my life. The smell of frankincense and myrrh announced him. Still maintaining his regalness, he wore a special garment trimmed in gold thread. Now he came to deliver a message about the child I carried. He was very concerned about my health, although excitement had brought a flush to my pale color.

We settled in the living room, warmed by the fire, with candles and incense appropriate to entertain the high energy expected to accompany the reading. My white caftan with silk embroidery was also befitting. Rama folded his shawl then placed *The Course of Miracles* on the table. He explained. "As the conductor, I began the inquiry, but the channel was not allowed to continue. We were told the nature of your questions was so delicate that before you would be allowed to hear the answers, you must first take an oath of commitment to God and the Divine Plan, for without this, the answers would have no meaning. At that point, I promised to receive your oath before you would be allowed to hear the tape."

How easy to say yes, like a marriage ceremony, one is overcome by the moment. Promises give meaning only as deep as the consciousness can bear. My commitment was given with pure heart, Rama satisfied, the tape began.

> The voice carried an impersonal monotone rhythm . . .
> "We have before us the records of the one, Mary Rosenbloom Golden. This one's part in the Divine Plan is a serious inquiry, one which requires commitment and responsibility."

A silent shadow slipped through my mind. Dear God, I haven't even read the Old Testament, let alone the New one!

"This one in the past has been many times the support system as wife or mother of great beings throughout your history. As in the time of David, King of the Jews, this one was Bathsheba, his wife. This union created a son, Solomon. Now this present life and time continues to work out this karmic triangle. Only the form and names have changed . . . Now Sydney, Mary and Peter. This is only one example of karmic pattern of relationship and is helpful to understand the lessons in present time yet unlearned and repeated life after life.

"This one before these records lived in that time of birth and resurrection of the Son. Known then as Mary of Magdala. 'She knew not, but on that day the sunset of "His" eyes slew the dragon in her and she became a woman.' After which time, she followed the Master and became his companion, as put forth in the *Pistis Sophia*. Your history has chosen to ignore the humanness of the man Jesus, known then as Yeshua. This is a mistake for there is much to learn from his struggle between awareness of who he was and why he came and its expression in your world of form.

"Together they knew the perfect love of soul for soul, though their loved remained unto themselves."

"Mary of Magdala in times to come will dwell in that maternal place in men's hearts. This is the wish of the Mother and Son."

"And so it is in this lifetime the one known as Mary Golden shall combine the energies of the two Marys. Mary Magdalene through Christ's forgiveness became the archetype for total commitment. And the Mother Mary, who represents for man complete compassion through love. These things are not yet fully manifested in this human. The waters are still muddy but beneath there is pure gold.

"Now as to the question of pregnancy. The seed was placed on the tongue, impregnating this being. It is to be thought of as an Immaculate Conception. There is no father on the earthplane. A most high being wishes to manifest at this time to be treated as though the very Christ were being nurtured in this womb. This one was chosen very carefully. The vessel has been prepared. The mother energy has been trying to make contact. It is unfortunate for the emotional human conflict, this need not be. It is simply mortal fuss."

The reading went on giving specific instruction for study and prayer in ancient scripture with Rama to aid me.

Click. The tape ended bringing us back to the living room. Still occupied with the magnitude of delivery, we sat in silence for a long while. My thoughts finally surfaced. "What would it look like if the whole cast of characters of two thousand years ago incarnated today? All changing roles -- like Pontius Pilate coming back as Jesus to forgive all judgments. What would they look like? Wearing long robes or Italian suits? What kind of work would they do? Would they be credible enough to be in the mainstream, to be on the Johnny Carson show? Is now the time to remember who we were along with knowing who we are? How would they be recognized, not only by others, but by themselves?

"If man has lost sight of who he really is, a God being, how can he recognize it in another? Surely I don't look like your everyday version of a virgin. And in Hollywood the great maker of images and illusions, one needs the proper packaging and marketing to make a star."

Rama sat listening then he grounded the spiritual reality in the present. "Ancient texts found with the Dead Sea Scrolls tell of seven women apostles. Mary Magdalene seems to have been His favorite. One of the apostles was always protesting why He kissed only Mary Magdalene on the mouth". Then he built a more scientific foundation bridging the mystical gap. "Parthenogenesis means 'virgin birth' in plants and organisms.

This has been known since classical times. Also *The Keys of Enoch**, a monumental work on the vastness of the universe, speaks of a seed planted on the tongue for a Christed energy to reproduce itself. Even dear St. Augustine wisely said, 'Miracles are not in contradiction to nature. They are in contradiction with what we know of nature!'"

"That's beautiful Rama, but truth can contort as it's acted out in this world of form. What profound irony in this cosmic joke, that God would choose a whore to conceive immaculately. It reflects man's own personal conflict -- wanting to respect a mother in the kitchen, but desiring to make love to a whore in bed. I've deeply experienced the pain of judgment and misunderstanding that comes with this duality. One can become a craftsman at this personal and archetypal weaving together!"

Past images flashed before me emphasizing, almost cataloging the set-up. Jake . . . my decision in that dark barroom about mothers and whores. Tahiti . . . the other side of the coin. Paris . . . the paradox of two Mary Goldens, Mary as mother, Mary as lover. A psychic reading . . . telling of my connection to Mary Magdalene. I couldn't hear it then. How much have I not heard? Not understood? Mary, Mary, who's Mary?

Now pieces of a more distant past puzzle shifted into place. Once, alone I frantically searched through my books, remembering years before after Tara was born being so captivated by *The Magian Gospel of Brother Yeshua**. Skimming it's pages, and that of the companion volume *Picture Windows on the Christ,** I realized that these had to be channeled works -- a story revealing the humanness of the man Jesus as told by Himself from the other side. Funny, I never realized that the first time. How many levels of understanding are there? Turning the pages looking for any reference to Mary of Magdala, my eye stopped, went back two pages and discovered it. He was speaking to her.

"Only one who knows all about love can satisfy a Son of

God. I know you love me. The world may never know, but in my eyes, and the eyes of God, you are my wife."

All levels of my being wept until there were no more tears. I slept. Fragments floated through my dream. The abyss, the black hole . . . to house all fault in my search for perfection. Sydney asking to keep secret our relationship. Deep sadness once again to keep my love secret. 'What keeps me from you,' the poem to myself. "I've been in love a thousand times. Been so close to it too. But whether it be this one or that, none of them were you." Oh Yeshua!

My prayers were answered through the reading and doubt lifted, leaving me the calming peace of no choice. Joyfully, I would have my child, live in the new community and all people problems would somehow be resolved. The instant of decision, my first challenge struck; Sydney called for the latest bulletin.

"You know how much I trust Peter. He's been my conduit to Spirit. I tried desperately to reach him but he was in Europe, so Joshua did the channeling for me. He works for the Brotherhood. I've just listened to his tape; Rama traveled across country to bring it to me." The calm clarity of my voice triggered Sydney's apprehension. "This is the third psychic who has confirmed again what I already knew -- I simply can't deny my own truth deep in my heart." The telephone wires relayed his anxiety as I continued. "It's beyond choice. I'm definitely going to have this child!"

Silence . . . then bombarded by need to protect his own reality, he defied my decision. "Mary do you know what this means, how it will affect your life and all of us around you? Think of your children!" He couldn't or wouldn't believe and his misunderstanding wounded me.

"If the world of money and fame force you to deny the mystic in yourself, how can I expect you to see it in anyone else? I'm so sorry my dear one. But I'm going to have this baby."

The mortal fuss created the human dilemma -- in our attempts to be understood ... and I had wanted *him* to share my spiritual experience with the world! Oh Sydney, Sydney wouldn't be. Sydney, Sydney denied the key.

Sydney didn't stop there. He betrayed my confidence. Next came a call from Helen. Gentle soul that Helen was, her persuasion at least compassionate and soothing; but I couldn't help wondering how much her concern was prompted by her own need to protect the first position as mother to Sydney's only child.

And then there was Anne. I should have known Sydney had to confide in all his women. Her tack -- typically confronting. "Mary, don't you think you're too old to have a baby? You're thirty-nine -- the chances are high he could be deformed!" I clutched my stomach to shield against her tirade. Anne surprised me by not questioning my menstrual cycles or accusing me of having slept with John ... and besides, God knows I'm thirty-nine!

Jonah brought in the morning mail. Just as he promised, a letter arrived from John Irvin the lawyer/metaphysician I met in New York. "How thoughtful, he kept his word." Recalling his knowing gaze as I opened the envelope, inside was a poem "An Ode to Mary Magdalene." Oh my God, did he really know?

There was also a letter from Jacqueline inviting me to Paris. The entire entourage was planning a holiday at the Club MED in Morocco and wanted me to join them. Can you imagine a combination of Paris and Tahiti? The thought of that lifestyle now, or better, if they knew mine, generated what I needed most -- a good laugh.

Ah, our world of man-made values! I could hear my mother, the kitchen philosopher saying -- "That's why there's chocolate and vanilla ice cream."

Sleep brought rest from mortal fuss and filtered past memories through my dreams.

> A desert scene in ancient time. I've been
> kidnapped by a band of Bedouins from my
> home in the Essene Community. On the horizon,
> vague from the ripple of rising heat, rode men
> on horseback. Rama leading the way was
> coming to save me. The escape led us to seek
> refuge in mountain caves. Within the dream,
> there was an overlay of present recognition.
> These were the same caves and location, seen in
> a documentary, where archeologists discovered
> the Dead Sea Scrolls, hidden there over two
> thousand years ago by the Essenes. "Why does
> he kiss only Mary of Magdalene on the mouth?"
> My sleeping mind tried to clean out cobwebs in
> the corners of ancient memory.

Clarity of past in dreams made the present turmoil unreal.
Sydney wouldn't rest. His protective anger that had devasted
Esther was again provoked. But now, a far more personal and
bitter attack came, long in the making. He placed a call to
Peter, catching him the night he arrived home from Europe.
His ensuing outrage was Peter's first awareness of Joshua's
reading. "How dare you be so irresponsible as to allow your
staff to support and indulge this kind of mystical madness!
How could Mary be carrying the Messiah? After all, we
thought you were!" No matter that Peter didn't know details
behind the harangue, Sydney's sarcasm riled him to fury as
they went at each other. Within privacy of the tent could
David and his son Solomon had fought over the mother? And
how I had dreamed of them working together. Through tears,
I turned my gaze toward the picture Peter had sent me of
himself as a child riding his pony.

Peter quietly ordered Joshua's reading stricken from the
Brotherhood files and demanded silence concerning any
discussion of it. Why did he do that? Peter must have a good
reason. The struggle between the two suggested need for each

player to protect his territory.

Lines were drawn -- now for mustering of armies. Even Generals had to be kept in line. This meant Peter needed to reprimand Rama, so now the wise man was placed in the humanness of conflict. And still, I remained -- caught in continuous crossfire. Friends like John followed their leader and distanced themselves from me as though I were afflicted with a spiritual disease.

The tension mounted for Anne had scheduled Peter to do a guest seminar with Sydney in New York -- and worse yet, to be his house guest. They met, the ground between them strewn with empty shells. With aid of an audience, the drama quickened and the stage soon a battlefield. Accusations developed into attacks. Words used as bullets bounced from protective shields -- all in the name of discussion on the "Responsibility of a Teacher."

After the public display, Peter, without returning to Sydney's apartment had his luggage removed and left immediately for Los Angeles.

Meanwhile as my guest, Peter wasn't asked to share the house, I was simply expected to move out. I didn't mind, for fever raged within me and to stay with Lenore would be so comforting. That afternoon, I sought refuge from the affluent noise pollution created by maid and gardener. I had wanted everything perfect for my teacher. Through all the recent turmoil, I hadn't seen him since we left Paradise. Each time a veil had lifted for me, he always made sure I went back to validate the lesson -- this was his mystery school. Learning wasn't easy, but perhaps neither was teaching. He was still the one human being I trusted to know truth.

Finally this day, I would receive Peter's confirmation and strength of his support. But it meant so much more to me -- knowing that at least one person on this planet understood what had happened, someone who believed me . . . and that might take another miracle.

Chapter XIV

The meeting with Peter changed my life.

Sam was flourishing as a live in father and eliminated all drugs and alcohol from his life -- it worked! I missed them more than I knew possible. And though my house was not yet sold, Lily Tomlin, the actress showed interest but made an offer which I refused. The next step seemed clear -- a move to the community.

There's a mystique and sense of poetry that blue mountains have as they surround and protect the Valley. Perhaps blue cast from the mountains mix with yellow of the sun to make the valley so green, meadows with proud stallions grazing, freshly painted white fences, a long road going up to the manor house lined with a hundred aged magnolias all in bloom, smells of pale honeysuckle and purple wisteria, and then the colonial mansion standing defiantly, longing to tell tales of the past. And there's something so southern about hearing a screen door slam out on the veranda that makes you thirsty for a mint julep.

Everywhere were sounds of hammering and smells of paint. One hundred and fifty residents each contributing something of themselves -- I felt proud to have seeded this.

My small, low-ceiling attic room in the ashram was shared

with two other girls. All three of us passed the prerequisite being under 5'5" to avoid eliciting the bends. Sparsely furnished in early Salvation Army, everything had a purpose to meet a specific need. I longed for this -- purity of a simple almost monastic life, stirred familiar feelings.

Much excitement brewed as preparations for a ten-day seminar finalized. The seminar on the cabala, astrology and tarot brought together over a hundred visitors from as far as Australia and Sweden. Peter's presence penetrated into the souls of many; but between us, a telepathic communication made our relationship special. Rama was here too offering the quiet strength of a spiritual pillar. He joked with me as I stood in the registration line.

"I'm going to keep an eye on you during meditation and my hand to keep you in your seat if necessary!"

Exhilaration generated a electricity in the air, settling as Peter started off with greetings and announcements. "Each night, instead of lectures, we will have an entertainment spectacular, performances to be given by that creative part in each of you. So search for what you do best."

Some irreverent remark turned my head, about Peter using the talent show as his personal platform to perform. My protective maternal instinct responded and righteously lashed out a piercing reprimand. "And why not, the man has extraordinary talents!"

Brilliance lay behind this staged mystery lesson. Amazing the internal challenge for everyone that this assignment caused -- a major confrontation with ego and fear. My mind instantly calculated the odds of fifteen minutes per person, for one hundred people over ten nights. Most likely time would run out before everyone performed; by waiting until the end to volunteer, I could possibly avoid exhibition.

As nights passed, the odds slimmed down and it seemed prudent to get something together rather than be caught actless. Some skits were quite ingenious as creativity in most stretched to new heights.

The tenth night brought mixed feelings for time had not run out. Deep down an old trooper dormantly waited to perform. Asking for a show of hands of those who had not yet shared, about ten hands lifted at half mast.

"Mary, you're on!" Peter called out. A sudden *deja-vu* flash of air raid and blackouts, Lenore and Jake, pink and black deco drapes -- made my heart pump in double time. I had planned the sequence with Jonah, who acted as stage manager. My goal was to tie the conference theme into the choreography. In the ancient Hebrew tree of life, the Cabala, Malkuth is the lowest point where physical energy lives. Through evolvement this energy rises to Tipareth, the pure heart. In astrology, Crystal had taught me years ago, a sign has many levels. When freed, my Scorpio base sexual nature could soar to the height of an eagle.

The lights went out. Jonah's melodic voice announced over the microphone. "Mary Golden in *The Dance from Malkuth to Tipareth* or *Scorpio Rising*. A whisper. "You're on Princess!"

A spotlight revealed me dressed all in black. As loud sensual music of *Saturday Night Fever* bombarded the senses at a primal level, my body responded with suggestive disco movements. Beyond the footlights, faces were distinguishable. My eyes scanned the audience instantly registering a common judgment. I felt thankful that Rama was absent this night. The women in their spiritual guise blushed and looked away. One who had been at Paradise turned to her neighbor apparently passing rumor with a righteous smirk. The men found it more difficult, but followed the female lead. Perhaps the same men who hurled foul words passing a brothel -- later slipping in the back door. Subtle negativity permeated the very air -- hardly, the 'Cousins Club.'

Childhood dancing allowed my mind freedom to escape

bodily confinement, dwelling in distant places and other times. Now, thoughts traveled from this pseudo-Essene community to the home of another Mary. Judgment was not a stranger there. Joseph her betrothed needed his own angel to announce the secrets of Mary's pregnancy before believing his young bride. Even the rabbis, whose lives were dedicated to nothing but the coming of the Messiah, had her cast out because of the presumption -- a dream of Christ becoming a reality within her mortal womb . . . Spinning around in dance, I felt the pain of stone-thoughts, stone-words and the first stone cast, thrown by a familiar hand; it was Sydney's.

The lights went out abruptly with the last beat of music bringing me to present. Now the spotlight returned to a new Mary all dressed in white. The poignant sound of *Pachebel's Canon* filled the room. Instantly, my body moved in rhythm and inspiration merging into the music's extraordinarily high vibrations. Remembering the feeling of hot sun, I closed my eyes and smelled the meadow and listened to the swing creaking as wind passed through the oak.

The dance of transcendence received mixed reviews. Another reason to be misunderstood . . . Who was this strange lady from Hollywood with a flamboyant style? My behavior was in sharp contrast to the low profile everyone thinks a higher life demands, for this spiritual mind-set has definite rules about what things should look like -- simple and demure. Outer design dismisses the magic and glorifies the mundane. Spirit follows form, just as much a prisoner of it as the material world. Definitely, this righteous group wouldn't recognize Christ unless he wore robes. Would they be first to cast a stone?

The conference ended and the month-long indoctrination program for new residents began. There were eight new people, all eager. Together we lived, working and studying from early morning to late at night, learning well the meaning of service. Joshua's reading had said I would learn about commitment by scrubbing floors in the Community. Commitment or penance, the work was more than I'd ever experienced stretching me out on the spiritual rack, as this little isolated ashram became the stage for a profound mystery school.

The pace intensified. Each person received an outside assignment. Given the prestigious job of decorating Peter's house, I was treated like a chosen one, not due to seed but rather coin. To make a beautiful home for Peter felt right, but I couldn't just drive to Decorator's Row on Robertson Boulevard. As Sam would have said, this was meat and potato country. Oh Sam, Sam, my gentleman. What are you doing right now? I closed my eyes and let his 'Aramis' scent wash over me.

For two hours each afternoon, I browsed through little antique stores filled with southern history. With his finished home, Peter could now pridefully demonstrate a more abundant approach to these people enchained in poverty consciousness, at my personal cost of seventeen thousand dollars.

My funding didn't stop there. Rama shared my genuine love for Peter and encouraged me. "Peter walks around with nothing in his pocket. Why don't you put ten thousand dollars in his personal bank account?"

I slipped comfortably into Esther's role. After all, why should a prophet be poor? Still living out a strong karmic memory, I needed to give to Peter and he countered with his own need to take.

My turn to be in charge of the kitchen and dinner was late. The menu varied from hor d'oeuvres to a carob souffle and special company had already arrived. Perspiration moistened my unmade-up face and a braid controlled my long dark hair. Riding on my hip, challenging all calmness was a ten month old baby left in my charge. A star struck voice announced through the swinging door, "Mary phone's for you. It's *Lily Tomlin*, the movie star!"

A futile attempt was made to put the baby down, but his cry demanded attention. He remained on one hip, leaning the other against the wall, I let out a sigh of thanks for the support.

"Yes Lily, how are you?"

"Mary I've just heard you sold my house! How could you do that?"

"Lily my lawyer tried to reach you for days. I wanted you to have the choice, but I've made a deal."

Lily's voice was sad, she loved the house as I did. "Listen Mary, if it's not too late I'll give you thirty thousand more!"

"I haven't signed anything yet, but I've given my word." The thought of all that extra money for the community tempted, but integrity wouldn't allow it. "Look the buyer hasn't signed anything yet either, why don't you offer *him* the thirty thousand? That way you both can win. Good luck, I hope you get it!" Feeling good about the decision, I hung up. Making real estate deals with super stars in a steaming ashram kitchen brought a smile in appreciation of paradox.

A final ceremony, a ritual of initiation, culminated thirty days of the servants' program. Preparation had the excitement of graduation complete with white gowns. With the chapel altar lovingly decorated with masses of white flowers, their aroma mingled with incense and burning candles -- the mood was mystical. The older community members swayed and chanted as the eight initiates were led to the altar. Peter began.

"Each of you must make a final commitment in service to God. All personal life end and material wealth placed on the altar." Even in the somberness of the moment, I smiled, imagining my fur coats amongst the flowers.

The community suffered from deep financial problems. In buying a piece of land far bigger than needed they assumed a debt greater than their ability to pay. Peter, a master at persuasion, was noticeably inadequate as administrator. Yet, power was relinquished only to people whom he controlled. On the board of directors besides Peter and Rama was Allan Chadwick, the community Master Gardener. Rama, although devoted to Peter, was not one to be ordered about. Allan

admired Peter but didn't like him and was idealistic and
stubborn -- not the correct combination for manipulation.
And so there grew three distinct camps in the community --
Peter's followers depending on his psychic channeling of the
Source, Rama's students looking for wise spiritual guidance
and Allan's gardeners who put their faith in the land.

As a young man Allan Chadwick had been Rudolph
Steiner's protege in bio-dynamics. Now in his late seventies,
Allan had gained a global reputation as the leading pioneer
horticulturist in methodology called the French Intensive.
Truly teaching about spirit through the understanding of
nature, he chose this particular community to live out his
dreams of a Garden of Eden. Tall and stately, the English
aristocrat and Shakespearian actor co-existed within a weather-
beaten exterior. He presented sharp contrast to the shorter,
stouter body Peter was forced to dwell in.

One might have thought, the donor of the seed money
would have been invited to sit on the board, but such was not
the case.

On this perfect warm day, I walked through Allen's garden.
Peter had sent word to meet him there. The orchards
abundantly mixed flowers and vegetables growing side by
side, plentiful enough to keep the hundred and fifty permanent
residents well fed. We strolled. Feeling a deep admiration for
so vital and healthy a garden, I stopped at one particular
flower, its aroma captivating me. Peter explained. "That plant
acts as a natural insecticide. The smell lures insects up the stalk
and intensifies at the top where the petals are activated by
touch, capturing its prey in a deadly grip." I shuddered.
"Something so beautiful and so lethal. Outrageous how nature
provides."

"Remember when you left Paradise Ranch, you came to say
goodbye and I acted as if you were invisible and walked away?
I wanted to discourage all personal thoughts you had about
me and maintain a student-teacher relationship."

We continued up and down the garden path. I smiled -- inwardly -- my personal thoughts or his personal thoughts? "Oh Peter, I thought you shunned me to let me feel the cutting edge of a potent mystery lesson -- Never give my power away, not even to you! Strange the individual intention almost doesn't matter the learning takes place at the level understood."

"You're wise Mary, I respect your judgment and need your help. You know the community is in deep financial trouble."

"Everyone knows about the problem; I've already given thought to a solution. You know it means more to me than just saving a project -- the whole concept is like my own child. Part of the difficulty is spiritual. There's such a deep rooted poverty consciousness here. People always asking for donations. That's like saying 'do it for me,' or expecting something outside of yourself to be responsible."

My entrepreneur experience with Sam came to my aid. "The first plan is to set up a limited partnership and sell portions of land to people who want to live here. Fill your need and theirs at the same time. That's real spiritual law -- everyone wins. I've already talked to different friends of mine with the kinds of expertise we need. They're willing to come to Kentucky, meet with the board and set a new direction."

"You're a strange combination of womanhood. I'm impressed."

I wondered what he really thought of me as rumors continued to keep me baffled, but my faith determined they were only teaching traps. One had to be wise and not too hungry to avoid snapping at his bait.

"But one thing Peter you must promise me, if I ask these people to help, you're obligated to listen."

"Set up the meeting as soon as possible and I'd like you to be there too Mary." Desire to keep the players happy usually kept my need to be acknowledged in tow, but I was grateful to be included.

Many of my close friends had expertise to save the community; beyond coincidence, perhaps group karma. The team included a lawyer, financial advisor, a Ph.D. in community planning and administration and Mark von Holt. As a writer in psychic research, along with his knowledge of community, Mark would be perfect to write the new by-laws.

Within one week, I managed to assemble the team in Kentucky. I paid for the tickets. And so began a five-day session of the board. We met in Peter's living room, the decor now as impressive as the assemblage. 'New servants' worked overtime to polish the black ebony furniture to mirrorlike reflections. Surveying the room, I thought surely these evolved beings could salvage the community -- a *deja-vu* feeling intertwined past and present -- perhaps another Essene community?

Peter graciously extended presiding reign of the meeting to Mark, who with a slight bow of the head acknowledged acceptance. Mark's manner as well as his clothes had gone from Protestant to Hindu. His hair was longer and glasses were replaced by secret sight of contacts. The package was made more attractive by his emerging maturity. Of course with Peter's mind being ten paces ahead of everyone else, I wondered exactly what his intentions were in giving up any authority.

After considerable rambling and feeling like a den mother, I made a suggestion. "If something's wrong in community, perhaps by understanding a portion, we can be more insightful about the whole. For example, there's hostility and rivalry between Peter and Allan that's creating a schism within the core. Let's see if we can begin by healing that!" My honest bluntness caused a deadly silence, but within that space, eyes darted around the room anticipating reaction.

My heros showed their feet of clay. Now with a total lack of communication and unwillingness to open this can of worms, I took a more personal tack, to light a fuse under hidden hypocrisy. "I can't understand you all!" My voice pleaded. "This is supposed to be as an Essene community full of love and peace to house a Christed being to come. Yet when one of your own had an experience not unlike that of the Mother Mary, instead of rejoicing, it was hushed and swept under the rug. The paradox here seems to reflect the same internal disorder in the community."

Rama bent his head as if in silent prayer.

Now even the darting glances stopped for fear of catching my eye. In finally expressing what had been eating at my soul, there came a peace to wash the wound. Peter called a lunch break. Walking out into the sunlight, Mark whispered in my ear. "So, you finally see that sacred cows have to shit too!"

By the third day all people problems had been sufficiently ignored and one basic reality remained to be dealt with. A payment came due on the land and the till was empty. Peter suggested, "We can go to the *Source*. I'll do a reading. If you all agree, we can reassemble later tonight. Through trance, we can get a higher perspective on the problem."

The Board meetings caused an even greater wedge in various camps. Gossip ran rampant -- everyone curious to know which of these men was my lover -- a celibate thrill. The emergency team went off to dinner. At a large round table in a funky Chinese modern setting, we over-indulged in oriental delicacies.

"And what do we talk about, food or sex?"

Mark wasn't amused. His researching mind grew stimulated by Peter's offer of a trance. Now mixing anxiety with determination, he planned, "After dinner, I'd like to examine the files on Peter's past readings to get a feel for his style. Then I'll prepare questions for tonight's channeling. The scientific method for research projects is to secure the questions in an envelope and once the channel goes into trance, the conductor opens the sealed questions and begins." Mark's new role as antagonist to Peter stirred protective overtones in me, like my children fighting. Immediately, I saw a deep conflict arising.

"You realize Peter always goes over the questions before trance and knowing him, he's going to take your scientific suggestions as accusation of fraud, very personally."

"Hey, I hear what he takes personally are all the young boys in his entourage!"

"Mark that's disgusting!" Rumors like these I choose not to hear. "He just likes being massaged."

Mark was adamant on his position to prepare the envelope. My feeling of impending disaster deepened.

Given the late hour some arrived in bathrobes accompanied by yawns. Anticipation coupled with mystery of a seance spiced the eerie flavor. The smell of cigar smoke turned my head, but no one was smoking. The old southern manor stairs creaked announcing Peter's late arrival with two young aides trailing. Even a midnight meeting required a three piece polyester suit. Peter's presence carried heaviness of internal pressure about to be unleashed.

"I hear you have set up the *rules* for my reading!" His glare landed in Mark's direction, his breathing deliberate.

I was right; Peter did take it very, very personally.

Mark quickly and loudly defended his position. "These *rules* are general procedure, eliminating personality or opinion overlay of the channel!"

Peter was furious. "The *Source* doesn't need my opinion!"

Feeling torn between them, I attempted arbitration, but only a few more heated remarks were needed and Peter's storm left the room -- the trance cancelled.

A rich polished mahogany railing guided my weary body up the stairs. Another night where sleep was long in coming; each turn stirring new questions and old memories. Undoubtedly, a heavy karmic connection existed between Peter and Mark, but what did it all mean? . . . Then pieces of this past-life puzzle seemed to fall from the sky into place. I remembered Maria Pappas' reading years earlier when I met Mark and all those mini-miracles. She was quite definite that Mark had been Alexander the Great and I, Olympia, his mother. Now, pages of history books leafed rapidly before my mind's eye, as I tried to recall this historic mother and son.

Alexander's hobby was bee keeping, learned from his teacher, Aristotle. Mark mentioned only tonight, bee keeping as a source of income for the community -- it had been his childhood hobby. What's more, Mark was planning a psychic research documentary, *The Search for Alexander's Tomb*.

Olympia, the mother, was Queen to Phillip of Macedonia. Legend told she had a visitation from the gods and proclaimed her son was of *virgin birth*. This infuriated Phillip, who never accepted his wife's religious ravings and ended their marriage, thus also creating a great split in his relationship with Alexander. My intuition put the final piece in the triangular-shaped puzzle. Of course, Peter had been Phillip of Macedonia! And my God, the synchronicity! Harry had been playing Alexander the Great on stage when my son was born and we named him . . . Alexander!

Mothers, sons, lovers -- all changing roles, each standing at a different point on the wheel of life. Lying there in astonishment at this extraordinary piece of history, I realized another part of the pattern within the Plan had been revealed.

The revelation seemed so outrageous in its perfection, the excitement it evoked kept sleep even further as Joshua's reading sifted back to me. "This one has been the wife or mother of great beings throughout your history." Remembering that the mother of Alexander the Great was impregnated by God brought my own memories rushing back.

I lay there reliving the time, *months ago* that I waited for Peter's arrival to confirm and celebrate my pregnancy. . . .

The doorbell activated my adrenals. Nervous, I still had a problem with an authority figure as powerful as Peter. He carried that same heavy internal disturbance as the first time we met, his body seemingly ill-prepared to carry the enormous energies ready to erupt.

"I want to talk to Mary privately. I'll have dinner when I'm finished." Jonah received his instructions, perhaps in order of importance or more likely so that he could establish reign over the household, after I left.

We found privacy in my bedroom, sitting on the bed rather than the sofa. Peter sat stroking the satin comforter, the elegance so foreign to who he was. He assumed his serious tone. "Do you know how many people are institutionalized after a mystical experience because they didn't understand its meaning or couldn't integrate it into their lives?" He shifted his weight and took pleasure in asking, "did you know your friend Sydney spoke to me of having you committed?"

I wouldn't allow myself to get involved in any emotional game of action/reaction, just sadly shook my head.

"No, I didn't know. I thought maybe Sam, but not Sydney."

"Well, I hear you're pregnant and the circumstances are *more* than unusual. I'm not going to give you a reading, there's been enough of that." He was still angry about Joshua. "I will simply tell you what I know." His powerful voice switched gears and droned on authoritatively, dominating, controlling . . . He gazed deeply into my eyes. I sat mesmerized.

"The fever you have has damaged the child. He will be born mongoloid and deformed! Your lesson is about commitment which you can learn by raising this child or you can learn it another way. The choice is yours!"

His words came crashing down on me like a volcano spreading molten lava in its wake, crushing my reality. My hands encircled my stomach, over and over desperately trying to heal it. "Oh my baby, my poor baby!" How cruel life can be. If I could give my own body to you, I would. In numbness I sat, barely feeling Peter's own hand on my shoulder, his single comforting gesture before he left the room.

Why, why, I sat alone with all my questions. Dear God, maybe you want me to have my deformed child so that you might work a miracle. Is this a never ending test? Have I failed it? Thoughts rushed through of the mongoloid child in Paradise . . . of Karma. Why punish my baby? Take me!

The conflict was beyond my coping. My cross heavy -- wavering to find balance. If I choose not to give birth, God will forgive me, but if I bear this child, would man be so understanding? I can't live in a higher realm all alone, when the consequences destroy everything around me, Alexander, Tara, Sam. My fever soared and my body ached. Maybe Sydney and Anne are right and I *am* too old. Hovering over my womb, tears falling on my baby. "What do *you* want? Can you live in a deformed body? Could I bear being the only one knowing such a spirit lived in you?" My sobs hushed any answer. Maybe I'm *not* ready. It's my fault! Oh God, please help me! Please help me! I feel nailed up against the cross, a dead end of no choice. Finally, a sense of relief swept over me, then a backlash of guilt. Oh humanness, you'll always find a way out of conflict. But surely, Peter above all men must know. There's only one thing I can do -- an abortion.

The memory of that decision brought tears to my pillow. The sounds locked inside, so as not to disturb my ashram roommates. Tossing and turning but I failed to prevent remembering what followed . . .

Having made the decision, I couldn't handle any more variables entering in, so the appointment was made for the next night. The clinic was staffed by young doctors who moonlighted by keeping unorthodox hours. God how I wanted my gentle Lenore with me or Esther or Eve. I really

loved Eve; but that wasn't a possibility. The next in line was
Crystal. I needed her compassion without any judgment.

Endless drive. Night lights and neon. Crystal avoided
asking questions or making small talk. I remember thinking
aloud, "I didn't tell Sydney. He and Anne probably would
have sent two dozen roses and praised my conscious
decision. Somehow, I feel caught up in that kind of two-
faced paradox."

The waiting room was crowded with women in various
stages of pregnancy; their exuberant enthusiasm contrasted
with my resigned despair, the light and dark of it. What
would they think if they only knew my story? Would my life
ever be normal again? How could that be, when normal is
not knowing? There was no unlearning what I now knew.
Physically depleted from weeks of fever and retching, still
waves of nausea persisted.

Realizing the utter finality of my decision, an enormous
sadness overcame me and released itself in a flood of tears.
"Oh dear God, what am I doing? Is it all simply mortal fuss?
Do you really want this child deformed so You can work a
miracle?" The words came out as I buried my head in
Crystal's arms.

"It's the only thing you can do! God giveth and He taketh
away. You know there is no death. It's simply not the proper
circumstances for this soul to enter. If it's to be, he'll find
another way."

"At least they let Jesus live before they killed Him. Today
we're all so separate from God, we can't even accept a divine
birth." Others in the waiting room smiled in embarrassment
as Crystal held me while I cried my heart out, as I once had
at the foot of the cross. Perhaps the unconscious Mary
Magdalene in me couldn't bear the thought of a Christ being
crucified again -- so denied the seed.

There was no Sam or Sydney waiting, only a picture of
Raphael's *Madonna and Child* over the tray of instruments.

The table was so cold. No blindfold . . . my feet slipped into stirrups. No pain could be penance enough; I heard the doctors commenting on how it was refusing to come out. Quieting a scream, going inward with my pain, flashing back to another time . . .

"An anesthetic would be too dangerous, after all, we don't want a corpse on our hands!"

"Oh God, please help me!"

"He didn't get you into this. A man did, call on him!"

My thoughts had but Sam refused to mount the white horse. Now I was refusing the gold ring. Oh God am I doing the right thing? Lying there silently in prayer, trying to contact this Christed energy, I released it with all my love.

Tears of remembering were not over, they would never be over, but exhaustion brought sleep nearer. Now my thoughts drifting, drifting . . . my first trip to Rome. Homage in coin to the Bernini Gods in the Trevi Fountain. Disillusionment settled in as the fountain was drained, exposing the Gods in the sunlight . . . St. Teresa said, "In a room full of sunshine, not a cobweb can be hid." What will tomorrow bring after Peter's dramatic attack against Mark? Was this man-made God of mine now beginning to stand in the sunlight revealing his imperfections? The thought crept in the door of doubt I now opened in my mind. *Oh no*, in my unwaivering trust, I never even challenged his words enough to have a medical test!

Why is it always easier to believe that someone else knows more than me? Could I have slipped back into my old pattern -- the controller and the controlled. By believing his prediction, I once again gave away my power and avoided responsibility for making my own choice. I created his power by giving away mine . . . Ah, the making of a guru! What a strange connection between Peter and myself if all these past life readings were true. Philip of Macedonia never accepted Alexander's *virgin birth* and Peter, if he had been Philip would never accept this immaculate child. What karmic irony that once husband -- that once son -- was destroying the chances of another son to live.

Now perspiration mingled with tears on my pillow. Did Peter deny a Christed being to keep control? And the young boys -- was that true too? The Apostle Paul denounced the Romans for sexuality between men. If Peter had been the Apostle Paul as *the Source* had said, must he now experience in life, his own judgment? Oh dear God was it my devotion to Peter that was deformed, not my child? And now do I replace conflict with guilt? Perhaps all this is happening as the mystery school of life presents its major lesson -- forgiveness. If Peter had been wrong, then I choose to believe the lie. Our needs intermeshed creating a situation for me to experience ultimate guilt. For how can we ever learn to forgive one another unless we have truly forgiven ourselves?

A new strength and clarity came with what went, still the memory of these times will burn within my soul forever.

Chapter XV

The next morning we gathered for the meeting and waited, wondering how Peter would handle the situation. Mark looked especially apprehensive, for another confrontation with Peter was an unattractive prospect. Finally Rama came in, his dark skin even darker under his eyes. I could tell he hadn't slept and was deeply disturbed; his silk clothes were wrinkled. Since my decision, he was under Peter's orders to erase the entire episode. His silent comments were penetrating.

Rama's eyes addressed the window and the floor throughout his announcement. "Peter has decided to step down as head of the community. He is a teacher, not an administrator to be caught in this human confusion. I too, feel the same. We leave the community in your capable hands . . . God bless you." He bowed to us, turned and left, his head not so high nor proud as usual. Even someone as strong as Rama can give away his power.

Our assemblage of faces expressed disbelief. "Jesus Christ, how irresponsible!" Mark spoke group sentiment. "Do you think he set up this whole fiasco to get himself off the hook?"

Peter had finally gone too far. My feelings were mixed with anger and embarrassment. And personally for me, it confirmed my unthinkable doubt -- Oh God, what have I done?

Mark by default and to demonstrate what a responsible person looked like, inherited the mess. He tried diligently to mend wounds and set new direction, but without paying the mortgage good intentions went down the drain along with the entire community.

Many skeletons now fell out of the closet. Mr. Penny, who owned the original smaller parcel for which I'd given the seed money, also owned the larger, grander piece that the community finally purchased. In the switch, Penny and Peter greedily denied the realtor his commission and in retaliation, the real estate company brought legal suit against the community. So the twenty-five thousand dollar donation, costing also my home, family and enormous anxiety had been held in litigation all this time. Mark arranged for a settlement, the funds were released and used to help members relocate. What irony the donation I thought would begin a community was finally put to use in its demise.

Fifty-five thousand dollars, but it was the best money I had ever spent. Where else could such learning take place so fast? A smile crept across my face thinking how Esther had set it up, so I could give it away. Maybe she owed me, I owed Peter, and so it goes, we all owe someone something.

Strange, I experienced no emotional involvement through this whole disaster. The gossip and bickering in every camp each protecting the reality they had put their truth in, for perhaps that's all the validity a truth has, its own integrity to the reality of the moment.

Not just the demise of the community, it was the death of a guru. The similarity between lovers and teacher/student, always asking another to do it for you. A solitary job this growth and everything a teacher in this mystery school of life.

Words spoken in my ear echoing through memory. "Take one step at a time as best you can." Destiny is like a giant carpet that unrolls before you, leading to exactly where you're to be. Life really is perfect; surrendering through ecstasies and despairs.

There was rain, but the dark clouds quickly dissipated exposing the sun. Mark drove me to the airport. I was going home. Holding each other in embrace, we said our goodbyes.

"This last week has been a real movie. Remember what Confucius says, 'the gem cannot be polished without friction, nor man perfected without trial.'" Suddenly, we both began to laugh and laugh and laugh. The release was healing. Passing on a final bit of kitchen philosophy as I boarded. "Just remember to show up and pay attention!"

First, I had to stop to see the children and Sam. His year now half over seemed more like an eternity to me. The vivid memory of Sam's letter when he left all those years ago. ". . . to see now . . . listen now . . . feel now. The only lasting values are those of the spiritual world, yet try as I might I can not make you see the way." Oh Sam my darling, could you have really known then what it took me all these years to find out? Oh Sam, Sam, you gentle man. I hope you've shaved your b. .rd.

Plane rides often induce a lulling trance midway between waking and sleep -- the twilight of a reflective place. Falling, falling together the puzzled pieces of my life . . . always placing myself in the role of victim. Then finally believing I had given up my victim status in spiritual pursuit where words became loftier, ego was referred to rather as destiny. My deep rooted decision as a child in that dank bar *Mothers are victims.* How could I accept . . . *The Crown of Motherhood* without unconsciously experiencing the ultimate despair of the victim? Lifetimes and lifetimes to perfect the set up . . . in order to so easily believe Peter who wears well *the Controller's Crown.*

But you can't give away power without asking to be manipulated. Now it all looked the same -- secular -- spiritual -- a lot of mortal fuss.

A retrospective smile flickered across my napping face, acknowledging I had done it all with passion and style. My mind running through romantic memories, behind closed eyes, the pattern of snowflakes fall, each pointed corner

touching another on their flight to the ground. The mosaic of
my relationships, one merging into the next, creating anew
what was unlearned from the last. Thank God, time for
chasing moonbeams is over.

Asking for commitment and fearing it at the same time, for a
commitment is not something you can ever ask of yourself or
another; like love it's either there or not. Longevity insurance
lies in the future made up of all the innocent little nows. I
wonder if God means for me to ever have another relationship.
The more you find out who you are, the greater you limit your
choice of a mate. Curiously, there's a paradox lurking in
shadow, for that same limitation magnetizes you closer to
destiny's choice. Surely, life itself is the ultimate art form and
relationship God's greatest gift.

The words of Joshua's reading of Jesus and Mary Magdalene
flowed through me. "Together they knew the perfect love of
soul for soul." All my relationships longing for this depth of
union and conflict creeping in when I tried to Christ each man
before his time -- lost in the abyss, for none of them were You.
The understanding brought comfort, as I shifted my position
in the airplane seat.

Once again, I slip off in the valleys of my mind. Around and
around the evolutionary spiral -- my merry-go-round. Flung
from one edge to another, in action, reaction. Emotions
creating conflict to give the momentum for the thrust around
another curve. For that moment of decision . . . the courage to
step out of this endless recycling, a quantum evolutionary leap
upward to the gold ring at the top. A release from karmic
imprisonment.

Memory resonating in my head of the voice and its message .
. . the meaning of the Immaculate Conception. Jesus and Mary
were of the same soul. Mary herself was conceived in the same
manner, to enter first, in order to house and give birth to Him.
Could I have denied the Christ seed to force myself away from
this continuing repeated pattern of a support system? Was I

stepping out of my karmic imprisonment? Does this denial mean I must now assume responsibility for the seed myself? The implication is awesome! Is it our own false humility that keeps us from our own greatness? Quickly my mind flashed to the LSD experience where I was giving birth to myself. Perhaps all of us must eventually fertilize our own seed with labor and give birth to our higher selves as we step out of this endless recycling. Tears began to fall from closed eyes. Surely faith makes the unknown an adventure and passion leads into the mystic.

The continually questioning human element asking how, wondering what I must *do* to fulfill my destiny. Even Jesus was a human who laughed, got angry and bled. Joshua's reading had said. "Your history has chosen to ignore the humanness of the man Jesus. This is a mistake for there is much to learn from his struggle between awareness of who he was and why he came and its expression in your world of form." He knew the uncertainty of the next step. After he received the Christed energy in his baptism he lived in solitude for forty days and forty nights, asking God in desperation what should he *do*, how could he best be heard?

As if given the answer directly, I knew. Only in being, doing finds meaning. If you keep the candle burning inside, the path will stay lit, and the next step illuminated.

A voice over the loudspeaker announced. "We're going through some turbulence, but don't be alarmed it's temporary. Keep your seat belts fastened . . . " I remember traveling with Sydney; he was so kind, always holding my hand and caring; I miss him. Yet slipping into deeper stillness, all thoughts seem to be in conversation with my higher side, feeding me answers as soon as the question appears.

Could all decision and choice just be a great cosmic joke? We believe we're given free will and in fact, we are, but the irony is, it doesn't matter. Free choice only computes in the same earthbound horizontal plane of reality as form, material, ego and results. No matter if you choose Sam or Sydney or Guru P. you still have to learn what you came to learn, in an endless array of stage sets, players and scripts—ancient, modern, science-fiction. Because the *master computer* in the sky doesn't compute form, it only registers essence, connection and process; so the cosmic joke is there's really no choice, the plan is already perfect.

The idea of a perfect plan dispersed any tension left in my body into oblivion, as I crossed the threshold into unconscious thought.

> **Standing in a field, minding children, I look up and see a foreign object in the sky. . .then another. Soon appears a fleet of space ships. A quiet, powerful realization comes over me. Could this be the perfection of the plan?**

"Time for dinner, even airplane food is looking good. Well you certainly seemed to be enjoying your sleep." An observation from my Southern neighbor in the next seat.

"I'd say it was more like a nap in the clouds. My name is Mary. Is that a pilot's uniform you're wearing?"

"Yes, I fly for another airline. I'm just pickin' up mah flight in Denver, en route to Hong Kong. M'name's Russ. Yeah, I've been flying for twenty-five years, started with the Air Force."

"It must be thrilling to fly so close to the stars. Have you ever seen a UFO?"

"Funny you should ask. Don't often tell this story. Ya know, people think you're a little touched. When I was flying for the Air Force, I saw one, plain as day, not two football fields away!"

"Interesting." I ask. "Did you report it?"

"Course not! First of all, I'd have jeopardized my credibility and second, I needed the courage to be responsible for the consequences." His answer ignited a spark, so alive . . . out of the framework of memory.

Fascinating, this is why it's so easy to accept something that happened two thousand years ago or to acknowledge the possibility of a miracle happening tomorrow. But to accept something *right now*, to be present and eliminate the gap between past and future, this requires commitment, courage and responsibility to the moment -- something that man avoids at all costs. Not living in the now is the same thing that keeps us from relationships, trapped in the limbo between memories and expectations. Life must be lived as a sustained beginning.

I remember Rama's story of three wondrous sisters, Past, Present and Future. "Past was adept in illusionary charm. Things seemingly insignificant in the hands of Present, became infatuation when viewed down the tunnel of Past. Future dwelt on the other side of the mountain, in the land of hope. She is inspiration for those tormented by Past. But unless the enchantment of Past and Future is overcome, it's never possible for anyone to behold Present in all her vital glory and wed her. He saw past and future merge in now and gazed into the eyes of eternity."

Somewhere between the *down side of up* and the climb to the up side of down lies heaven here on earth.

The Swan is dead. Long live the Swan!

EPILOGUE
By
Neil Freer

As a new paradigm of humanity comes into focus, the yet shapeless vision begins to manifest in precocious individuals; those who somehow know that they are supposed to know. The dislocation is internal. We are not nurtured nor educated to dance to rhythms of our private genetic harmonics. The isolation is external. The cultural deafness to those molecular drums stunts the child and contracts the adult. We should not do that to ourselves anymore. No longer live lives "stringing and unstringing" our bow because we have been denying the reality of the target. We no longer need to recycle the tales of the confused warrior heard around the cultural fire. No longer are we wrenched and torn by the eruptions from our collective unconscious, haunted by the suppressed archetypes of our ancient mind. **We now have a map.**

We have, and will constantly improve upon an inadequate language to describe and share supraconceptual experience. The elegant crystal of precise western physics couched in the alluring mysteries of the East does for now. **We have a language.**

The overwhelming archeological evidence for our genetic creation as Homo-Erectus-Nefilimus by the 'Gods of Genesis' has afforded us the last pieces of the collective puzzle of our beginnings, and restored our history to us. Within the expanded perspective of the new paradigm, 'religious experience' is clearly the dynamic leading edge of humanity's obessive probing for self-comprehension, independence, nobility and transcendence. For the individual, it is positive growth, the essential activity of human sociobiology. This dawning genetic enlightenment is accelerating our metamorphosis. The grip of that ancient godspell can be dispelled now, as surely as adolescence can be passed. Religions give way to an unlimited quest for whatever ultimates we can conceive as human beings. The genetically created species shakes off its racial amnesia, and arises from its cloud of unknowing. Prometheus reaches Satori.

In the future we shall see education redesigned as realization. One may pass under wise guides selected by the student, through the Dark Night of the Soul 1A and 1B in Junior High. The Cloud of Unknowing and the Philosophical Experience courses passed by sophomore year, while receiving a non-grade for exploratory Satori by junior year. 'Enlightenment' will be reached by graduation. One will basically be prepared to live a life span of at least 200 years, with an open option for relative immortality, and unlimited information access as an inviolable civil right.

WE HAVE A CONTEXT

But what of those prematurers who have been waiting all night in line, on the strength only of persistent rumor, before the tickets have arrived? The naturally noble, sensitive precocious child who refuses to close the doors of perception on parental command, feels "dropped off at the wrong house", early homing towards "someone I knew, evasive but familiar, divine but human. . ." demanding ". . .from where did this history come?", a "Princess". . .providing she conform? Regal femininity of the bannered desert tent thrust roughly into the harsh role of solitary hero-explorer. Walking the eerie boundaries between two ages, the focus of the quest ignites an incandescent consciousness which blazes deeply into the core of our being, reaching our genetic reality with laser-like intensity.

But one must integrate, communicate the experience and turn desperately to the old words, the antique concepts, the metaphors absorbed in childhood. . .Conversion only has meaning if we have been conditioned to self indite. It is not the experience that is lacking but the cultural context: no adequate maps, communication system, vocabulary, support systems, no toe hold in the dark. In anguish one projects the few unquestioned stereoarchetypes one has left. . . The vulnerable suspension between identities invites patronizing by the expert, the ruthless manipulation of the powerful, and misguided pity. And "Mary, Mary, who's Mary?" The survivors stagger from that scorching reentry in dazed glory. But how many have we lost in that lonely, unnecessary fire. . .

We Need Never Do That To Ourselves Again.

TEN YEARS LATER
By
Marian Greenberg

A decade of time can change even beliefs about beliefs. For years the seed of thought has been growing inside me, trying to decipher these archetypal models that each of us carry some aspect of, as every leaf tells the story of the tree. These symbols are the macrocosm of our humanity, filtering down through time their essence. Yet, they only represent a *key* to our vaulted memories.

The archeological research by Sitchin on the origins of Man as a genetic hybrid, engineered by humanoids from another planet, has taken mysticism back to its roots. *The key has been turned, the door opened. . .* But this still leaves us with the question: Could all 'mystic models' be advanced extraterrestrial technology simply incomprehensible to us at the time? And miracles therefore created by a misunderstanding due to a scientific/historical gap?

The research of Bud Hopkins on current UFO abductions (as presented in the introduction) projects this astonishing hypothesis: "That extraterrestrials are indeed abducting individuals, to collect sperm and ovum samples. It appears that their purpose is to create — a genetic hybrid!" In most of

these abduction cases there are some major pertinent character-
istics they share which occur over and over again. It is startling
how they correlate with my own 'mystical experiences' at
Paradise Ranch:

Commonalities in UFO Abduction Cases	My 'Mystical Experience'
1. shown a cataclysmic event	shown destruction of New York and San Francisco
2. a violent quaking of the room	just before the 'voice' came the room violently shook
3. a voice or telepathic communication	told of the immaculate conception & origins of man
4. red & blue flashing lights	what I saw in the night of missing time
5. a period of missing time	awoke in bed not remembering how I got there
6. recurring dream as a child	hiding deep in the earth from something terrifying
7. collecting sperm and ovum samples	impregnation

It is significant as well to review Dr. Hyatts' fascinating
theory that "depth sex can release archetypal memories of
our historical roots." He goes on to speculate ". . .that a
profound sexual experience can link us to our memories of
extraterrestrial origins." Could my strong sexual drive be a
genetically predetermined necessity to jolt my ancestrial
memory?
    "And now we have a language. . ."

    The foundation has been laid for me to reveal my deeper
understanding which bridges the historic gap between Sitchin
and Hopkins: What if the Gods or Nefilim left this planet but
at key times, in order to influence human destiny, incarnated
'one of their own'? Not as simply a hybrid, but as more of a

thoroughbred, by placing a specifically programmed God-Seed in the Birth Goddess, referred to by us as . . . Immaculate Conception . . .

The Bible explains much of this in what may have been chronicled naivete, but our literal interpretations distorts further the original meaning.

"And the angel of YHVH appeared unto the woman and said: you are barren and have no child, but you shall conceive and give birth to a son." And it continues ". . .and no razor shall come on his head, for the child shall be a Nazarite unto God from the womb." "And the angel of Elohim came again to the woman, who was sitting in the fields, *her husband was not with her.*"

An advanced scientist traveling in a spacecraft (an angel of mercy, a forerunner to todays physician, who remains God-like) could easily have healed her infertility and artificially inseminated her womb. This would give the Gods, or extraterrestrials a son or Prophet of their own directly on Earth, in this case, Samson.

Perhaps the purpose of star-gazing is to find in the heavens answers to affairs here on earth. Or could it be a yearning for our parents? For part of separating ourselves from our birthright is to deny the inheritance of the 'God' within.

We believe that we must colonize space, yet we are the colony. If extraterrestrials created man, can not man become extraterrestrials and recreate himself elsewhere? Sitchin says that Adam and Eve ate of the Tree of Knowledge, thereby learning about the secret of procreation. It seems the destiny of the species is to reproduce itself. Now man is going after what he was denied by the Gods. . .immortality, but aging is a model so ingrained into our DNA, we would first have to de-program ourselves before accepting the gift. Are we ready for this 'divine formula'?

Nostradamus predicted, "There will be a complete revision of the basic concepts of religion about the year 2150 and a new world order will arise, possibly one understanding for all." Maybe this cataclysm of consciousness destroying the very foundation of our belief system about ourselves can prevent us from having to experience a physical Armageddon.

So planetary or personal, past or future, all only variations on the same theme, recycled and always ending up in our own lap. As Freer aptly put it, "Because we all know in our most private thoughts that we can't go off into space looking for contact with other races until we know who and what we are."

Compassion and understanding are essential to arbitrate the internal war waged in each of us before "Star Wars" can be launched. We must come to terms with that innate morality where the heart knows the answer. An intuitive instinct which at its core is immaculate. I hope this story has spoken to that part of you.